THE WALKING TREES

Published in the United States by
Dymaxion, an imprint of Earthlight Pictures, Lake Oswego, Oregon.
Cataloging-in-Publication data is available from the Library of Congress

ISBN 978-0-578-42680-8

Cover Design by John Teton, Michael Ray Allison, and Justin Mikkelsen

This book is a memoir. While the events it consists of happened essentially as described, certain names have been changed.

Printed in the United States of America
First Edition

to
Peter

THE WALKING TREES

A Memoir
by
Chloe Scott

Prologue

On the edge of the Ten Thousand Islands, fringing the southwest coast of Florida, there once was a magical island known as Duck Rock. Covering little more than an acre, this small clump of mangroves rising out of the waters of the Gulf of Mexico formed a roosting and nesting habitat for an astonishing number of exotic and endangered bird species. Upwards of one hundred thousand herons, egrets, ibises, spoonbills, anhingas, and more inhabited the thick, leafy tops of the protecting branches and raised their families on the untidy piles of sticks they built for nests. The mystery is why, out of all the myriad islands in the Gulf, the birds chose to make this one their home as year after year they returned to raise their families.

Situated near the mouth of the Chatham River, one of the outlets of fresh water moving slowly from the Everglades into the Gulf, Duck Rock sheltered few ducks and was no kind of rock. There is no land as such on most of these mangrove clumps; mangroves grow right out of the water on long reddish, tangled, claw-like roots covered with barnacles. The tepid, murky water laps around these roots at low tide exposing them so they seem to grow longer, but when the tide is up, only their trunks show. From a distance they appear to move across the water—living up to the name the Seminoles gave them, "the walking trees."

Not only birds call the Ten Thousand Islands home. This vast mangrove swamp region is a vital transition zone between the interior Everglades with fresh water seeping down its rivers, and the salt water with which it mingles in the Gulf. The result is a marine estuary whose brackish water supports a dazzling profusion of life including crocodiles, alligators, manatees, sharks, and snakes as well as myriad crustaceans and fishes. Mangroves—ancient, primordial—are sometimes called land builders, as all manner of silt and debris becomes entangled in their gnarled root systems. Much as the earth must have gradually risen from the sea in prehistoric times, the land here is slowly building, so that a few of these islands actually do have solid ground under them. To go onto one of these slightly forbidding mangrove keys is an eerie experience of silent strangeness. There's an uneasy feeling of trespass and even danger—which is true. These mucky, murky islets are inimical to humans, with hidden hazards ranging from cottonmouths in the branches to alligators underfoot.

Over two thousand years ago, the first humans to take up residence in the Ten Thousand Islands were the Calusas. They helped to build high ground with the shucked oyster shells they discarded in piles. The Calusas are credited with (or blamed for) having slain Ponce de Leon, in 1521. Then, in the mid-18th century the Calusa Indians died out and were replaced by Muskogean and Creek tribes. These tribal refugees, driven from Alabama and Georgia by the white settlers, eventually joined together and called themselves Seminoles, from a Creek word meaning "runaways." In 1946, when my husband, Peter, and I came there as wardens for the National Audubon Society, they had not yet signed a peace treaty with the U.S. government and technically were still at war with the "white man." Their descendants live hidden away in small villages, or "chickees," in the Everglades where they eke out a subsistence living fishing and farming. Over the years, the Ten Thousand Islands had attracted many runaways: escaped slaves, convicts, outlaws, hermits, and other miscreants who found refuge and some kind of living in the swamps and backwaters. In the late 19th and early 20th centuries, many of the descendants of these lawless denizens took to gator poaching and plume hunting, causing grievous harm to the animal and bird populations. The plumes came mainly from the snowy and American egrets, which, during breeding season develop showy, filmy white feathers on their crests and chests. Herons and cranes also were targeted for their wing and tail feathers.

In 1900, the Lacey Act was passed. It was the first piece of legislation that had any effect on the plume-hunting business by making it illegal to ship bird skins or feathers interstate. In 1901, the state of Florida made plume hunting illegal, but the bill had no real teeth as there was no effective way to implement the new law. At the urging of local Audubon Societies, the first warden was hired in 1902 by the American Ornithologists' Union. Guy Bradley was his name, and he faced a formidable task. Here he was, a Florida local, protecting the birds he and his cronies had only recently been shooting for considerable profit. Why he took on the job is something of a mystery. His life was threatened by his cohorts, who realized their livelihood was in jeopardy, but despite the danger he persisted. In 1905 he was murdered by plume hunters as he tried to prevent them from shooting up a bird colony.

By this time the Audubon Society, which until then had been a loosely affiliated group of state-based societies, had incorporated and formed the National Audubon Society. This group hired two more wardens to try to stem the continuing depredations against the birds. In 1908 both of these men were gunned down by poachers. None of the perpetrators of any of these murders was ever caught.

The Audubon Society didn't give up, however, and hired more wardens to continue the brave attempt to save the plume birds. In 1910 the then president of the Audubon Society, William Dutcher, was instrumental in passing a bill in New York state which banned the "sale or possession of feathers from birds…already protected in the state." This effectively crippled the plume trade, as most of the feathers were sold to New York's fashion market. Ladies' hats now had to do without their feathered adornments. The final blow to the feather merchants came in 1913 when the NAS helped pass a federal law banning the importation or sale of any wild bird plumes, thus making the killing of birds a felony. These acts and bills were among the earliest conservation legislation in the history of the United States.

In the Everglades and the Ten Thousand Islands, however, the locals' habits were slow to change. Even though there was no more market for the plumes, it was still considered good sport to drive over to one of the nesting colonies and shoot it up—thus the continuing need for the presence of wardens.

By the end of the 1940s when Peter and I arrived, because of the Audubon Society's perseverance the birds had made a comeback, although they were not in as great a profusion as they once had been. Though the danger that anyone would try to shoot us was probably slight, still, we were warned by our employers in New York to be careful and never go onto an island or key if there were poachers in the act of shooting birds.

"They'd just as soon shoot you as the birds," the senior warden told us solemnly. "It's a felony either way."

In general, it was a lawless society. The descendants of the original refugees still squatted on various keys, living an anarchic, anti-social life, hunting and fishing and poaching for a living. It seemed that every male over the age of fourteen carried a gun and knew how to use it.

It was part of the old American frontier mentality, when everyone felt the need to protect himself from everyone else. In that watery environment, violence was more commonplace and easier to get away with than in most places. Not only was there almost no law enforcement, it was dangerously easy to dispose of a body in the mangrove swamps. In the maze of hidden creeks and rivers up in the backcountry, a body could be dumped almost anywhere by a perpetrator confident that it would be quickly disposed of by carrion-feeding crabs or alligators that act as the region's highly efficient clean-up crew. Even if a body were found, it would be difficult or impossible to find out how it had gotten there.

The law traveled by boat and consequently it was slow. For instance, it could take hours for the sheriff from Everglades, in Collier County, to arrive at the Chatham River to answer a call. The sheriff from Monroe County, in Key West, was a couple of hundred miles south, so he wasn't much of a threat either.

It was easy enough to evade the law—just cross the county line, hole up in the swamps, and you had a good chance of getting away with whatever you did. Moonshiners ran stills hidden up in the backwaters without interference, and if you happened upon one of them accidentally, you'd be met by guns.

(Please note that, while the story to follow happened largely as described, certain names have been changed.)

We toted a small gun, something slightly above a BB, which I was never sure would actually fire. It was more a stage prop than a real threat, but it looked real enough from a distance, resting in the gun-rack as we drove our boat around. The gun was part of the image we strove to live up in to our role of wardens in this new life. We didn't have much in the way of role models. I wonder how we must have appeared to the locals—Peter, six feet tall in his socks, with his dark good looks, wearing his Goki snake boots, and me with my red pony tail and lithe dancer's body. Here we were, a couple of green kids from the distant and alien urban Northeast, from a privileged background with private school education and upper-middle class cultural values. What could they have made of us? What would bring us all the way to this untamed, uncharted wilderness?

They never would have imagined the truth. Peter, who was George Drake Scott Jr. from a social register St Louis family and who had just come back from driving ambulances with the American Field Service in World War II, was a genuine naturalist and eco-scientist. He was happiest when he was wandering around with his field glasses checking out birds, searching fields and bushes for signs of mice and hedgehogs and other little mammals, making notes of his findings, keeping logs, and drawing conclusions about his discoveries.

Nor would they have believed that I was born Miss Chloe Keighly-Peach from an English family with a distinguished history, who had been evacuated to America at the beginning of the war to live with a family of complete strangers, my American guardians—guardians whom I had fled from 4 years later into this marriage, and that l, although I did have an adventurous and curious temperament, had no background whatsoever in any sort of nature studies or natural history.

But whatever they thought about us, they looked upon us with suspicion. In our own small way, we represented law 'n' order, something many locals had little respect for. Our job was to try to allay their suspicions, win their acceptance, and with a bit of luck, to persuade them to a different way of thinking.

Chloe and Peter Scott Aboard the *Audubon*
in the Florida Everglades, 1946

Part I

Duck Rock in the Florida Everglades

1

"This here boat's a floatin' coffin."

These were Art Eifler's opening words to us. The old Audubon warden emerged from his boat, the *Spoonbill*, which was tied to a piling a few yards upriver from us, and, with hardly more than a casual hello, launched into his monologue.

"There's these old gas tanks, y'see, just sittin' in the bilge, full of fumes," he continued. "One spark and up she goes. It's a miracle it ain't happened yet." His deeply creased, suntanned face showed concern and a certain relish. He liked having these two greenhorns to lecture to. He went on, "I can't git the Society to do nothin' about it, neither. I've written to 'em and told that Mr. Baker, he better pay some attention, but all they say is they'll look into it. 'Look into it.' Huh," he snorted, "by the time they get around to it, she'll be sittin' on the bottom with a hole in her you could walk through, and where'll you be?" He looked at us almost triumphantly. "I tell you, them Audubon folks up there in New York City have no idea. They just think all we got to do is sit around in the sun chewin' the cud. They ain't got no idea how much work it is just to keep these goldarn boats runnin', old and rotten as they is."

He pushed back his old yachting cap with a long yellowed fingernail and scratched his head. "Why, I just come from up Naples. I was there tryin' to get my hothead engine a-runnin' again. It's always breakin' down and the boatyard here in Everglades ain't worth a nickel. Them crackers don't know their ass from their elbow, if you'll pardon my French." He paused for breath and shot a glance at us out of his rheumy eyes to see if his language was going to shock these northern newcomers, especially the lady.

He was about to plunge back into his monologue, but Peter forestalled him. "Does this boat run?" he asked, pointing to the *Audubon*—the subject of the old warden's cautionary forewarnings and the boat that was to be our new home.

"If you can start 'er up without blowin' 'er up," he replied, "she'll run you out into the Gulf, sure enough. What you gotta do, see, is to take up that there hatch over the bilge and let them fumes air out before you start 'er up. That way, at least, if you get a spark it won't blow you to Kingdom Come."

By this time all my alarm systems were fully activated. I looked at Peter in dismay. Where had he brought us? What were we doing here in this strange, literal backwater of a place? Peter didn't seem particularly fazed by Art Eifler's dire predictions. In fact, he was looking with a distinctly pleased expression at the boat in question, as she floated on the Barron River, here at the southern end of the Florida Everglades, on the edge of the Gulf of Mexico. But then, Peter had a stronger predilection for adventure than I had, plus a great confidence in his ability to handle challenging situations. I was much more tentative about it all, and I definitely didn't have his self-confidence in the wild.

Becoming a warden for the National Audubon Society was a perfect situation for Peter, a naturalist by nature, a birder from childhood, and a man quite ahead of his time in his interest in ecology and environmental issues. This was 1946, a time when only a few prescient scientists and thinkers had become aware of the growing threats to our natural world. He had been hired six weeks before, a few days before Christmas, just as his temporary job in the ornithology department of the American Museum of Natural History in New York City had come to an end. He'd jumped at the chance to be a warden. It had all sounded glamorous and desirable to me too, while we were still in New York in all the cold and slush, but now I was wondering what we'd gotten ourselves into.

My mind wandered as Art continued to go on about his concerns and problems with life on a boat in the Ten Thousand Islands, not to mention the major task of protecting the birds, which was why we were all here in the first place. Peter and I had arrived in the hamlet of Everglades City only that morning, and after the long drive from New York City I was feeling quite disoriented. Before we had found our way to the Barron river bordering the western edge of the village, we had driven up and down the few blocks that made up Everglades City proper in about five minutes. We'd passed a small grocery store and a drug store that seemed to double as a bar, a post office, and a primary school. The dirt streets were lined with palm trees—date palms clustered with orange buds, spreading fan palms, leathery banana palms, and, with their tall heads high above the rest, a few feathery royal palms. On either side of the streets, small wooden houses crowded together with masses of purple bougainvillea, scarlet trumpets, and white scented jasmine climbing up their screened porches. In front, small plots were filled with tropical shrubs and flowers crowding up to low fences or blossoming hedges. The effect was dazzling in the subtropical light. Although it was only January, the air felt moist and warm on my skin.

In the stillness and silence of early morning, we saw no other cars and no people about. Finally, we had come to the dark green river, its banks lined with pilings and a few boats tied up here and there. This was the edge of the wilderness, one of the last outposts of civilization for hundreds of miles. On the opposite side of the river were thickly growing mangrove, oak, and cypress trees. Hidden in that dense, rich mix of trees and undergrowth, orchids grew high, Spanish moss hung from the branches and cottonmouth moccasins coiled out of sight. Countless herons, egrets, fish hawks, and myriad birds large and small, sheltered there. Even panthers still roamed the darkest thickets. A few eastern brown pelicans sat motionless atop the pilings, their long bills tucked into their breasts, while overhead, gulls and terns wheeled and squawked as they flew up and down the river. I stared across, trying to see into the density, attracted and repelled in equal parts. Art Eifler's monologue was running down.

"Well," he said finally, "we'll be goin' out to Duck Rock before too long. Got to get so's you can find yer way around these islands. We'll have to get these here boats runnin' and you'll need supplies 'n' all. Tell them

Monroes at the grocery store yer with the Society and they won't cheat yer too bad." He retired to his lair aboard the Spoonbill, where he lived with his elderly wife and pug, both of whom were near deaf.

"We'd better unpack the car and get our stuff on board," Peter said.

"Okay," I answered, "though I have my doubts about this tub. It looks a bit small." "Oh well, we'll get used to it, I expect," replied my cheerful husband. "She looks kind of grimy, but we'll paint her and clean her up. She'll be great." I was not entirely convinced.

The *Audubon* indeed looked small and dilapidated as she lay there tied up to the pilings, definitely not the handsome yacht I'd been led to expect when Mr. Baker, president of the National Audubon Society, told us we'd be living on their "flagship in the Everglades." She was a houseboat, built not for speed, but with a wide, flat bottom to navigate these shallow waters. She was actually only thirty feet long. There was a main cabin aft, screened all around rather like a porch. I couldn't see into the rest of her, but there were round portholes up towards the bow, which I took to be in the sleeping cabin. The boat, originally painted white, had become discolored and dirty with rusty stains running down her sides like sores.

"What are these two other boats for?" I asked Peter. "Are they ours, too?" Tied up behind the *Audubon* were a small inboard launch with a forward cabin and a skiff with an outboard motor.

"Yeah. I guess they'll be for transportation and errands and stuff," he answered. "This big one will be tied up at Duck Rock most of the time while we guard the birds."

"But not yet?" I wanted to get it clear.

"Well, I don't think the nesting birds have arrived yet. We'll be moored somewhere else for a while, I think Mr. Eifler said. At least while I'm learning about navigating and driving the boat. Anyway, we'll find out soon."

We're going to have to learn a helluva lot about running boats, I thought. I hoped I was up to it, and actually it did seem like it might be fun.

The tide being high, we easily stepped down from the bank into the stern well and in through the screen door to the cabin, where I took stock of our new living arrangements. Near the door was a dilapidated old-fashioned icebox. As I opened it, a musty smell of mildew assaulted me and I saw that the whole interior was covered in patches of black mold. A couple of director's chairs stood by a folding table on one side of the cabin and a folding canvas camp cot was against the opposite side. Towards the bow end was the steering wheel with a brass compass on a ledge above. A shallow companionway of three steps led down into the minute galley, right up against the sleeping cabin. Two narrow, hard bunks, one on each bulkhead, were separated by a narrow aisle leading to the head, tucked right up under the bow. Above the sleeping cabin was a glass hatch like a skylight, hinged on each side to allow much-needed ventilation down below. No bath, no shower, only a sink in the galley and a pump for water. Close quarters. I pressed on the thin pallets on the bunks—hard as the heart of a loan shark, as my mother would say. Not conducive to long lie-ins in the morning. And not too comfy for lovemaking, I thought. Too many hard surfaces to bump your knees and elbows.

Peter was unloading our small blue 1946 Ford, the first new model since before the war and his pride and joy. For the next couple of hours, we carried our gear aboard and stowed it as well as we could in the limited storage space. Once we'd set up housekeeping, the interior looked more cheerful, but still dingy and in need of a good scrub and a coat of paint.

Next came a trip to the family grocery store that we'd passed on our way here. The screen door banged behind us as we stepped into its dim interior, smelling of salami and pickles. Barrels of flour and cornmeal stood on the floor, a big open pickle jar on the counter along with boxes of penny candy. Flies buzzed everywhere, and long sticky paper traps hung from various vantage points. The crammed shelves, and variety of items reminded me of neighborhood stores in the Village in New York, where we'd so recently lived. Except here, we had to get used to some basic differences in food customs. Many of the things on the shelves I'd only vaguely heard of-- grits, hominy, okra, chitlins. I had no idea what to do with any of them. The Monroes, a middle-aged couple who owned and ran the store, were eager to help. We told them we were working for the National Audubon Society, and that Art Eifler was our colleague.

"Savin' the birds, are ya?" said Mr. Monroe, who was large-boned and squashed into his old jeans, his beer-barrel belly hanging over his belt. "Well, ya got yer work cut out for ya. Some folks around here don't care much for the law protecting those birds, they think shootin' the birds is their right. Some of 'em, that is," he amended. "There's folks think otherwise, too, though." He had much praise for Art Eifler, in which his skinny little wife joined enthusiastically.

"Yes, indeedy," said Mrs. Monroe, "them Eiflers is sure fine folks. That Art, he'll talk the hind leg off a donkey, but he sure treats that old wife of his kindly. Deaf and sickly as she is."

They were quite unabashedly curious about us and asked dozens of questions about ourselves (*Where y'all from? How long y'all been married?*) and about our lives in New York (*New York must be a real bad place to live. I hear tell they've got black folks and white folks livin' next to each other. How do you like that?*) Everglades City was the back of beyond, and although I knew the Monroes were a product of a still-segregated South, and no different from most residents in their attitudes and prejudices, I found their questions upsetting and had to curb my tongue. We filled a dozen grocery bags and went back to the boat.

By the time we'd located the ice house and wrestled a block into our ancient icebox, the setting sun was firing up the tops of the trees across the river. Red light silhouetted the arching fronds of the palms, motionless now in the early evening. Small ripples of the river, dyed red and pink, lapped against the boat. I was hungry. Climbing into the Ford, we drove out of town and back to the Tamiami Trail—that scar across the southern end of the state stretching from Miami to Tampa which we'd driven only that morning. It seemed ages ago. A few miles to the west, in the hamlet of Ochopee, we found a hamburger joint. It was dingy and smoky, but the juke box was cheerfully playing country music, and although the hamburgers were leathery, the beer was cold, and we relaxed after our strenuous, and for me, somewhat stressful day. Here we were, thrown into this alien environment which was to be our home for at least the next year. Unknowns abounded, and although it was exotic and exciting, I felt a little uncertain. I looked across the table at Peter. His dark, handsome face, with its high cheekbones and deep brown eyes, had an expression of anticipation and aliveness, despite his being tired after all the exertions of the day. I knew he was excited about being here.

"What an adventure," I said. "I can't believe where we are. It's really pretty amazing."

"It sure is," he agreed. "I can't wait to get out and explore everything."

"What do you make of that old Mr. Eifler?" I asked him.

"It's too early to tell, really. The Monroes seem to think well of him. He's certainly full of dire warnings, but no matter what, he's someone we've got to get along with. I gather he's supposed to be retiring, but I guess he's going to wait until he shows us the ropes."

"There's really a lot to learn. Driving the boats, and keeping them running and everything."

"Oh, I don't believe it's that hard," said Peter optimistically. "It's just a matter of practice. Shouldn't be much harder than driving a car."

"Except for the navigating. I don't think it's so easy finding your way around on the water, I mean, there are no roads or anything."

"Yeah, but there're buoys, and we just have to learn to recognize landmarks and so on." From what I'd seen, it didn't look that easy, but we'd find out soon enough. By the time we'd had a second beer we were ready to call it a day, and we went back to the boat. We lit the Coleman lanterns, and in their yellow flaring light we climbed into our hard little bunks. Peter was on the port side, and I was on the starboard side, for no particular reason. Through the portholes above the bunks, I could hear the river murmuring past on its way out to the Gulf, gently rocking the boat, and soothing my tired muscles and mind. The squawk of a night heron on its way to feed upriver accented the silence. Peter reached across the narrow aisle and we held hands for a while as we fell asleep. The strangeness of it all made us feel closer, and I was glad we were together.

"Tomorrow, I'll have to figure out how I'm going to take a bath," I thought as I fell asleep. "Maybe we can swim in the Gulf."

2

The next morning, we looked out at dark skies and deep shadows under the palm fronds. Across the river on the pilings along the bank, the pelicans still sat hunched, their eyes half-closed. The night heron flapped back to its roost in a nearby cedar tree to sleep for the day. The ever-present terns, with their long bills and forked tails, dipped and wheeled above the water, swooping on their elegant wings.

Aboard our boat, all the humdrum tasks required a set of new skills that I didn't have, and everything took much longer than I was used to. The tiny galley had very little storage space, and I had been forced to put things in odd places. Storing dry goods under the sink and keeping vegetables in the pots and pans. We had no electrical convenience gadgets either, no toaster, not even an oven.

Since there weren't any faucets, water had to be pumped out of the tanks below. If you wanted it hot you heated it on the gasoline stove. First order of business became figuring out this diabolical device and getting us some breakfast. Learning to master such a hazardous contraption took the skill of a prestidigitator, and the patience of a saint. That morning, there I stood, trying to synchronize a series of knobs to pump the stove's air pressure up until the fumes billowed forth at the right speed. Sometimes they got too high for safety, and I had to shut it down, or while I tried to light a match (damp, of course), striking it over and over, the pressure went down again by itself, and I had to start pumping again. Then the match would go out, and I had to turn it all off and start over. At six o'clock on a chilly morning, in bare feet and my blue two-piece shortie nightie, desperate for a cup of tea, I already wanted to jump overboard.

After burning my fingers, and holding back my hysteria at the damned stove, I managed to get one burner lit. It turned out only one was working. We had to settle for hot tea and cold cereal.

While I struggled, Peter wandered off to check out our other two boats to make sure they were still safely tethered astern and to look for birds along the river. He was eager to begin to document his sightings. Even this near to our little village, there were many exotic creatures. Egrets and herons sat in the mangroves, showing off their white plumage, occasionally squawking and flapping off to another perch. Peter came back after a few minutes, and we sat at the folding table in our screened cabin looking out across the river. The water appeared dark green and still. Occasionally the plop of a jumping fish broke the surface. I felt soothed despite my burned fingers. Peter didn't seem to mind the skimpy breakfast, but I missed my soft-boiled egg and toast.

"What happened to your hand, hon?" he asked, noticing my Band-aided fingers.

"Oh god, that stove," I moaned. "I'm scared of it, it seems really dangerous." I wanted to complain much more, but I also wanted to be a good sport, so I stopped. Peter picked up my hand and inspected the damage.

"Doesn't look too lethal," he said lightly and kissed my fingers. "I'll help you next time, if you like."

I felt the need to assert myself. "Oh, that's okay, really, I'll get the hang of it," I said, not feeling as confident as I sounded.

I changed the subject. "When do you think we'll get to go out into the Gulf?"

"I don't know," Peter replied. "I can't wait to get going, but we can't do anything without Art. We're completely dependent on him for now, so I guess we have to wait for him to be ready to show us around. It's going to take a while for me to learn to run the boats and find my own way."

"What about me? Don't I get to run the boats, too?"

"Oh sure, of course, hon," he reassured me. "You'll definitely need to. We just have to go a little slow, one at a time at first."

Actually, this was fine with me. I wasn't in any great hurry. I found the whole enterprise quite daunting. I could imagine myself tooling around in our two smaller boats, which would be used for short trips, like getting ice from the fish house. I wasn't too intimidated by the rowboat, that had a small outboard motor, or the medium sized boat that had an inboard motor and a small cabin, but I had serious doubts about navigating our big houseboat. Fortunately, it would spend most of the time tied up to Duck Rock. This new reality of traveling everywhere by boat was going to take some getting used to, and some practice.

Here on the edge of the mainland beyond Everglades City, there was no land as such, no roads, and hardly any solid ground. With the exception of a few old Indian shell mounds, where land had slowly accumulated, and a couple of natural keys with sandy beaches that had stretched inland forming small, low-lying islands with nothing between them but mangrove clumps and water, there was no place to get off the boats and walk.

As we already knew, the *Audubon* would be moored at Duck Rock most of the time. We would move it only for special trips like refueling and getting water. Art informed us the journey from Duck Rock into Everglades City was at least three hours in the big boat. We now found ourselves on a very different timetable from our city life. Would I ever be able to cope? What was I doing here? All my old familiar anxieties—fear of the unknown, of not being equal to the task—derived from a mixed-up childhood spent in English boarding schools, and from the war which had made me a refugee, began to arise from within. I tried to stifle them.

A little later, the sun came out and my confidence and spirits rose. Art Eifler appeared and announced we were to start preparing for departure.

"Great," said Peter, "we're ready any time."

"Well, no you ain't," was Art's reply. "We got to do a lot of supplyin' and readyin' before we're set." It turned out he meant in a day or two, not right away.

First, we had to meet "the Missus," Art's wife, Frieda, so we were invited aboard their boat for coffee that morning. Of German descent, she was a garrulous old woman, but as she was extremely deaf, communication was difficult. She seemed to be glad to have someone new to talk to. As many deaf people do, she tended to shout.

"Vere do you live?" she yelled.

"New York City," I screamed back. I couldn't go into all the business about being English and coming here during the war. Besides, I thought, she might have relatives still in Germany and it could be awkward.

Peter bellowed, "How long have you lived on the *Spoonbill*?".

"Art has bought us this boat twenty years ago." With that she was off on a long tale about their life aboard the *Spoonbill*, how much she really wanted to live on land and how they had some property on one of the Keys, and some day they would go and live there. Peter and I nodded and grimaced, pantomiming a trumped-up interest.

It was all rather tiring. I was aware of the closeness of the atmosphere aboard the boat, and the smell of their old dog, stale dog food, and enclosed people. I longed to open all the portholes and hatches and let in some fresh air. The dog, a small misshapen old pug, was also deaf. She had overgrown toenails from never getting to run on dry land, and consequently she clicked everywhere she went. She was clicking now as she paced restlessly back and forth, as we drank our coffee, listening to the Missus tell us what to expect from our new life in the wilds.

"You won't have all your comforts here no more, this ain't the big city," she shouted triumphantly. "You'll have to become used to doing without now."

We were glad to escape. "Phew," Peter murmured to me, "that was a bit of an effort."

Then he and Art had to go off and talk to the operator at the Ways, where Art's small outboard was being repaired.

"You gotta meet these Ways people," Art told Peter. "You'll probably be spendin' a lot of time with 'em, the way these old motors is always breaking down."

I was glad to be returning to the *Audubon* with its open screens and airiness. Walking back along the grassy bank to our berth, I noticed the tide had turned and the water was flowing rapidly out towards the Gulf. Small leaves and twigs, paper trash, even garbage from the boats, whirled along on the surface. Several seagulls sat on the pilings, one with his beak open squawking his raucous challenge to the others, all of whom looked quite unimpressed. A sinewy anhinga, black as pitch, locally known as the snake bird because of its long, twisting neck, flew swiftly up-river and out of sight.

As I reached our boat, I discovered a little girl, about six or seven, squatting on the edge of the bank and peering in through the screens.

"Hello," I said. "What's your name? Mine's Chloe."

"Rosamaria," she said, smiling. "Your boat is right in front of our house."

And indeed, it was. All that separated the boats and the houses was a grassy bank, and a narrow dirt road onto which the small wooden cottages faced. Rosamaria's house, with its tidy patch of grass, was opposite our berth.

"Well, would you like to come on the boat and see it?"

"Oh yes." She jumped aboard eagerly, her bright black eyes taking in all the details. Her dark hair lay in two long braids down her back and she displayed a charming, self-confident air. She was quite at home on the boat. When she smiled, she showed small, even white teeth with a few gaps where her baby teeth were missing. Within a few moments, a dark-haired woman appeared from the house calling for her. The little girl jumped up, saying, "That's my mom—I'm over here, Mom," and started out the screen door.

Her mother approached. She was young, in her thirties, I guessed, though at that time I saw anyone over thirty as "older." She had the same dark eyes as Rosamaria, and her face was friendly and expressive as she told me, in a melodious and lilting voice with a slight accent, that her name was Rosa Leighty and she was from Puerto Rico. Her husband, Ralph, was at his job teaching at the local school. I was delighted to have found such compatible neighbors.

The Leightys became our fast friends. The little family had been there only a couple of years, and hoped to return to Puerto Rico soon. Rosa turned out to be wonderfully generous and kind. In fact, she solved one of my major problems almost right away. The Laundry.

Laundry. Another of those ordinary chores we take for granted, here it was a huge problem. First, I needed something big enough to do the wash in, because everything—sheets, towels, blue jeans—all would have to be done by hand. Scrubbing such big items, not to mention wringing them out to dry, would require a lot of space on our little boat. Hot water, every bucketful, had to be heated on our small stove, taking ages, and then toted from stove to tub. And finally—a major obstacle—where to hang it all to dry? The whole enterprise seemed impossible and ever more daunting. Maybe I could enlist Peter to help sometimes, I thought hopefully. Then there was another possible solution.

I had heard from Art that there was a laundry service in town. The laundry man drove his truck in once a week. Your task was to flag him down and give him your bundle, but you had to guess at which corner he'd stop, and then lie in wait. If it proved to be the wrong corner, and you saw him several blocks away, you had to run screaming, waving your bundle, and try to catch him. A further twist to this already tricky process arose when the laundry was returned. If you happened to be out on the high seas at the time, what was he supposed to do with it?

Here was where Rosa so generously helped me, and just like that, my problem was solved.

As we stood chatting, she suddenly remarked, "How do you do your washing? You have not space on this little boat. Is very difficult for you, no?"

"Well," I answered her, "I haven't really done any yet. I'm going to have to figure it out."

"Oh," she told me, "there is a laundry man in town. He comes by in his truck to pick up my laundry up and leave it off. You could leave yours here if you like." I was saved. Delighted, I thanked her profusely.

"Oh no, no. Is nothing. I have a line, too. You could hang things to dry, if you need." I vowed silently that the first time we went into Miami I would bring her something really nice for a present.

During the next couple of days, Peter and I prepared to leave the shelter of the Everglades City berth, and venture forth into the mysterious Ten Thousand Islands. Art had told us we could tie up for a while on a shell mound at a homestead, several miles south up the Chatham River. The couple living there were friends with Art, and were willing to let Audubon people tie up at their dock. From there, we could begin to learn the most important skill we had to acquire, that of navigating around these treacherous waters. Before we could leave, though, we had to make sure we were fully provisioned. If we forgot anything we'd just have to do without. There was no corner convenience store out there. It was a lot like camping.

We filled the water tanks from the marine water supply faucet nearby. Another trip to the grocery store, and we were set for ice and basic food supplies, not forgetting the all-important case of beer. Then came the scary business of filling our gas tanks. This was one of the things Art had warned us about.

He had told us that, when you are filling the tanks, the bilge tends to fill up with fumes. These fumes are highly explosive and a spark, or any small friction, could ignite them and the tanks would blow up like a bomb. We had to be very careful to open up the hatch over the bilge and give it plenty of time to air out before starting up the motor. Even worse, according to dour Art Eifler, were the two old tanks still left in the bilge which, though empty now, were probably also full of fumes. Between the old tanks and new fumes, I thought we'd be lucky to survive even one trip down the river. When Peter moved the boat in line with the gas pump, I kept my distance, positioned on the bank nearby, watching anxiously as the ancient pump, like a relic from an old-time gas station, delivered our fuel. We stayed off the boat for an hour or so before venturing aboard again. I held my breath as Peter started the motor. The engine gave a cough and a splutter, puffed out a cloud of black exhaust, then settled down into a noisy thrumming, exhaust burbling out into the water astern. We were ready to begin the journey down the river and out into the Gulf.

3

As Peter revved up the engine, I ran along the bank to cast off the bowlines holding us to the piling, dashed back to let go the stern ropes, then jumped into the stern well to check on the small boats we were towing. A little shove away from the bank, and we were off down the river. I was feeling quite nautical and competent.

The morning was perfect and calm as we moved slowly and smoothly through the water in the wake of Art's boat, leading us on our first trip out to the Gulf. Passing closer to the sides of the channel, we could look deep into the recesses and dim leafy ranks of the trees, mostly mangroves, but with an occasional cedar. They were festooned with gray-green moss, and covered in ferns. While in their tops, every now and then, we spied some of the herons and egrets we were to be so closely allied with. Even without their breeding plumes, these birds were so large and so white that sitting in the trees they appeared as ghostly apparitions sitting in stark contrast to the deep greens and blues of their surroundings.

Still filled with pleasure over my recent display of seamanship, I suddenly realized that I had a legitimate connection to things nautical. My father was a career officer in the Royal Navy and I had grown up around shipyards and ships. We lived always near water, in a series of seaports around the British Isles and in the Mediterranean. We moved to a new coastal town almost once a year, as my father slowly climbed through the naval hierarchy towards ever higher rank.

Some of my earliest memories are of the excitement of being taken to the harbor when the fleet was in, to the quay where one of "Daddy's ships" was berthed. Looming huge and high above me, its great anchor holes filled with enormous chains, each link as long as my leg, they made me feel like a little ant as I peered down into the water where the anchor was plunged deep into the harbor mud. The smell of tar and ropes was always strong as we would climb up the gangplank and step onto the wooden decks, there to be piped aboard by that hellacious Navy whistle they've used for a hundred years. From there, we would be taken down treacherous perpendicular ladders ("backwards, Chloe, go down backwards") and into the wardroom, where my brother and I might be given wonderful crisp chocolate cookies wrapped in red and blue foil, while the grownups drank tea or sherry. Aboard Her (or His) Majesty's ships, alcohol was always available in the officers' mess, except during combat, and the ratings still got their daily tot of rum. Everything was always tidy, "shipshape," with polished brass, creaking wood, and low ceilings. You had to step high over the doorsills, all made of metal, because the heavy doors had to be able to seal in case the ship began to sink.

Rousing myself from my childhood memories, I joined Peter at the wheel of the boat up in the front of the main cabin. We stood up to see better over the bow, but later when we'd had more experience, and when the going was easy, we perched on the high stool to rest. This was our first voyage and we were both keyed up. The engine was so noisy that conversation was almost impossible, so we just stood together, looking out after Art's boat, leading us steadily along.

What a day! Sunny and clear, the horizon beyond the mangroves a clean straight line, visibility infinite. I felt elated, optimistic to be riding along on top of this beautiful water, green and clear close by, dark turquoise farther out, small choppy waves blowing across the surface. "O, a life on the ocean wave!" I sang the old song. Coming through the screens, the sun was warm on my face, and the breeze blew freshly through the cabin.

As we came out of the channel and entered the Gulf proper, the water kicked up a little and the boat started to roll gently. We had to steady ourselves, spreading our feet apart. "Getting our sea legs" it was called. I hoped I wouldn't be seasick.

Since the birds had not yet arrived to take up their summer residence, and raise their families on Duck Rock, we wouldn't be going there until later. I felt disappointed. I was anxious to see this famous mangrove key, where more than a hundred thousand birds roosted and bred within its leafy confines. We passed by it a sea mile away, and it looked just like every other mangrove key squatting on the water on long, spindly roots.

Overhead, a man-o'-war bird with deeply forked tail and huge wing-spread, sailed high above, looking for food in the water below. The strange thing is, man-o'-war birds can't swim. They don't land on the water at all, but dive down and scoop up some tasty morsel. Unable to sit and float, as pelicans do for instance, to eat their meal, they are forced to eat "on the fly."

For now, we were headed for the Chatham River, which, like all these rivers, flows from the Everglades proper, out through the mangroves, to the Gulf. We were on our way to an Indian shell mound, where a couple named Tooke lived in an old farmhouse.

Some of the shell mounds here were at least two thousand years old. They were left by the first human inhabitants of the area, the Calusa Indians. The high ground was built up gradually from centuries of oyster shucking. Overtime, soil accumulating on the piles of shells, resulted in mounds that have become small islands, and to this day many remain above sea level. They have withstood many serious hurricanes and are considered a great archeological resource.

The Tookes, we had been informed by the ever-forthcoming Mr. Eifler, were old-timers in the region. Mr. Tooke (I never learned their first names, they were always Mr. and Mrs. Tooke) was a fisherman. They had a couple of grown children—a son, also a fisherman, lived with them when not on his own boat, and a daughter who had her own family and lived somewhere on the mainland. They also had an adopted boy living with them, who was much younger than their biological children. We were to tie up at their place because it was closer to the rivers and creeks that we would be learning to navigate, and it also gave easier access to the keys and islands Peter was interested in studying.

Suddenly we saw Art's boat slowing way down and a telltale stain of muddy water appearing from under his keel. Art had hit a sand bar on our narrow course towards the mouth of the Chatham River. Running aground was always a risk when the tide was low, and now we felt it too, a sudden jarring and juddering as we crept along. We just had to hope we could scrape by. Otherwise, we'd have to spend the night in the exposed, choppy waters of the Gulf, waiting for the tide to bring in enough water to break us free to navigate the rest of the way.

Getting stuck wasn't the only problem, we were also in danger of damaging the propeller or the steering mechanism as we ground along hitting bottom. I was holding my breath hoping we'd get clear again. I did not want to get stuck there overnight. Then, just as suddenly as it started, the grinding ceased, and we floated on deep water again. Hallelujah, I thought in relief. Art's boat sped up and our little convoy continued on.

All around us the mangroves sprang up out of the water, resting on their tangled red roots, each green top home to its hidden cache of birds, from which every now and then, one would separate itself from its roost to go flapping off. The clumps and groupings of trees on the water were so numerous, and all seemed to look so exactly alike, that I couldn't imagine how in the world we'd ever learn our way amongst them.

The river became wider and I felt safer. The water looked deeper and more reliable. Still, even here, we had to be aware of underwater hazards—submerged logs, unexpected sand bars, you never knew. At last we came around a bend and saw, on a sudden high bank, the peaked roof of a house half hidden in its setting of palms, papayas, avocados, and guava trees. At waters' edge was a small rickety dock with several pilings, room for berthing a couple of boats. Hanging above the dock, seeming to teeter over the bank, was the most enormous poinciana I'd ever seen. One of Florida's glories, this tree grew everywhere and, with its graceful, widespread arching shape and feathery leaves, it was always breathtaking to look at. In the early summer when it bloomed it was glorious beyond belief, with rich bunches of flaming red blossoms clustered thickly all over. It was so bright it sometimes appeared to give off its own light.

As we approached the dock, I scrambled onto the forward deck and grabbed up the lines. When we were near enough, I reached for a piling and lassoed it loosely to hold us while I jumped onto the dock and ran to the stern. Taking hold of the sheets, I secured them to another piling. They would probably need some adjustment if there were a big tide here, but for the moment we were safe enough.

Peter cut the motor and sudden silence enveloped us. This was something of a signal event for Peter. His maiden voyage, as it were, and we'd made it without a hitch. He was properly pleased with himself.

I looked around. The shell mound rose steeply above us, covered with banana trees and coconut palms. I couldn't see the whole of the top, it was too high, curving up and out of sight. More extensive than it first appeared, we were told later that it was about forty acres of mounded land that had formed on top of the shell deposits.

I turned to look across the wide and slow-moving river to the dark, thickly clustered trees—mangroves and more mangroves. The river was nothing more than a channel running among miles and miles of them.

Turning back, I looked up at the steep path leading from the dock to the house, and there standing ready to welcome us were the Tookes. They looked like Tweedledum and Tweedledee, both round and cheerful, wearing big rubber boots, their twinkling eyes smiling out from behind little spectacles.

Art and Frieda climbed out of their boat, and the group of us stood on the dock a little awkwardly, the others eyeing Peter and me. Art pushed his sailor's cap back from his sweaty forehead and made some garbled introductions, which the Tookes gracefully acknowledged.

We were so alien, coming as we did from suspect northern climes. Young though we were, both just twenty-one, I felt we nevertheless conveyed that indefinable air of being from a privileged background, though we were both slightly apologetic about it. We were ardently liberal thinkers, and were anxious not to appear snobby or superior. We were also well aware that our social standing was of little use in the wilderness and that we were the "tenderfeet." My jeans and sweatshirt, my long red hair and my English accent set me apart immediately, and Peter, handsome with his dark crew cut, looked like the Ivy League candidate which, of course, he was.

But the Tookes, bless them, with their natural gentility, were utterly comfortable and unfazed by any of this, and we were immediately enveloped in Mrs. Tookes warm, welcoming version of Southern hospitality.

"Well, welcome, welcome," she cried. "Come on up to the house. You're just in time for supper. We can get acquainted whiles we eat." and Mr. Tooke, with a slightly more reserved manner, (which we later came to realize covered his shyness), added his welcome, saying, "We been expectin' you. Art's been telllin' us he'd be bringin' you by soon. We's glad to have you."

"We'll get et up by sand flies if we stand around out here," said Mrs. Tooke. "Art and Frieda, you too, come on up to the house."

As we walked up the crunchy, shell-covered path, I became aware of clouds of dancing black sand flies, some of which had begun to attack. As we stepped into the screened porch, Mr. Tooke's two hound dogs and a favorite mutt of indeterminate breed, got up from their sleeping places and came wagging to greet us. Entering the kitchen, we were met by the delicious smell of hot cornbread and frying fish. In the middle of the spacious old room, as much family room as kitchen, an enormous rectangular table, covered with a red and white checked oilcloth, stood on the wide, uneven planking of the floor. Against one side, taking up almost a whole wall, was a giant old-fashioned wood cooking stove, its chimney pipe disappearing through a hole near the ceiling. Unmatched chairs were set around the table, and a large old rocker took up one corner next to a huge brick fireplace. The kitchen warmed the whole house during the short Florida winter.

The table was already set, and Mrs. Tooke immediately began filling serving dishes and bowls with mounds of food. In addition to the fish and cornbread, she'd fixed greens from the garden and grits with bacon in them. Without refrigeration, all their food had to be eaten as soon as it was gathered and consequently everything was always fresh. Mrs. Tooke was an excellent cook. I enjoyed learning from her about cooking, what she called "cracker" food, something I'd never been exposed to before.

The men did most of the talking. After the preliminary grumbles about the low price of fish, and the shockingly high price of gas, Mr. Tooke asked Peter about his wartime experiences.

"I was an ambulance driver for the American Field Service," Peter started.

"What's that?" Mrs. Tooke interrupted.

"Oh. Well, the Field Service is a volunteer organization started by the Quakers, who are pacifists and didn't want to be in combat, but still wanted to support the war. So, in the First World War, they founded the American Friends Service Committee, and the Field Service is part of that."

"Are you Quakers, then?" queried Mr. Tooke.

"No, but I was too young, you see, to get in the army or anything, so I just signed on for ambulance driving. I wanted to get into the war."

Our hosts looked a little baffled, but at the same time seemed impressed.

"How long were you overseas?" Mrs. Tooke wanted to know.

"I was away altogether about two years."

"And where were you?" Art asked.

"Well, we started out in North Africa, but just as we got there, old General Montgomery, you know, the leader of the British Eighth Army, had defeated Rommel at El Alamein, and the fighting was over, so they decided to send us to Italy instead."

"So, did you see a lot of fighting while you was in Italy?" Art questioned. "Oh yes," Peter replied, "it got pretty hot sometimes."

I could tell he didn't want to talk about those experiences he'd had, picking up the wounded and dying after an engagement. Even after three years, the memories were still too raw. I tried to deflect the course of the conversation.

"We were all waiting to hear from him all the time," I offered. "But the mail was so slow and sometimes the censors cut bits out of the letters or after nothing for a month, sometimes we'd get three or four letters at once."

"Where were you, then?" asked Mrs. Tooke.

"Well, I was still living with my American guardians, who'd been my family since the beginning of the war when I was sent over from England," I started. There was so much to explain. These new people were curious about us, and friendly, but I felt daunted whenever I had to try to explain my situation because it seemed so complicated.

It was time for dessert and I jumped up to help Mrs. Tooke clear the table, but she wouldn't hear of it.

"No, no, you stay put. I c'n do this just fine," she said firmly. I sat down again. A little later, after dinner was over, we started to take our leave.

"Here," said Mrs. Tooke, "How about some eggs? We got too many," and she gave both the Eiflers and ourselves a bowl of eggs. "Now, you need anything, be sure to just holler, and just come on up any time, we's always glad to have comp'ny."

Mrs. T was wonderfully open-hearted and hospitable, and I was very grateful for both of them. Peter and I returned to our boat. I got out my little Olivetti typewriter and started on my journal. I was determined to keep an account of this adventure. Someday I might want to write about it.

4

A few mornings later, I again set off up the path to the Tookes' house. Wide and stony, it was strewn with broken shell fragments from the ancient mound on which the house stood. In addition to the magnificent poinciana growing at the edge of the river, the whole place was covered in banana palms, palmettos, guavas, avocados, citrus, and papayas, all producing abundantly. Overgrown and weedy, the yard in front was chicken heaven for a happy flock that ran around scratching for bugs.

The house itself was impressive. Constructed out of sturdy pine, it stood two stories high with a steep, peaked roof. It was badly in need of a paint job but otherwise looked to be in good repair, with intact screens on all the windows and doors, a most basic necessity in this mosquito-and-sand fly- infested state.

Known as the Watson place, the farm covered most of the island, and it had an interesting and varied history. Built at the turn of the century, it was farmed by its earliest owners. There had been many inhabitants since those days, among them outlaws and renegades of all stripes who, we were told, had used it as a perfect hideout. I never learned how the Tookes came to be there, but they certainly were the opposite of any kind of outlaws, being just a kindly, hardworking fishing family.

The night before, as we had sat around the Tookes' large dining table once again, Mr. Tooke had regaled us with tales of local history. Thirty odd years ago the place had been lived in by a notorious outlaw and murderer, E. J. Watson. He seems to have been an extremely wicked character. Everyone was afraid of him. It was said he killed the blacks who worked for him instead of paying them. Then, one day the body of a woman supposed to be his housekeeper-mistress was found floating in the river, and as Mr. Tooke said, "That was different." It appeared that in those days it was considered okay to murder a few itinerant black men, but the murder of a white woman couldn't be overlooked.

There are various versions of how he was eventually shot and killed by a posse. The question of who fired the first shot, or whether he was killed here on the Watson place or on the dock of the notorious Chokoloskee Island, the answer seemed to depend on who was telling the tale. However it happened, the story continued to be a big deal to the folks who lived in the area, and the legend had been growing ever since, people never seeming to tire of telling their version of it.

As I walked up the path this brilliant, sunny morning, I mulled over all that miserable history, glad it was far in the past. I also knew there were lingering unsolved problems in the area. We had been warned there were still plenty of people ready and willing to flout the law. In particular, Art had told us many scary stories about "that godless bunch" on Chokoloskee Island. A large Indian shell mound, it sheltered an enclave of people most of them related to each other, living in what amounted to be a small village. The island was situated in the Gulf, just off the mouth of the Barron River at Everglades, so we had to pass it any time we went into or out of town. Once we had seen a boatload of rough-looking men driving along in one of their speed boats. No one smiled or waved at us, and I was definitely nervous about their presence.

My errand today was to see if I could borrow Mrs. Tooke's big galvanized iron washtub. I had an enormous amount of cleaning and washing I needed to do. Mr. Tooke was sitting on a tree stump by the well in front of the house, repairing his fishing nets with stubby but nimble fingers. His round face creased into a smile as I came up.

"Mornin," he greeted me.

Mrs. Tooke opened the screen door.

"Well howdy," she smiled. "Come in and get you a cup of coffee. I just made a fresh pot."

We chatted a little, and she readily agreed to lend me her tub. She also offered to let me use her long clothes line that was stretched between two banana palms. So now I had solved the laundry problem here too, at least to some degree. Mrs. Tooke loved a good gossip, and she was pleased to have a new audience. She was curious about our relationship with Art and Frieda.

"How do you get along with 'em?" she asked bluntly. "That Art can be cranky. He's got his ways."

"He's been very helpful to Peter and me," I answered warily.

"And Frieda, she's turnin' into a real old fussbudget," Mrs. T continued. "I swear, she's got complaints runnin' off her like a dog sheddin' in spring."

"Maybe she's fed up, living the way they do, and Art does leave her alone a lot." I wanted to be diplomatic and not get into their tricky, complex relationship.

"He leaves her alone, all right. She never stops with her fussin' at him, and she's as deaf as a post. Poor old thing." Mrs. Tooke wasn't meaning to be unkind and I imagined she was trying to feel me out, to see where I stood.

"Well, I'd better go get my laundry," I said, deciding to avoid the whole situation. I stood up from the table.

She looked at me. "You and Peter been married folks for long? It's goin' to be a little bit lonesome for you two, I reckon, without none of your friends or nothin' here."

I was grateful for her friendliness, and she had a motherly way about her that gave me comfort. I'd been without my own mother for much of my life, and I felt reassured knowing I would have Mrs. T to help with navigating my way though this alien landscape.

Returning to the boat, I decided to clean it up first before doing laundry. There was still grime and grease in all the corners. The floor, or I should say, deck, was stained and scratched, and both the galley and the head were a disgrace. The head smelled bad, and I needed to wash the whole cramped little space with Lysol. As for the galley, the shelves were covered in old grime, and though I'd managed to scrape off some of the cooked-on grease, the stove still needed a more thorough cleaning.

Eventually the whole boat would need painting inside and out, but for now, all I could do was try to clean up the interior.

First, I gathered up all of our belongings we had so recently packed aboard, and piled them on the dock, out of the way. They sat there rather forlornly, like leftovers from a rummage sale. Then, gathering mop, pail, scrubbing brushes, and sponges, I set to work. The air outside our screens blew in, redolent of mangrove mud, fishy and organic. At low tide, when more of the banks and roots were exposed, this smell could be very strong. Now it mixed with the soap and bleach, and I felt close to elemental stuff. As I scrubbed away years of neglect, the boat began to look habitable and even inviting. When I'd finished, I stood back admiring my work and imagined how I would paint it. It would be blue for the ceiling, orange-buff for the deck, and the rest white. Quite an upgrade for the old girl.

While all this cleaning was going on, Peter and Art were struggling with the engines of our two smaller boats. These we would need to use locally, going to Turkey Key for ice and fresh fish or checking out the birds at other bays and local keys. There was plenty of exploring to do, but neither the *Snowy Egret,* nor the *White Ibis* was currently serviceable. They were always having engine trouble. The men were forever having to tinker with their motors, with varying degrees of success.

Now I had the boat cleaned up and put back together, it was time to face the laundry. All this cleaning and laundry entailed a lot of pumping of water from our tanks and then heating it on the miserable stove (at least we finally had both burners going). Dunking and scrubbing in Mrs. Tooke's wash tub didn't get things very clean, but it did get the worst of the dirt off.

Now that one of my major difficulties—that of drying everything—had been solved by Mrs. Tooke, I was feeling more optimistic, though it was still my most daunting task.

By the time all that had been accomplished, I was exhausted, and I needed a wash myself. That meant MORE pumping and heating of water. A bath aboard the *Audubon* meant standing in a bowl of water and taking what we used to call a "bird bath." Most unsatisfactory and standing naked in the bowl trying to sponge off the soap could get quite chilly.

When I first arrived, I had thought, naively, we could just jump in the river or the Gulf. We did try it a couple of times, but the water was salty and hard on the skin. Even the river was estuarine and brackish, and there were too many nasty things sliming around on the bottom—little sting rays ("stingarees" the locals called them), small harmless sharks (but a shark is a shark), the occasional water moccasin, and other nameless squishy things. The bottom itself was thick mud, and who could tell what might be hidden down in it? Better the known drawbacks of the standing sponge bath than the unknown perils entailed by immersion in muddy waters.

Now I was clean, the clothes were clean, the boat was clean—and here came Peter, covered in grease and dirt from his encounters with the boats' engines.

"Ready for a clean-up?" I suggested.

"God, yes," he said, peeling off his filthy jeans and standing there looking like an ad for Jockey underwear. Peter was a very good-looking man. He had graceful proportions with long, shapely legs (I always had a weakness for good legs). He had been an athlete when he was at Andover, a track star. Since his ambulance driving days, he'd kept his dark, straight hair in the short buzz cut required of service men. Personally, I liked it better when he grew it longer and combed it straight back, as he had when we'd met in the early forties in East Hampton, on Long Island. Peter was an upbeat person, when I had first seen him, it was his expressive dark eyes and wide grin, which he flashed often, that had attracted me to him.

He had a ruddy complexion and was one of those people who have only to be in the sun for half an hour to get a great tan. In fact, there's a story told in the family of how, when he was a young child, he was so tan, that once, when crossing the border from Tijuana to Coronado, where they had been visiting, his blonde American mother was questioned by the border guards about his origins! They thought she might be kidnapping him.

Peter's family had moved from St. Louis to East Hampton, where his mother's family owned various properties. The Scotts lived in a white, two-story house called The Box (because of its box hedges) across from

Town Pond. Peter had gone to elementary school locally, and in the (then) unspoiled countryside of eastern Long Island he had developed his lifelong passion for natural history. He was guided and encouraged in all of his explorations by his uncle, Will Helmuth, a well-known ornithologist and chronicler of the flora of the region.

When I came to East Hampton in 1942 as a student at the Rollins Studio, a local theater school–cum–summer stock company, I met Peter backstage. He and his cousins preferred building sets and painting scenery as volunteers, rather than hanging out at the highly social Yacht Club or equally snobby Beach Club. Peter was instantly smitten. I fell in love not only with him, but with his whole family, who welcomed and accepted me into their midst. I felt a strong affinity with them all and they made me feel completely at home. A feeling which, most unfortunately, I was never able to feel with my American guardians, we just didn't "click," though they were nothing but kind to me. So, the Scott clan became my unofficial, surrogate family.

Now, going to the sink, Peter started to pump, but all he got was the raspy, choking sound of sucking air. Thunderstone! I had used up all the water! It was supposed to last a month and I'd run through it in five days. Unfortunately, the Eiflers, tied up just ahead of us, had no extra, so putting his pants back on, Peter dashed up to the Tookes' to beg some water from their well. The well was old and deep, and apparently never ran dry. There were terrible tales of bodies having been flung into it in the wake of past evil doers, but that was in the bad old days. Now the well water was pure and sweet, though it bred a hardy strain of huge mosquitoes.

Peter returned shortly with enough water for washing and immediate needs, but my profligacy meant we'd have to take a trip back to Everglades City, to replenish our supply. It was too late this evening. We would have to go the next day. Luckily, the small boats had been repaired, and we could take one of them, much better than running the *Audubon* back to town, which would take four hours round trip and use up a lot of fuel. Art would have to navigate as Peter wasn't yet familiar with the channels. Well, good enough. Every time we set forth, we were learning our way around.

In the morning the tide wasn't right, so we waited till later, taking off in the *Snowy Egret* after lunch. It was the fastest of the small boats and could make it to Everglades in an hour and a half. The trip turned out to take more like three.

The first ten minutes were splendid. The sun shone, the air was crisp, though the breeze came up a little stiff. We sped downstream in the middle of the dark green river. I was seated in the bow facing forward, exhilarated, the wind blowing my hair. Within a few moments I was soaked from the spray flying over the bow. I huddled into my cheap plastic raincoat, which promptly tore in several places.

In desperation, I turned around, faced backwards, and managed to keep my legs dry. Then the engine, which they had worked on so hard the day before, started acting up, maddeningly stopping and starting. We were all three wet and disgusted by the time we tied up near the Leightys' house.

Rosa came out of her back door. "Oh, you poor things," she cried in her lilting voice. "You are all so wet. What has been happening to you? You must come inside quickly and get dried up."

I was very happy to see her and go into her cozy little house to get warm. She gave us coffee and home-made cake. Rosamaria was jumping around wanting to go for a ride in the boat.

"Why can't we go for a ride? Just a little one? You said we could," she insisted. "We'll all go on an outing another time, honey, but you see, now we have to hurry up to get water and be on our way. It's getting late. We don't want to have to drive that long way home in the dark."

She was disappointed. "Well, soon. Next time you come, okay?"

I assured her we'd go soon. The possibility of getting stranded in the dark on our way back was on my mind. We'd listened to many horrendous tales of unfortunate travelers unwary or unlucky enough to be caught out on a sandbar overnight. How they'd died of exposure and insect bites, or foolishly left their boats and staggered off into the terrible, unforgiving mangroves to be bitten by snakes or eaten by alligators. Even though I realized these stories were undoubtedly greatly exaggerated, I was still uneasy about the prospect of night navigation in these unmarked waters.

The men went off to the marine hose near the dock to fill the containers we'd brought with us, and it was not long before we started homewards with an hour of daylight left. Gliding down the flat-calm river, loaded to the gunnels with water tanks, I was afraid we'd sink if we encountered rough water, but we sped on into a sunset of pure rose and gold, the water reflecting the colors one shade deeper. So far so good, I thought, but lurking in the back of my mind was the fear of losing our way in the fast approaching night. It was hard enough navigating these endless channels through the mangrove islands by day, let alone in the dark, unable to see any landmarks. "Hey, Art," I spoke loudly over the noisy engine. "How can you tell where you are at night like this?"

"I done it a hundred times, young lady. Know it like the palm of m' hand," was his reassuring reply.

As we journeyed on, the night sky became filled with stars, many more and brighter by far than we'd ever seen in town. Every ripple reflected star shine. Dense mangrove clusters surrounded us, at times far-off black silhouettes and at times so close we'd be slipping between them and I could have reached out and grabbed a mossy root. They seemed full of mysteries waiting to be discovered. The sound of our motor, miraculously restored to full working condition, thrumming as we flew along on top of the water. The air so balmy, blowing over us, adding to the thrilling, visceral sense of speed. All of these elements combined to create an ongoing moment, timeless, without dimension, an experience which, even as it unfolded, so perfect in its immediacy, was breathtaking, as fleeting and impermanent as it was exalted. Life, after all, is neither more nor less than a series of moments endlessly flowing into one another, with us always poised in the shimmering present. Even as I was feeling the glory of this special moment, I was also aware of an underlying anxiety roiling around somewhere inside me. That we wouldn't make it, that we'd be stranded, that a disaster could happen. I felt trapped in a constant struggle between these two opposite feelings, the effect of being caught in the duality of earthly existence, and unfortunately my anxiety very often got the upper hand.

We continued to zip on up the Chatham River until, coming around a bend, we could see the dim outlines of our boats tied up at the Tookes' dock, waiting faithfully for our return. I felt a surge of relief that we'd made it, even as I was briefly sorry our trip was ended. I had a sudden burst of affection for the old *Audubon*, because for the moment, she looked like home.

5

I woke up early in Peter's bunk. We were snuggling against the cold.

"I can see my breath. I don't want to get up," I grumbled.

"Well don't then," Peter said. "I don't mind, I'll do it," and a little later, yawning and stretching, he got up and made tea. He could be very satisfactory at times.

We'd been in the midst of a cold spell for a couple of weeks. Outside, the rain pelted down, splashing watery pits on the surface of the river, drumming on the roof and blowing in our faces when we opened the door. We had put the wooden panels into the frames of the screened windows of our upper deck, but they were old and leaky, and when the wind blew hard the rain came in around the edges. We had no heat of any kind, and the temperature dipped to freezing on more than one morning. Despite piling on layers of our warmest socks and sweaters, we were still chilly. I tried staying in bed as long as possible and getting on with my reading. As that was one of my favorite activities, I had brought an ambitious supply of books with me. At the moment I was plowing through all of Proust. *Remembrance of Things Past* made a perfect counterpoint to my present living situation.

The boat rocked and heaved, testing our balance and causing the overhead Coleman lantern to swing wildly. At times, when the wind gusted particularly strongly, the boat banged jarringly into the dock. That was alarming at first, but once I realized we weren't going to sink, I got used to it. It was not dangerous, as the rubber tires hanging from the pilings acted as bumpers to fend us off. The constant bumping had become mostly a nuisance, but still it was unnerving, and the jolt could pitch you off your feet if you were taken unawares.

The landscape had taken on a dark, lonely aspect, the leaves of the mangroves dripping and shivering or blowing and whipping in the wind, showing their silvery undersides. Any birds we saw seemed equally miserable, their damp feathers plastered to their sides, shoulders hunched, sitting hunkered down on a branch just waiting for the weather to change.

While it was cold and miserable out, we spent as much time as we decently could with the Tookes. Their house was a haven of coziness with their big fireplace and the old wood-fired kitchen stove. After a visit, I found it hard to tear myself away and go outside into the rain to splash my way down the chalky path back onto our chilly boat. But at least the rain filled our water tanks. An ingenious system of gutters had been arranged to catch the rain and channel it into the tanks below the deck.

Then just as suddenly as it left, the balmy air returned. The sun gained warmth and brilliance, sparkling on the green surface of the Chatham River, and we took the shutters down. While idling over our cups of tea on that first good morning, listening to The Breakfast Club on our unreliable battery radio, someone mentioned it was February 23, and I realized with a start that it was our second wedding anniversary! I'd lost track of the date. Days and dates were meaningless out here. We lived day to day and the days were all alike. Even Sunday was the same as the rest. But this date was important.

Peter and I were married, both aged nineteen and over everyone's objections, at the beginning of 1945, the last year of World War II. I had been living with my American guardians in Pennsylvania ever since that tumultuous day in 1940 when I'd left England, my family, and my childhood behind, and been sent to live in America. Peter and I had known each other for three years, but for the previous two years he had been in Italy driving ambulances for the American Field Service. Then he'd returned and we had wanted to be married before he was drafted into the army and sent off again. To be legally married in Pennsylvania while under twenty-one, it was necessary to have the written consent of both parents. And there was the rub. My father was off fighting the war aboard a carrier in the Mediterranean and my mother was dodging buzz bombs in London. It would have meant an endless delay to get the needed documents. What to do? Then it was discovered that anyone, of any age, could get married in Maryland. Elkton, just across the state line, was the place to go for eloping couples, unmarried mothers-to-be, underage truants, the lot. No problem. Except, we did have a problem. A large church wedding had been planned in Haverford, where my guardians lived, with invitations sent out, minister engaged, and catering laid on. It too late to cancel. Besides, I didn't want to, I wanted to have a proper wedding. The church ceremony would satisfy the religious, spiritual, and social aspects of marriage, but not the legal. So, it was decided we would go to Elkton to satisfy the state requirements and then have the church wedding the following day.

In some excess of propriety, my well-meaning guardians decided that Peter and I could not spend the night together after the first wedding. We would have to wait for the consummation of the bond until after the church ceremony because, heavens above, I had to walk down that aisle in my white dress a virgin (and of course it was assumed I was one, this was the '40s, after all). Despite our objections, we were kept firmly apart until after the wedding in the church. As it was wartime and we had only a couple of weeks before Peter would be called up, we couldn't go far for our honeymoon. We drove to East Hampton, to Peter's family's house, The Box, a place we knew and loved. We always counted the date of the second wedding as our anniversary.

Reminding Peter of the date, I said, "Let's go somewhere special. Let's go on a real expedition. We need to do something to celebrate."

"Okay, good idea," Peter replied. "I've been wanting to try to find Gopher Key and see if any birds have arrived yet. That would be an adventure."

"We could take a picnic and make a day of it. It really looks like the weather is going to stay nice." I strongly wanted to get off this boat for a while.

Peter decided to take the skiff as it was the only one of our boats small enough to navigate the small creeks that wind amongst the mangroves.

While I cleaned up the breakfast dishes and made a picnic lunch, Peter went to see if the skiff was actually going to run. We were still plagued with motor troubles, the main problem being that everything was quite antiquated and in need of refurbishing or replacement.

As I finished packing up some cheese sandwiches and a couple of beers to take along with us, I heard the outboard start up with a snort and a sputter, and Peter yelling to come on before it died again. I clambered up onto the dock and walked back to where Peter waited in the skiff and stepped down carefully as it rocked and vibrated, waiting to take off. He let go the stern lines and I untied the bow and we started up the river.

Gopher Key was a large, dense mangrove island at the edge of the Everglades, with a bay on its farther side bordered by an open savannah, and with a small beach on its' near side. It was reputed to have a prodigious number of birds frequenting it, as it provided shelter and food for a wide variety of species.

We went slowly, to diminish the spray as the water was still a little rough. The sun shone warmly on our backs and the rain-washed air smelled only slightly of mangrove mud. As we dawdled along the mangroves at the river's edge, we became aware of dozens of small birds—warblers and finches—darting to and fro in the trees. There was an excited chittering and twittering amongst them as they flew. They too seemed to be celebrating the change in the weather.

At low tide the mangroves lived up to their Indian name, "the walking trees." Their roots, gnarly and barnacle-covered, rose out of the water giving the impression that the trees were walking along through the water on strange spindly red legs. Our first problem was to find the entrance to the narrow creek that would lead us to Gopher Key. Looking like any other small break in the thick mass of trees, it would be easy to miss. Luckily, Peter's navigational skills had improved by leaps and bounds and his confidence had risen accordingly.

We cruised along peering into the trees, and at last, an entrance showed itself. Peter nosed the boat cautiously into the narrow opening and began to ease upstream. We didn't know for sure if we'd found the right creek—we just hoped for the best. The channel was narrow, dark, and silent except for the soft putt-putting of our motor. The sun could not penetrate the thick canopy of the mangroves, twenty feet above our heads, it could only hit the very tops of the trees, which were tipped with a golden light. We were in a tunnel of trees, mysterious, yet inviting. I had my usual anxieties about unknown hazards such as submerged logs and unexpected shallows, which could sink us or strand us in this totally isolated spot. Peter slowed the motor until the boat was just barely moving along.

As we drifted around a sharp bend, suddenly another boat glided silently towards us. It was a dugout canoe, and standing in the stern, polling it down the creek, was a tall, dark Seminole, wearing a characteristic patchwork multi-colored shirt and head-band. Sitting in the bow was a woman, also dressed in full Seminole attire, with a long skirt and a sort of capelet over her rounded shoulders. Although they passed within inches of us, their faces gave absolutely no sign they had seen us or were aware of our presence. We were invisible as far as they were concerned. We just sat there, holding our breath as the two boats slowly passed by each other. We were absolutely mesmerized, staring at their dark, impassive faces and colorful clothes. In moments they had passed downstream and out of sight. We just looked at each other, speechless.

At last Peter said, "You know who I think that was? I think that was Billy Tiger. I saw him in Everglades one day when I was there with Mr. Tooke. He knows some of the local tribe's people. He said Billy Tiger's their chief."

"I guess they don't think much of us white people, and I can't say as I blame them."

"Well, technically they're still at war with us," Peter reminded me. "They never signed a peace treaty."

"Her skirt was beautiful" I remarked. "I would love to have a skirt like that."

"Their canoe was really interesting too, it looked like it was hand-hewn," said Peter.

We continued on our winding way towards Gopher Key—we hoped. The channel was gradually widening now until finally we emerged into the open water of a wide bay, and we realized we'd found it, that this was indeed Gopher Key. We looked across its large expanse, with savannah grasses fringing one side and a small beach edging the other. The bay, about half a mile across at its widest point, narrowed and merged into the Gulf on its far side.

Although it was still early in the year, there were scores of birds feeding amid the long grasses of the savannah and along the water's edge. Four or five wood ibises, those great big storks, stood on their spindly legs, focusing intently on the water as they scanned for food. There were egrets—both Snowy and American—the birds that develop such incredible showy white plumes in the mating season and are the prime target of the hunters. Great blue herons and a couple of green herons were also standing in the water intent on a meal, and on the branches of the mangroves, anhingas and cormorants basked in the sun. There were not yet the hundreds we would see later, but still a respectable showing for this time of year.

Peter was happy. He cut the motor, and I slowly and quietly got the oars, one by one, from the bottom of the boat and started stealthily rowing us closer, trying not to scare the birds into flight, while Peter was glued to his field glasses. Farther off, out towards the edge of the Gulf, we could see brown pelicans feeding. Wheeling overhead, a large flock had apparently discovered a shoal of fish swimming beneath them. These rather ungainly birds, one after another, transformed themselves momentarily into spears, pointing their long heavy bills towards the water and elongating those ponderous bodies into taut javelins as they plunged, missile-like, upon the hapless fish below, whereupon they bobbed up again to sit on the water with their catch, transferring it to their capacious pouches with a shake of their uplifted heads.

Closer by, we spotted a flock of white pelicans, rarer and more skittish. We could hear their occasional grunts as they sat crowded together on the water. They were bigger than their brown cousins, with a wingspan that could sometimes stretch up to nine feet. At our approach, as slow and quiet as we tried to be, they took flight in alarm, and with a great flurry and commotion, flew up into the sky, climbing higher and higher, until they became virtually invisible as their white undersides blended with the sky. Then they would wheel and turn, suddenly showing the black edges of their wings, clearly etched in the sunshine, as they circled above us. I rested on my oars while Peter scribbled notes into his quickly expanding record book. I was hungry.

"Let's go over to the beach and eat lunch," I suggested.

"Okay. I'm dying for a beer," agreed Peter.

I rowed us slowly across the lagoon to the shady side and the narrow strip of sand. I unpacked our picnic and spread it out on our old striped blanket. Cheese sandwiches, pickles, an apple, and chocolate cookies for dessert. Everything tasted especially satisfying out on this wild beach. The beer and the warmth of the sun made me sleepy. Lying on the soft white sand reminded me of the beaches in East Hampton, where until just a few months ago, Peter and I had spent so much time, it made me a little homesick to think of it.

In those days, all the beaches were open to everyone, we had our pick of ocean or Sound beaches, the Coast Guard Beach, Ocean Avenue Beach, Louses Point, or Three Mile Harbor. Best of all them was the beach in front of the family's Dune House. It was built in the early '20s and was the first house to be built on a dune. The local people had shaken their heads, everyone knew you couldn't build a house on sand. But old Grandpa Keck, the family patriarch, set the house on huge pilings reaching deep down into the dune. As sturdy as a rock, the mansion came through the great hurricane of '38 with only sandblasted windows to show for it. We'd had many a splendid picnic on the wide expanse of beach in front of the "Dune house," drinking beer, eating hot dogs and swimming in the breakers as they rolled up the sand. Now I thought of all my friends and relations left behind in New York with a twinge of melancholy. I wished they could be here to see this amazing place and share in our adventure. I wanted to talk to them about all we were experiencing, to explain, to discuss, to share. There was no one here I could really talk to apart from Rosa, and, of course, Peter.

Peter had gone off to explore, prowling around the key, observing, counting and noting. I was alone, as I seldom had been in my life. Here, except for my husband, there was not another soul for miles and miles around. What a lovely spot. Even the sand flies left me alone. I dozed.

Peter came back and woke me up with a kiss. He lay beside me and nuzzled my ear. He started stroking me, kissing and petting.

"Wanna do it?" he murmured.

I was still drowsy and I really didn't feel like making the effort, but he smelled of sweat and the outdoors, and he seemed strong and sexy, and I began to feel more like it. Besides, here we were, alone on a tropical island. It would be a shame not to take advantage of such an opportunity. We quickly flung off our clothes and made love on the blanket, drawing it out, savoring every pulse and shudder. It was very romantic, almost a cliché, the stuff of movies and novels. We lay for a little while quietly holding each other. But it was hot, the bugs were beginning to bite and we couldn't go into the water to cool off because it was shallow, murky, and muddy on the bottom and wouldn't have helped much. I stood just on the edge and splashed water over me before I put my clothes back on. What freedom it was to be naked and have no concerns about propriety, or shocking anyone. Americans are rather prudish. In England, as in Europe in general, people are much more relaxed about nudity.

Although I preferred this solid ground that wasn't rocking up and down all the time, it was time to head back to the Audubon, moored and waiting for us at the Tookes' dock. On our way along the darkening tunnel of trees, Peter spied an inviting half-hidden channel.

"Let's see what's up there," he said, starting to turn the boat into the entrance.

"Oh, I don't know, Peter. It looks awfully narrow. What if we get stuck?"

It was just the sort of thing that made me anxious. I started to imagine the myriad disasters awaiting us.

"We'll get lost, I know we will," I wailed.

"I promise you we'll be okay, honest, hon," he persuaded me. "Tell you what, it won't take long and if it looks at all hazardous, we'll call it off and turn around."

As we chugged slowly up the channel, it began to get narrower and narrower. I could reach out my hands and touch the trees on either side. It was also getting more and more shallow, and even though this boat drew very little water, I was afraid we'd get stuck. I started to protest, but Peter—ever the explorer—wanted to go on a little bit more. Just as it seemed we must run out of water and navigable space, we came to a slight widening in the stream, and up ahead, standing in the shallows, was a flock of roseate spoonbills. They are about as big as a flamingo, but with shorter legs.

These rare and wondrous pink birds were feeding in their pool with the characteristic back-and-forth head-wagging motion they use to filter small crustaceans through the wide, flat, spoon shaped bills that give them their name. There must have been at least thirty of them. They rose up in alarm at our approach, but after circling above us about half of them glided back down and settled in the water again. Peter had shut off the motor and we sat motionless and silent, watching in awe as they calmly continued with their afternoon foraging.

Finally, we had to leave. As there wasn't enough room to turn the boat around, we had to pull ourselves along backwards by grabbing roots and branches until the creek was wide enough for us to turn and progress down the main stream. Then we sped on by the last light of a deep red setting sun. Our trip had been a wonderful anniversary adventure, and I was glad Peter had helped me overcome my anxieties and persevered in taking us up that little creek to culminate our day with the magical flock of spoonbills.

In addition to all the birds we'd seen, there had been the mysterious encounter with the Seminoles in their canoe. I couldn't help feeling somewhat uncomfortable about it. Were we seeing them in the same light as the other wild creatures we came across? Were we putting them in the category of rare and exotic sightings, to be catalogued in our note books and put on our life lists? I hoped not, but it was something I wanted to think more about.

6

Turkey Key was a small mangrove clump, not far out of the mouth of the Chatham River. Joe and Nellie Tompkins, a middle-aged couple from Tampa, ran an ice house there on a rickety dock sticking up on stilts out of the water. They also had a gas pump and kept a few staples on hand. Local fishermen could ice their catches, gas up their boats, and buy a can of beans without having to go all the way into Everglades. It was a vital link in the survival chain out there in the Ten Thousand Islands, sort of the equivalent of the neighborhood corner grocery.

One morning, being out of milk, short on gas, and very low on ice, Peter and I made the forty-five-minute run there in the skiff. Buzzing along on the sparkling surface of the river on a clear, sunny Gulf morning, I was driving and Peter was looking for birds through his trusty Zeiss binoculars, a serious birder's most important possession. Every now and then I had to slow down as we passed a particular mangrove clump, so he could better observe the new spring arrivals.

The birds were appearing in ever larger numbers. We were starting to see not only the big herons, egrets, and ibises which came for the summer to Duck Rock, but beautiful little warblers and finches, such as the Florida yellowthroat, goldfinches, white-eyed vireos, and myriad kingfishers, woodpeckers, and sparrows. There were dozens of sea birds too, pelicans, anhingas, terns, and gulls. As we came out of the mouth of the river into the Gulf proper, four frigate birds with their eight-foot wingspans sailed serenely and indifferently above us, each long scissor-like tail now closed in flight, pointing out behind them like a single, slender lance. Looking south we could see Duck Rock on the horizon, a perfectly smooth rounded clump. Its trees, shaped by continuous use of so many birds, seemed to have been clipped into a topiary sculpture. Soon, we'd be moving out there to protect those birds from unruly locals, who still found shooting dozens of helpless, peaceful birds a worthy sport. It wasn't as if they were killed for food, they were just shot and left, their sad, limp carcasses floating amongst the banyan roots of the island. Even more distressing, since most of the birds were nesting, their nestlings would also be doomed to die of starvation.

I was more than ready to make the move. I was feeling a need to be on our own for awhile, away from the ever-watchful eyes of our neighbors, no matter how kindly, up at the Tookes' place. At the same time, I wondered how I'd manage being constantly on the boat, with nowhere to get off. At least at the Tookes', I could walk around on dry land, help in the garden, and get a little exercise. Having space to move mattered to me, because, as a dancer, movement had always been such an important part of my life. After all, the *Audubon* was only thirty feet long, not much dancing space. As we zipped along, heading for the ice house, my mind continued to wander. My thoughts turned to another major hitch in our whole situation here—the condition of the boats. As Art had warned us upon our arrival, the *Audubon* in particular was in need of extensive repairs. The state of the gas tanks was a serious hazard. Recently, we had been in touch with the VIPs in New York, who had told us to expect a visit from someone who would assess the situation and authorize the necessary repairs. Soon, we hoped.

Once past Duck Rock, we still had a fifteen-minute run before we reached Turkey Key. I shaded my eyes from the sun's glare as I looked across the water. From a distance the fish-house appeared quaintly picturesque perched up on its high pilings, with a sharply angled roof and surrounded by a commodious deck. Dozens of pelicans, terns, and gulls swarmed around it competing for fish scraps and garbage. Their high-pitched squawks and screams carried clearly across the narrowing expanse of the Gulf. As we approached, we could see several boats tied up alongside.

"Looks busy today," said Peter. "We'll probably have to wait."

"Oh, well, we don't have anything else to do and it gives us a chance to get to know some of the locals," I said lightly, but actually I was a little nervous. I had yet to find a comfortable way to relate to all these folks from such a different culture. Peter was good at it though, and knew how to talk to the men, at any rate.

We found a spot to tie up and climbed the steps to the deck. A group of fishermen stood around the gas pump talking about the weather and the price of fish. Several of them were familiar faces that we had met in Everglades and chatted with at the gas pump there.

The gas pump in the everglades seemed to be the equivalent of the water cooler at the office, the place to see people and hear the latest local gossip. Recently, the main source of buzz and speculation was about the soon-to-be Everglades National Park. A huge project, it would turn the Everglades south of Okeefeenokee Swamp and all the way to the Keys, into one major conservation area. The coming changes were bound to have a big effect on the lives of everyone who lived here.

The local people were mostly friendly towards us, even though, in a way, we represented the law, something which the majority of folks were distinctly leery. But everyone we met liked Peter. He had the "gift of gab," and was friendly and non-threatening, not the sort of person to throw his weight around. They bantered and joked with him easily as we came up onto the dock. They seemed willing to give us a chance, even with the controversy over the notion of conservation in general, and protection of the birds in particular.

I recognized Dutch Futch, an older guy in an ancient yachting cap whom I'd seen in Everglades and who was a friend of the Tookes'. He mumbled in an unidentifiable accent, "Hey there, Scotty boy. How's the bird business? Haw haw." Peter grinned good-naturedly and asked Dutch, "How's the fish business?"

No one knew quite how to relate to me. Of course, I was in the position of "the wife," a second-class citizen, politely greeted but mostly "seen and not heard." But I was disconcertingly beautiful in those days and I had a social presence that was quite different than they were used to. I had been brought up to have good manners and make conversation, though I was having trouble with that part of things. The men seemed to be torn between doffing their caps and tugging their forelocks—or making smutty jokes, so I became somewhat tongue-tied around them.

Leaning on the rail behind Dutch Futch was a grizzled old-timer wearing a knitted watch cap and smoking a pipe. He looked half-asleep, but he woke up when he saw me, took his pipe out of his mouth, and waving it vaguely in the air said,

"Ah-ah. Must be the new warden and his missus. Well, howdy folks, and how do you like our neck of the woods, hey?"

His name, it turned out, was Darwin. He told us that he lived alone on an Indian shell mound up a creek near the Chatham River. We learned later that he was as independent and "off the grid" as a person could be, growing his own food and fishing for his keep. Peter struck up a conversation, and after talking for awhile, Peter asked if Darwin would mind if we came to visit him sometime and explore his shell mound.

"You come on, young feller, and be sure you bring your purty missus," he said.

One of the other men standing around I'd also seen once before, a sinister-looking, toothless fellow with one eye that didn't look straight at you. His presence made me nervous and uncomfortable, and I was afraid to look at him. I had been told by Mrs. Tooke that he was one of the Browns from the notorious Chokoloskee Island. They were reputed to be outlaws, running a still back in the mangroves somewhere making moonshine. He also smelled strongly of liquor even this early in the morning. When I sneaked a look at him out of the corner of my eye, the words "scary and depraved" came to my mind. I thought he looked capable of anything.

Nellie Tompkins was behind the cash register. She was sort of a mousy woman, shy and unassuming. I thought she appeared downtrodden by her husband, Joe, who was a large, surly man who seemed to be in a permanent bad mood. It was clear she was nervous around him.

They had a rambunctious and overly friendly mutt named Blackie and a rescued raccoon named Molly that was quite tame and unafraid of people. When I fed her a fish head, she would take it politely with little black paws that looked as if she were wearing gloves, then delicately rinse it off in her water bowl before holding it up to her mouth and chewing. All her movements were graceful and gentle. Nellie clearly loved her. I sympathized with Nellie's plight trapped out here on this key in the middle of nowhere with a disagreeable husband. I just hoped he wasn't violent.

At last it was our turn. We picked up milk, some spare gas, and a big block of ice. Then we said our goodbyes and left. I wanted to talk to Peter about the fishermen and the Tompkins' odd ways, but the outboard was too loud for conversation. Peter was driving this time and, running before the tide, we made good time.

"I want to fish," I shouted over the motor. "Let me get the gear out of the box." It was under Peter's seat. He pushed it over.

"Okay," he replied, "I'll slow down."

"Well, we aren't in any hurry, and maybe I'll catch something right away." I stuck a piece of fish head onto the hook and threw it over the stern, paid out the line, and began trolling. We'd hardly gone a hundred yards before I felt a tug and Peter slowed down even further as I began to pull the fish in. It was a beautiful yellow jack and fought hard, but I managed to land him into the bottom of the boat, where Peter dispatched him with a single blow to the head. I was relieved. I could never bear to let fish flop around, gasping as they slowly expired, their eyes seeming to roll reproachfully up towards you. Anyhow, we had our supper for that night.

Back at the Tookes' place, we discovered Art had been into Everglades and had picked up the mail. We had two letters. One was from the National Audubon Society, from the president himself, Mr. John Baker, and the other from my oldest and dearest friend, Donna. I handed the one from Mr. Baker to Peter and quickly opened Donnas' letter. I'd known her from our student days five years before, when we went to the American Academy of Dramatic Art in New York. We'd lived together in a series of scruffy apartments while we both tried to break into the "theatah," making the rounds and answering casting calls. Through it all, we'd remained close. Although I'd given up on a career in the theater, she was persevering.

"Hi, darling," she'd written. "You won't believe this, but I've joined RBB&B Circus and we'll be in Florida in two weeks!!! I'm so excited. I just couldn't stand this cold weather another minute, it's been so freezing. Making the rounds is completely depressing and there're no jobs anyway. So, I'm about to become one of the "50 GORGEOUS GIRLS 50" and flaunt my body hanging from a rope 30 feet up in the air. If I think about it, I get cold feet, so I don't. I'm going to have to ride an elephant too! I had a big fight with Bob about it. But I told him it's only six weeks and when we get back to New York I'll quit. I have to pick up some money somewhere. Sarasota's not far from you, is it? We'll get to see each other— I can't wait."

"Peter," I said, "guess what? Donna's joined the circus and they're coming to Sarasota for six weeks to train, won't that be wonderful? We can go visit her. I'd love to see Sarasota. And she'll visit us, too." Thinking about seeing Donna made me realize how much I missed my friends and my New York life.

"What's she going to do in the circus? She can't do trick riding like Bunny or be a clown like Walt." He was referring to two other friends who had recently done a stint with Ringling Bros. Barnum & Bailey. It seemed to be the fashionable thing.

"Well, she'll probably wear some skimpy, glamorous outfit and be in the chorus," I guessed. I was a little annoyed with him for doubting my friend's abilities. "She's very talented, you know." Though if truth be told, Donna had never been much interested in physical activities of any kind except sexual adventures. But I was sure she'd learn quickly enough for the circus.

"What did Mr. Baker say?"

"Well, now YOU guess what. Mr. Baker is coming to see us. He wants to get a first-hand look at everything here, and I believe he really is concerned about the boats and we'll finally get the go-head to get them fixed."

"Well, thank the good Lord for that."

The news of Mr. Baker's impending arrival threw us all into a bit of a tizzy. For Peter and me, it was just the usual slight dither induced by the necessity of making a favorable impression on the boss, but Art and his wife tended to be paranoid about such matters. Art often seemed to think he was being spied upon. For all of us it meant we had to put everything in order. I was pleased to know the bigwigs cared enough to send the president himself and I was glad he would see first-hand how dilapidated our boat really was.

Peter and Art were conferring.

"Looks like you'd better take the *Audubon* and go out to Duck for the night," said Art. "That way, you can give Baker a first-hand report."

"Sounds like a good idea," Peter agreed. "I've been wanting to go out there and stay, anyway."

I was elated. I was ready to leave the Tookes' place. Even though Mrs. T and I had struck up a friendship, I would be glad to get away from dour old Art and Frieda Eifler. They were hard to be around for long periods, she with her heavy deafness and complaining, and Art always trying to be boss and telling us, or at least Peter, what to do. Out in the Gulf next to Duck Rock we'd finally be doing the job we came to do, and even though it was just for the night I felt excited. When we'd been to Duck Rock once or twice before, we'd stayed only long enough to check out the bird activity and see if the place had been disturbed by any of the local poachers. We had never stayed overnight.

The next day we cast off and started downstream heading once more to open water. The day, which had started out cold, had warmed up and was ending in a typically brilliant sunset.

As we neared Duck Rock, we could see the birds beginning to come in for the night, flying in long undulating lines, landing in the tree tops and settling out of sight. With no dock, our mooring was three large stakes tied together, stuck into the mud on the bottom of the shallow Gulf about a hundred yards from the key. I stood on the bow as Peter eased us closer to the stakes. Finally, I could grab hold and, working quickly, loop a rope around them to tie us up. I was becoming adept at roping and knotting and secured us without a problem. I left enough slack in the line to allow for the boat to lower in the receding tide. If there wasn't enough extra rope, either the stakes would be uprooted or we'd be hung up by the bow.

Once we were safely tied up, Peter turned off the motor and we climbed onto the top of the cabin to watch the birds coming in for the night. Peter was counting them for his report, noting numbers in his little book. They flew in from the Everglades savannahs off to the east, where they had been feeding all day. Since they hadn't started nesting yet they would spend only the night here and return in the morning to their feeding grounds. Hundreds of egrets, herons, ibises, and roseate spoonbills, were coming in, flying low, each with its own kind, alighting with a flurry amidst cackles, gurgling rattles, and squawks. Out of sight amongst the branches they could still be heard muttering and gargling as they settled down for the night. They were almost never completely silent so our nights were accompanied by a constant murmuring lullaby.

As the last of the purple light on the horizon faded to darkness, we reluctantly went below and lit the lamps. We had a few small electric lights, but we used our Coleman lanterns to conserve electricity. As I made supper and Peter wrote up his bird notes, the tide ebbed, leaving us to settle gently into the muddy Gulf bottom. It was so soft that the boat sank straight down, where it would stay until the morning tide floated us free again. I was thrilled by the romance of being alone on our boat in such an extraordinary place. It was the first time Peter and I had been by ourselves for weeks. It seemed special, almost illicit. I had fried the yellow jack I'd caught, and along with Mrs. Tooke's greens, it made a delicious supper. We sat in the lamplight and Peter raised his glass of beer to me, saying:

"Well, here's to us, hon. I'd say we're doing all right."

"Yes, here's to us," I toasted him back "What a place. I can't wait for Mum and Will and everyone to come visit and get to see it."

The water lapped gently outside, but the boat, resting on the bottom, was still. A full moon rose over the mangroves and a sense of peace enveloped the moment. I was infused with the rare and wondrous feeling of the essential rightness of things. The ordinary became illumined by the extraordinary and I was filled with an unquestioning acceptance and gratitude to be part of it, to be here, to be alive.

The moment passed, but a lingering peace remained with me as I finished the evening chores. Peter and I climbed contentedly into our narrow berths for the night. We made love by the light of the moon slanting down through the skylight, the sound of the of the birds mingling with the soft rippling of the water in that otherwise-silent vast place.

The next morning, we were up before dawn to watch the birds' spectacular departure. It was still half dark and the air was chilly. We took our steaming mugs of tea and again sat on the cabin top. All was hushed, expectant. Suddenly, as if at some secret signal, the birds erupted out of the canopy of trees with an incredible whirring and thrumming of wings and in a huge cloud began streaming away to their feeding grounds. On and on for many breathless minutes they kept pouring into the sky, dispersing in a long, thinning stream until finally they had all gone except for a few late-rising stragglers. And this, we knew, was just the beginning of the congregation. Later there would be even more thousands coming and going and nesting on this small islet. Why it had been home to such a huge population for so many decades was a mystery. Why of all the Ten Thousand Islands was this one chosen? No one seemed to know. Even though it had been shot up by poachers many times over the years, the birds still favored it for their breeding and nesting site.

After breakfast, as soon as the tide had risen enough to release us from our muddy resting place, we started back to the Chatham River, to the Tookes'. Peter was pleased with the bird count he would be able to report to our eminent boss, the high and mighty Mr. Baker.

Arriving at the dock, we'd hardly tied up before a seaplane, with its large ungainly pontoons, appeared and zoomed along the river flying low. It circled up over the Tookes' house before landing lightly on the surface of the water and taxied up to the dock. The Tookes and Eiflers had come out and we all stood gaping at this unexpected apparition, waiting to see who would emerge from the cockpit. Mr. Tooke guessed, though.

"It's that Mr. Baker, I'll be bound," he said. He was right. It was none other than Mr. Baker. I'd met him once briefly with Peter in his big New York office after Peter had been hired. I guess they had wanted to look me over. He was hearty and confident with that Ivy League assurance of his unquestioned right to his place in the world. He climbed up onto the dock, greeted us expansively, and told us to meet him with the *Audubon* in

Everglades in two days. He was here, he said, to get to the bottom of these equipment problems and clear them up once and for all. He also wanted to spend the night at Duck Rock and check things out for himself. He stayed about five minutes and then he and his pilot flew off again. We were duly impressed.

7

The next morning, we were up early to prepare for the trip into Everglades to meet Mr. Baker. Art came over from his boat and we sat around having coffee, talking about the condition of our boat, and what we needed to make clear to Mr. Baker. The boat was in need of a thorough renovation. Not only did she need a paint job inside and out, but the head, the shutters and the roof leaked, the engine needed an overhaul, and worst of all, those wretched empty tanks in the bilge (just waiting to blow us up) had to be removed. This would be a major undertaking. It meant we'd have to be out of the water and up on the ways for at least a couple of weeks.

"Now when Baker gets here, we got to make him understand you gotta go up to Naples. This here boatyard ain't worth a nickel." Art was in his role as senior warden advising the new boy.

Peter agreed. "Well, that's certainly true about Jackson's Ways. I've had the Ibis in there three times and the motor's still not fixed right, plus which they nearly dropped her off the cradle when they were copper-bottoming her."

Naples was a fishing village up north along the Tamiami Trail that catered to commercial as well as sports fishermen. They had more advanced facilities and, we hoped, more reliable mechanics.

"Why does he have to be persuaded?" I ventured the question. It seemed pretty obvious to me we would have to go there.

"Well, the society don't like to throw money around," Art replied. "In fact, you might say they's downright tightwads."

"But in the long run," remarked Peter, "surely it's to their advantage to keep the equipment in good order."

"Yer'd think so. But look at it. Old, falling apart. Don't make good sense." Art was about to get up on his high horse and go into one of his railings against the Audubon Society, which he both feared and needed as an employer.

But he was forestalled by Frieda's querulous German voice calling, "Art, Art, commonze, commonze!"

He took his departure, but not without a parting shot. "Reckon we'd better go into town after lunch. Give you time to clean up the boat a bit."

I started to bristle. Our boat was relatively shipshape compared to his messy old tub.

But I let it go—it wasn't worth getting annoyed with the silly old thing.

Mrs. Tooke had recently acquired a second-hand gasoline-powered Sears washing machine with an automatic mangle. It sat, vast and round, on stubby little legs on her front porch. Its noisy engine, sounding like a cross between chain saw and lawn mower, buzzed and chugged as the wash swirled round and round in its soapy stew. Since she had unconditionally invited Mrs. Eifler and me to use it any time, I felt comfortable about asking to do my accumulation of dirty jeans and tee shirts before we went into Everglades.

After drawing a bucketful of water from the well, I dumped it into a large galvanized tub which was raised high enough to light a fire under. Once you had started the fire it didn't take long for the water to heat up. Two people were needed to lift the wash tub and pour its contents into the washing machine. Then all you had to do was pile in the clothes and start up the motor. Of course, you had to do this all over again for rinsing.

While waiting for this marvel of modern technology to do its work, Mrs. Tooke came outside and we sat on the grass under the palms eating coconuts. She used an old machete to whack the green casing open and extract the hard, hairy brown nut from inside. Then she'd whack the nut open and we'd drink its thin, sweet milk before scooping out the succulent, white, meat and chewing to our hearts' content.

"So, you're going back over to Everglades," she said. "Art says you need a lotta work done, says you're goin' to Naples."

"Yes, I guess so," I answered. "What's Naples like?"

"Oh, it's bigger'n Everglades. Got more stuff. Got a movie-house, open all the time in winter. Iffen you like movies. Got a real laundry, too. Hamp, he keeps his boat up there most of the time. Likes it better 'n Everglades." Hamp, a fisherman, was the Tookes' son. We hadn't met him yet.

"I hear the beach is really special," I offered. "I love to swim. We used to go to the beach a lot back home."

Mrs. Tooke looked at me, "You sound a little homesick," she said. "Reckon you miss yer friends 'n' all."

"Well, there are a lot of new things to get used to," I admitted. "I'm a little lonesome for my friends now and then. I really like it here though," I hastened to assure her. As we all often are, the natives are protective about their place. "I really want them to come down here and visit us. I know they'd all love it, too."

The three dogs, never far away when food was handy, came sniffing hopefully closer and we threw morsels to them from time to time. They all loved coconuts, especially Berry, the old coon hound. He couldn't get enough. This feeding frenzy in turn alerted the chickens, who were pecking and scratching nearby to come over and join the party. They pecked closer and closer till they were practically pecking between our bare toes, which made me a little nervous. I hoped they could distinguish coconut from toes. Mrs. Tooke just laughed at me.

I was happy sitting barefoot on the grass in the warm sunshine, eating coconuts with dear, jolly Mrs. Tooke. It was so peaceful and unhurried, without a single twinge that there was something else that ought to be done. We ate at least four coconuts before the wash was finished so I could mangle it and hang it out to dry.

I wasn't really hungry for lunch after all those coconuts, but Peter, who'd been getting the boat ready all this time, was making sandwiches as I returned to the dock.

"Eat up, we have to leave," he said, anxious to get going.

"Isn't Art coming?"

"Yeah, he'll lead us through the passes, though I think I could probably do it myself by now."

"When are we coming back?" I was thinking about collecting the wash.

"In a day or two, I guess," I went up to say a brief goodbye to the Tookes, who came out of their house, and we all stood around the well.

Perched on the crumbling bricks, I idly brushed my fingers along the side. Suddenly I felt a sharp, jabbing sting on my finger. Snatching up my hand, I looked down and saw a small brownish scorpion scuttling away. Thunderation! I had been stung by a scorpion. As Peter and the Tookes crowded around me and inspected the growing red swelling on my finger, I waited anxiously, not knowing if I would pass out or stop breathing or what the symptoms would be. My little finger had been stung and it throbbed and tingled electrically much like a bee sting only worse. Mr. Tooke found the scorpion in a crevice in the bricks, and he was reassuring. He told me that most scorpion's stings aren't all that dangerous and even though there's a lot of fear and folklore around them, there's only one species in the United States whose bite could be serious and it's not found in Florida. As there didn't seem to be much to do about it and apparently it wasn't going to be fatal, I tried to ignore it. At the moment though, my finger was throbbing and it really hurt, much worse than any bee sting I'd ever had. I didn't say anything because I didn't want to seem like a wimp, but I wished I had an ice cube. It took a long time to stop hurting, and for days after, whenever I touched it, it sent off a strong electric shock up my arm. I promised myself, that from then on, I was going to pay more attention to where I put my hands and feet.

Casting off the boat lines, we started downriver on the trip to Everglade. We had good weather and made our way there without incident. The usual crowd of pelicans and cormorants were sitting on the pilings outside the Leighty's house, where we tied up.

We'd arrived on washday. Rosa called out hello and I went over and began helping her take the wash off the clothes line. In a few minutes we carried two baskets of delicious-smelling dried laundry into the house. Rosamaria and Ralph were at school, and the house was quiet and tidy. She offered me some coffee and we sat down in her sunny living room. It was full of colorful artifacts from Puerto Rico and some local Seminole fabrics and carvings.

"Where did you get your beautiful Seminole things?" I asked. "I think we passed two Seminoles up near Gopher Key a couple of weeks ago. Peter thought it might have been Billy Tiger and his wife."

"Yes," she said, in her charmingly accented voice, "the Indians here have such hard life. There is this woman, a deaconess, she is missionary here. She help the families in the villages. She has teach the womans to sew on little sewing machines so they can make more easily their clothing and also she helps them to sell it. You can visit the villages. They call them chickees."

"Oh, I'd love to do that sometime."

"Well, we could go tomorrow." Rosa was not one to let the grass grow under her feet. "Oh dear, I can't," I answered, and I told her about Mr. Baker's imminent visit. She was instantly curious, wanting to know all about him.

"He is important man, no?" she asked. "Has he the wife and children? He is living in New York City?" I explained as much as I could, but I didn't have the answers to most of her questions. All I could tell her was that he was an investment banker who was also an amateur ornithologist. He had been the Audubon executive director from 1934-1944, and then was promoted to president of the Audubon Society.

I also knew that Mr. Baker was an ardent conservationist and had helped fund research studies on two endangered species of birds, the California condor and the roseate spoonbill. These were landmark Audubon research reports, the first of many he'd done. Together with the current vice-president, Carl Bucheister, they had been initiating various public education programs to help raise awareness about the need for more and better conservation methods. Environmental considerations and management were almost unheard of in those days. Rachel Carson's groundbreaking book, "Silent Spring," was yet to be published, and most people were blissfully ignorant about the heavy damage we were all inflicting on our environment.

One of the programs Mr. Baker and Mr. Bucheister had started was over on the east coast of Florida, where they had made it possible for boatloads of people to venture into wilderness areas of the Everglades. In a letter from Mr. Baker not long ago, we'd been alerted that something similar was being considered for our area this summer. Trips out to Duck Rock, which would include evening suppers while watching the birds come in—I had mixed feeling about these plans. It sounded like a lot of work.

"You'd have to entertain all these tourists?" Rosa questioned.

I wasn't sure, but I hoped not. I was expecting Mr. Baker to clarify our many questions when he came. Meanwhile, there was work to be done to get the boat ready and have everything in order for this important visit. Reluctantly, I took leave of Rosa and went back to our boat.

Peter was sitting at the table working on some notes to give to Mr. Baker. He looked up with his broad smile as I came aboard.

"How's Rosa?" he enquired, but without waiting for an answer, he asked me to look at his notes and check his spelling. He was a good scientist but a poor speller. He had been keeping a detailed account of his observations of the bird populations and where they were to be found. He wanted to be able to take Mr. Baker to the best places for bird watching.

He had recently discovered the typewriter (a fever I predicted would pass in a week) and he was trying to type up his notes. It was an old Olivetti and I was used to it. Besides, I had taken typing one miserable year at business school when my guardians decided I had to learn to do something practical. I could type well enough, but I'd refused to learn shorthand because I never wanted to have to take a job doing it. But Peter was of the two-finger hunt-and peck-typist, and the mistakes in his notes were as much typos as poor spelling. I took pity on him and offered to type them up for him.

"But how will I ever learn if I don't do it myself?" he said.

"You can practice on something else," I told him. "These notes have to be ready by the time Mr. Baker gets here and you won't be able to finish them, and do all the other stuff we have to do, to get the boat set for his arrival." He agreed with obvious relief.

We spent the rest of the day cleaning and fixing, and by the end of it we both wanted to get off the boat altogether and go somewhere. Peter wanted to go get a beer, and I vetoed the drug store as being too dull.

"I know," he said. "Let's go up to the Alamar. It's supposed to have good hamburgers." "It's also supposed to be really rough." I said a bit skeptically.

In the old days, we'd heard, the Alamar Cafe had been a hangout for all sorts of nefarious characters, a really rough crowd of drunks and lawbreakers, poachers, plume-hunters, bootleggers, smugglers, and even some of Dutch Schultze's gangsters from Miami. Nowadays it was considerably tamer, although still rumored to be favored by a shady element.

"We probably should ask Art to come along," said Peter.

"Okay, if we have to." My response was lukewarm, Art could be a mood depressant at times.

Maybe he won't come, I thought hopefully. But when we asked him, he seemed eager to come. So, we drove up to the Loop, off the Tamiami Trail, found the place, and parked in front. It had a dilapidated air—there was a defunct neon sign "BEER HERE" and the screen door was tattered. Loud cowboy music vibrated over the parking area. As we got out of the car, two men came out—or rather, fell out the door, one staggering backwards pushed by the other, equally unsteady—arguing loudly. I was discouraged by this, but the argument didn't escalate and they both stumbled off to their pick-ups.

Inside it was smoky and dim and smelled strongly of booze and unwashed men. Still, it seemed quiet at the moment. Everyone looked at us when we came in and Art greeted one or two acquaintances, but no one else took much notice. We sat in a booth and I looked around the large room. A space had been left in the middle for a dance floor. I saw only one other female customer and no one was dancing. The juke box was so loud that conversation was hopeless, and we drank our beers and ate our hamburgers without talking. I wanted to dance, but I was afraid of being conspicuous. Just then, a noisy foursome banged through the door, and after a while began to dance. Now I would feel all right.

"Come on, Peter, I want to dance." I jumped up and went onto the floor. He followed me, and we managed a low-key jitterbug-honky-tonk combination. No one paid us any mind and there was plenty of room. Peter was an okay dancer, not inspired, but at least he would get out on the floor with me. And I did so love to dance, to get that exhilarating feeling of my whole body from toes on up moving without conscious thought, responding to impulses sparked by the music spiraling up through my being, feeling every particle of myself involved and connected to the whole incredible network of nerves, muscles, skin, and breath. For me, it was unsurpassed delight.

After about half an hour, we were thirsty again and went back to our booth. Art was talking to a skinny red-headed fellow he introduced only as "Red." He was young, perhaps our age, and he seemed less rough-and-ready than most of the men around. He had mild blue eyes and a way of ducking his head when he answered a question as if he were doubting his own answer. He told us he lived in Ochopee and crewed for different fishermen, sometimes with Hamp Tooke. He asked Peter if it would be okay to ask me to dance.

"That is," he ducked his head, "iffen she wants to." His smile was nice and his diffidence appealed to me, so we went out on the floor.

More people had come in and it was getting crowded. He held me rather gingerly and we twirled around the floor a few times in silence. He was concentrating with all his might. When the song ("I've got tears in my ears, from lying on my back, in my bed, while I cry over you") came to an end, we sat down again.

"Well, did he stomp yer toes?" Art smirked.

"Not at all." I was annoyed with Art. "We had a fine time." We all had one more beer and then decided to head home.

The next morning, Peter had a hangover and we got a rather late start. We were expecting Mr. Baker later in the day, but he surprised us and came early. The boat was shipshape, but we were still in our dirty work clothes looking like a couple of tramps. Not the impression we wanted to make. However, he was unfazed, and after giving us time to tidy up, he swept us off to lunch at the fanciest place in town, the venerable Rod and Gun Club.

8

Mr. Baker turned out to be as forceful and dynamic as his reputation predicted. A man in his early fifties, he was solid and robust, without appearing overweight. He sported a carefully tended mustache and his still-black hair was retreating from his high forehead, giving him an air of lofty intentions. There was something vaguely 19th century about his appearance. He reminded me of pictures of some of the early financial barons of that era, with his waistcoat and a fob watch on a chain draped across his ample front. He wheezed when he laughed (infrequently), showing neat, regular teeth. He wore a signet ring on his little finger which he twisted absently from time to time.

Lunch at the Rod & Gun club made a pleasant change for Peter and me. We had been eating all our meals on the boat or at the Tookes', except for once or twice at the hamburger joint up at Ochopee, so having lunch at the Rod and Gun club felt very "uptown." The club was actually well known throughout the state, having been built in the 1920s by Barron Collier. Scion of the powerful Collier family, he pretty much ran the state back then and their descendants were still influential in Florida politics. Over the years the club had been patronized by many of the rich and famous, including Ernest Hemingway, several presidents, and various movie stars. Decorated in a style to appeal to its huntin', shootin', fishin' type clientele, there were stuffed alligators, tarpon and even a black panther skin mounted on its paneled walls. Potted palms stood in the corners of the lobby and the dining area, and the bamboo tables were covered with white tablecloths. Over it all, three large ceiling fans rotated slowly.

Not many other patrons were present when we came in, and Mr. Baker chose a table by the huge window looking out on the Barron River as it made its way down to the Gulf. Across the river in the thick mangroves and swamp oaks we could see a heron drowsing on one leg and could hear the usual accompaniment of squawking gulls and terns.

"Now, what will you all have to drink?" Mr. Baker enquired expansively.

After some consultation, the men opted for martinis and I went for a daiquiri. Then we ordered up a three-course luncheon including onion soup, broiled local jack, and Key Lime pie for dessert. The chef was famous and we weren't disappointed.

"Are you finding your way around all right?" Mr. Baker wanted to know. "Art being helpful?"

We assured him all was well.

"How're you managing with the boats? I understand there've been some problems." Here was Peter's chance, and he took full advantage of the opening to run through the litany of complaints about the shortcomings of the equipment. Mr. Baker listened, nodding. "Well, yes. We'll see," he answered non-commitally. "It's true the boats are all pretty old, but they're seaworthy nevertheless, and I should think they've a few good years left in them."

Just you wait and see, I thought darkly. I wished we might have some bad weather while he was here—then he'd understand. Be careful what you wish for…

Meanwhile Mr. Baker was telling us how to deal with the locals.

"Gotta let 'em know you mean business," he advised, "but at the same time you need to be diplomatic about it. If they respect you, they're more likely to pay attention. But, you know"—he continued, now well into his second martini—"these people are abysmally ignorant and backward. You really have to deal with 'em like children."

This sounded like the old paternalistic line I'd heard so often about the "Negro problem" and I didn't like his attitude. "Well, we've made friends with some of the people here," I spoke up. "The Tookes are wonderful, and there're some people in town who've been very helpful and friendly. A lot of the folks here may not have a formal education, but they seem very generous and kindhearted." I was surprised at my temerity. Must be the rum, I thought.

"Well, yes. Good, good," Mr. Baker replied vaguely. "You seem to have made a good start, anyway. We've decided to give you a raise."

Peter and I shot a glance a each other. This was exciting.

"Yes," he announced, "I think we can now pay you fifty dollars a month." He made it sound like a princely sum, when it wasn't much, even in those days. Still, as Peter and I had said to each other more than once, we weren't in it for the money, and it was nice to know we were appreciated by the powers that be.

Mr. Baker then suggested we take a trip out to Duck Rock, as he wanted to count birds. After some discussion, it was decided we would go that very evening so he could watch the birds come in. As soon as we'd finished our pie and coffee, he gathered his gear together and we all went aboard the *Audubon*.

We cast off and started down the river. The weather, which until now had been fine, if a little windy, started to change. As we got under way and headed into the Gulf the wind picked up considerably, and as soon as we came out of the lee of the river mouth, we began to hit increasingly rough water. The boat started rolling and pitching and everything that wasn't secured began to slide around and fall to the deck.

Standing by Peter, who was at the wheel, Mr. Baker was hanging on to the dash rail, looking a little green around the gills. Suddenly he excused himself and went outside to sit on the roof of the cabin. Peter and I looked at each other. We were both feeling rather sick ourselves. Thunderation! Were we all going to lose that wonderful lunch we'd just had? I got us some lemons to suck, which had always been my own personal remedy for seasickness. We managed to hold on for what seemed an interminably long two hours, and I don't think I had ever been happier to see Duck Rock then when it finally came into view.

By the time we were tied to the stakes in the shelter of the key, the water became calmer and the wind was dying down. The sky was still dark with heavy, threatening clouds and the waves swelled and sank around us.

The wind was blowing small whitecaps on some of the waves and it couldn't have been a less propitious evening for bird viewing. It was such an extreme contrast to the first night Peter and I had come out here and tied up under the tranquil stars and watched the birds fly in. No one was very hungry, but I made a pretense of cooking up some supper, while Peter and Mr. Baker sat on the cabin roof and counted the birds as they came in for the night. Even in this weather it managed to be an amazing sight. As the sun slowly moved lower, its last rays shone suddenly from under the cloud cover, sending scarlet light across the water. It gleamed on the birds as they flew in—line after undulating line of herons, egrets, ibises, and even a few roseate spoonbills—circling over to the other side of the island.

We were all tired after our adventures and went to bed early, Peter and I to our hard little bunks and Mr. Baker to a makeshift bed on one of the camp cots used as settees in the main cabin. The boat continued rocking and rolling all night and none of us slept much. Far from being lulled to sleep, I felt as if I might be pitched out of my berth at any moment.

In the morning no one felt very well. The weather was still bad. A cold wind raking across the Gulf kept the water dark gray and roiled-up. The sun came up behind thick clouds which were moving swiftly from the east, presaging rain. We struggled gamely through breakfast, then watched the birds leave in their spectacular mass exodus from their mangrove sanctuary. Mr. Baker, looking a little the worse for wear, declared his wish to go to Buzzard Key, a mangrove islet a few miles to the south where Peter had described his discovery of many different species of birds.

The weather looked ever more threatening and we could see a squall approaching across the dark water of the Gulf. It filled the whole horizon with a thick gray wall of rain, seeming to connect the water to the heavy clouds above, kicking up whitecaps and blotting out our view of the keys farther out to the west. Mr. Baker wanted to go anyway, and he was not a man to be denied when he'd made up his mind. Peter tried to discourage the idea, but as Mr. Baker seemed determined, we reluctantly untied the lines and headed south.

Hardly had we come around the lee of Duck Rock, when the squall hit us. We tried to keep going, hoping to get through to the other side of it, but it was too big and too intense. I started to rush around putting up the wooden shutters over all the windows in the main cabin. The wind was blowing so hard, the rain was coming in almost horizontally around them, leaking through every possible crack and misfitting joint. The roof, too, which had recently begun to show signs of leaking, now began to drip in earnest. I was secretly glad of all this. Just as I had hoped, Mr. Baker would get to experience first hand the dilapidated condition of our boat.

He wanted to help putting up the shutters, but—as we had done before we learned the trick of it—he merely pinched his fingers and dropped things. Peter was wrestling the wheel, trying to keep us headed into the wind which seemed to be getting stronger. The waves were rolling heavily and bucking us up and down without mercy. Fortunately, we all seemed to have gained our sea legs and no one was seasick, we were all too busy coping. The last straw came when, with an almighty crash, the icebox fell over and lay face down on the deck right in front of the screen door, blocking our exit from the cabin.

It became obvious we were not going to get past this squall, and Peter announced we were going back. Turning the boat around in the midst of the terrific wind gave us a scary few minutes as we came broadside to it and it heeled us over, but the *Audubon*, despite her shortcomings, was a sturdy old tub. Once turned towards Everglades, we headed home with the wind and waves pushing us from behind, hurrying us onward. Damp, cold, and miserable, I was glad to be heading for the shelter of the river and our berth along the bank.

Once we were safely tied up, it took all three of us several minutes to right the icebox and it took me more time than that to repair the damage inside. However, nothing was broken except the eggs, which had made a great mess. Just as we had gotten settled, the weather, as it so often did, changed rapidly back to being fine and sunny, with dripping palms and sparkling grass the only reminder of the recent maelstrom. Mr. Baker retreated to his room at the Rod & Gun club to collect himself, but not before it had been decided that we would all go up to Naples that very afternoon, to talk to the people at the boatyard and find out how soon they could take the *Audubon* for refurbishing.

This was a very encouraging turn of events for Peter and me. I was happy that, beyond having the dangerous empty tanks in the bilge fixed, we were going to get new windows and a roof that didn't leak. It was with high hopes that we collected Mr. Baker a little later, and the three of us set forth up the Tamiami Trail to Naples.

Peter and I had been up there with Art a few times on boat business. I found it more appealing than Everglades, if only for the lovely beaches. Naples has since become a major tourist destination, and today it has block after block of condos and huge hotel complexes chock full of every imaginable luxury. But in the late '40s, there wasn't much there at all, only the big white beaches, a few streets lined with small homes, and of course, the boatyard. Small as the town was, it was still more of a "place" than Everglades, and was a regular destination for fishermen and boating enthusiasts.

The boatyard was a large, untidy sort of place. There were all kinds of boats tied up in the water and lying out in the dry dock, plus a couple suspended up on the ways. There was something disquieting to me about a beached boat, lying on its side, looking so helplessly out of its element. Several men in greasy overalls were working on a few of them. It was hard to see what they were actually doing, but saws were whining and there was a continuous clattering and banging going on. The sun shone on everyone and the pace seemed leisurely.

Mr. Baker found the foreman, a wiry, ginger-haired little Scotsman whose name was George, and arranged for the *Audubon* to be delivered into his hands within ten days. George swore once they started, they could finish it in two weeks. During that time, we'd be up on the ways, while they removed the tanks from the bilge, redid the deck, re-roofed the cabin, and remade the shutters. Two weeks on the ways. My heart sank. Had I known how long it was actually going to take, my heart would have been in my boots. Luckily for my peace of mind at that moment, I didn't.

It seemed to be taken for granted that Peter and I would continue to stay on the boat throughout the repairs. The explanation given was that we needed to be around to oversee the workers and keep up the pressure on them. The birds were beginning to arrive in ever greater numbers daily, making it even more important for us to be out at Duck Rock or at least in evidence there, as soon as possible, to discourage raids by the local sports. So, while I did believe it was all true about keeping an eye on the boat job, I also think, in the wisdom of hindsight, that the Audubon Society was saving money on us.

9

As soon as we got back to Everglades, Mr. Baker called a planning meeting aboard the Eifler's boat, the *Spoonbill*. The weather had turned hot, and the mosquitoes and no-see-ums were out in force. I got our bug repellent from the *Audubon* and we sprayed ourselves thoroughly before we started the meeting. No-see-ums can go through any screen and I didn't want to sit there itching all through the coming pow-wow.

Art and Frieda, Peter and I, and Mr. Baker crammed ourselves into the Spoonbill's stuffy cabin. The old dog sat panting in her corner and everyone seemed rather uncomfortable. I don't know why Mr. Baker wanted to meet on Art's boat. I think perhaps he wanted to make Art feel included. Art and the Missus had been getting rather touchy, and Art had been making negative insinuations to Peter about "the Society" and his feeling that, for some reason, they had it in for him. (He meant the Audubon Society of course, but at first, when I heard him, I thought he was referring to some paranoid invention of some shady non-existent organization out to get him.)

Mr. Baker spoke firmly on behalf of his agenda. "Now that the birds are beginning to return, it's of the utmost importance for at least one of you to be here at all times for the remainder of the summer."

Art looked discomfited and shifted in his seat. He scratched his head, then spoke up. "Well," says he, "the missus and I have to go to Tavenier to pay our property taxes and we was hopin' these here"—he gestured towards Peter and me—"would be able to drive us down there and back before the end of the month."

I tried not to look surprised. It was the first I'd heard of it. I looked at Peter, who gave an almost imperceptible shrug, meaning he hadn't heard of it either. We said nothing and let Mr. Baker handle it. He was unmoved and suggested they go on the bus. I could see this did not please Art, but without further discussion Mr. Baker went on to his next item.

"I'm leaving for New York the day after tomorrow," he informed us. "I'd like you, Peter and Chloe, to come to Miami with me tomorrow morning. We can purchase some of the items you need for the boat. It'll be a lot cheaper there, I can assure you. Your expenses will be paid, of course."

This sounded promising. A night in Miami, on the Society. Could be fun.

"Also, it will give you a chance to meet Charlie Brookfield, he heads up the local chapter in Miami and he's been leading tours into the Everglades. They've been very popular and we would like to implement something similar here."

The idea was to bring tourists out to Duck Rock, where they could watch the birds come in and then have a picnic supper aboard the boat before they went back to the mainland.

So, it seemed these trips might actually happen. My heart sank a bit. I wasn't at all sure I wanted to be invaded every weekend by boatloads of strangers. But after all, it was for a good cause, and who knew—perhaps we'd meet some interesting people.

All this time poor old Frieda had been sitting there not hearing much of anything. Now suddenly she began pressing iced tea on us. We accepted glasses of lukewarm, weak tea though no one really wanted any. The meeting was then adjourned, and I for one was grateful to get off that airless boat.

Mr. Baker retired to the Rod and Gun club, leaving Art, Peter and me standing on the riverbank.

"Phew, he doesn't waste much time, does he?" said Peter.

"That old so-and-so." Art was fuming. "What's he mean, 'Take the bus'? Does he have any idea how long that bus takes to get to Key West? No, and it's hotter 'n the hinges of hell. The Missus'll be broiled alive."

"Listen," said Peter, "don't worry about it. I'll drive you. Won't hurt to leave for a weekend this time of year. Just don't talk about it any more to Baker."

The next morning was hot again. The gulls across the river were sitting quietly on their pilings and an anhinga, its long snaky neck tucked up, observed us from the top of a mangrove. Mr. Baker emerged from his hotel after a quick breakfast and the three of us climbed into our little Ford, Peter and Mr. B in front and me in the back. As we set off along the Tamiami Trail, the day was brilliant and sunny with little traffic. The road was only a two-lane highway, running almost dead straight all eighty miles to Miami.

Running along one side was a small canal full of that scourge of the South, the ever-present swamp lilies. Beautiful but deadly, they filled up all available space, suffocating everything under the surface. Ducks paddling around amidst the white and yellow lilies were watching out for the alligators lurking, floating as still as death, with only their slitted eyes showing. Herons and egrets contrasted, breathtakingly white against the dark green trees and amidst the yellow grasses. Through the open windows of the car (no air conditioning in those days) the chorus of frogs was a continuous, joyous celebration of sound.

We stopped a couple of times so Peter and Mr. Baker could look at warblers in the thick vegetation lining the road. They got very excited about a black-whiskered vireo. I got out of the car as well, as it was too hot to stay in it. Not being much of a birder myself, I was content to poke around on the edge of the canal hoping to see an alligator up close. Peering into the tangle of cypresses, pines, and great oaks, I imagined all the animals hiding in their depths. Were there perhaps panthers still in there? Or wildcats? Certainly there were snakes—rattlers and cottonmouths. I decided I wouldn't want to be wandering around in there for any reason.

Within two hours we arrived in Miami. In 1946 Miami was a much smaller, quieter town than it is today. Side-by-side hotels along the water front were slightly shabby and run down. The Cuban presence was minor. The general tone was relaxed and easy-going. Still, it was definitely a city, and Peter and I had been in the boondocks for three months. It looked like the big time to us. Just to see sidewalks lined by shops, with people walking up and down looking prosperous and busy, was exciting.

Mr. Baker directed us to the Columbus Hotel, a comfortable, old-fashioned place with a rather grand lobby, which boasted marble floors and large marble pillars. There were even bellhops. Of course, it was completely segregated, as was everything then, including restaurants, bars, movies, public toilets, and drinking fountains. I never got used to the signs that were everywhere, No Coloreds, Whites Only. Every time I saw one, I felt guilty because I was white.

Our room faced the water, which was nice, but hardly a novelty for us. My main interests were the size and softness of the double bed and the amenities in the white-tiled bathroom. What luxury. Big bath towels, sample soaps and shampoo, and even hand lotion. Of all the shortcomings of living aboard the Audubon, the lack of a bathroom was the hardest for me. I longed to run a bath right then and lie in it till I wrinkled like a prune.

"I've time to take a bath before we meet Baker, haven't I?" I asked Peter.

"Well, if you don't take too long. He said to meet right after lunch, and he's got a shopping list a mile long. Why don't you take a shower, that might be faster?"

But I was from the old English tradition where everyone takes baths. Hardly any household had a proper shower and if there was one it was likely to be the hand-held, hose-with-a-nozzle arrangement, which was far from satisfactory. Peter didn't quite understand, but he saw it as one of my English idiosyncrasies and didn't really care anyway.

"How about this bed?" he said, lying on it and bouncing a little. "Come over here and feel it. It sure beats the hell out of the bunks."

Suspecting an ulterior motive in his invitation, I was tempted. Was there time for both a bath and a little amorous dalliance? I joined him on the bed. A bed—how wonderful, how could I ever have taken a bed for granted? This one was covered by a blue and white striped coverlet with crisp white sheets underneath—and room to spread out and roll around on its soft, receptive mattress. I decided there was time for both lovemaking and bathing if I took a shower. I could save my long soak till later. Peter had his arms around me.

"I want to take a quick shower, I'll be right back," I said, removing myself from his hug.

"I need one too," he replied, taking his clothes off. "I'm coming in." The shower was in the tub and there was plenty of room for two. We soaped each other up, a delicious turn-on, and we were still damp when we got back on the bed. It turned out we had plenty of time and we made the most of it.

We were dried and presentable when we met Mr. Baker down in the lobby to embark on the great shopping expedition. Except we didn't exactly go shopping with him—we trailed along behind him while he dickered and bargained and generally fussed about everything. We walked up and down several streets lined with white stucco, some with art deco fronts and fan-shaped windows or glass-brick facades. Most were in need of paint and repair. Bars were open doing a brisk business and we passed a couple of seedy burlesque houses displaying lurid posters of women in various stages of undress. It was all a far cry from the mighty towers that have since replaced them.

At last we found what we were looking for, the Marine Hardware Emporium, where you could buy everything you could ever want or need for your boat, be it a dinghy or a 100-foot yacht. It was the apex, the acme, the Taj Mahal, of marine hardware stores. It was a forerunner of the modern-day megastore like Wal-Mart or Home Depot except that it was specialized and much more upscale. Its wide glass storefront took up half a block. Over the entrance spread a stained-glass transom with golden sun rays slanting up from behind a splendid white-sailed yacht. Inside, the smell of rope and canvas and brass polish enveloped us. The parquet floor squeaked decorously beneath treading feet. Ceiling-to-floor shelves were crammed, albeit neatly, with ship's pipes, fittings, sails, ropes, paint, tools, anchors, buoys. Drawers opened to disclose nails, screws, hinges, brass fittings, nuts, bolts, and copper wire. Above our heads, canoes and dinghies hung from the ceiling, rope ladders dangled, netting draped, ships' lanterns lit dark corners, wading boots stood on shelves, and flags and pennants waved. Behind glass-topped counters alert clerks awaited our desires and answered questions.

Mr. Baker was the customer from Hell. It took three-quarters of an hour merely to buy the brass letters A U D U B O N to put on the stern. Then we had to get spare engine parts, paint, a new generator and fenders for the sides of the boat. He also enquired about a bottled-gas refrigerator, which sounded wonderful, but alas, they were not yet available since they were such a new invention. Undeterred, he announced he would write to the factory and order one for us. (It finally came months later, two weeks before we were to leave for good.) All of this shopping took up the rest of the afternoon and when we finally got back to the hotel, I just wanted to collapse and take that long soak. But we did have a lot of good loot for the boat.

We were expected to meet Mr. Baker for dinner, and Peter rousted me out of the bathtub a little later.

"Come on, hon. We've got to get going. Old Baker will be waiting for us."

"I hope this Charlie Brookfield will be a good guy," I mused as I dressed. "We're going to have to get along with him."

"Well, we'll see soon enough," Peter replied.

"I'm not sure I like the idea of these tours much," I remarked.

"Why not?" asked Peter, "I should think you'd like to meet some people." "Well, but they'll just be going away again. It won't be like making new friends or anything."

"It'll be a change of pace, though."

"Yeah, I know, but it'll also mean having to be sort of hostessing and making conversation and taking care of people. It could get to be a bit of a strain."

We met Mr. Baker in the hotel bar, and after a couple of drinks we went around the corner to what turned out to be a good Chinese place. We were joined there by Charlie Brookfield. He seemed a nice enough young man, with blond hair cut bristling short, bright blue eyes, and a just-ever-so-slightly camp manner. Later, when we got to know him better, we learned he was gay. He sometimes brought his partner along on the tours when they weren't full, which was unusually open for those days.

The tours were a part of the Audubon Society's laudable effort to educate the public about the essential need for conservation and preservation, an unfamiliar idea then. If people were exposed to "nature," the theory went, they would come to love it, and if they loved it, then there would no longer be any question about recognizing the need to preserve it. Over the decades the Audubon Society has done a great deal to promote this idea and still does.

Charlie's manner towards Mr. Baker was deferential, but he treated us as comrades-in-arms. "How's life aboard the old *Audubon?*" he asked Peter.

"We're having a great time." Peter told him. "I'm really amazed at all the birds. Got a new one for my life list this week: black-whiskered vireo."

With that, they were off on a bird discussion, comparisons of where was the best place to see what and when were the best times, all dear to a bird lover's heart. Mr. Baker chimed in with a few of his own observations and theories. I was by now used to being left out around birders and was content to drink my wine and think my own thoughts. When they finally noticed, Charlie politely asked me what I was interested in.

"I've always been involved in the theater," I answered, feeling slightly awkward. "I used to dance."

The phrase rang around in my head. Was it true? Was dance over for me? I would have to think about it later.

Meanwhile Charlie said, "Oh, if you like dance, Miami has a ballet company that's pretty good, and the Cubans come over and perform a few times during the season and they're terrific. We get some good theater from New York from time to time too."

I began to like him.

The men went back to their discussion and started on the whole National Park conundrum, and I tuned out again. The phrase, "I used to dance," kept coming back to me. It had just popped out of my mouth when I answered Charlie's question, and I began to wonder about its meaning in relation to my present life situation. Did I really believe dance was over for me?

All my life, from the tender age of two when I was in a kiddie class and we marched around the room to a tinkly upright piano, I had been dancing. I knew very early on I wanted to dance. Dancing was my outlet, my own expression, my way of interfacing with the world. It was the one thing I did really well. I was usually the best in a class. Teachers singled me out. I was considered talented, "had promise," "could have a career in dance." And I loved it, loved the flow of movement through my body in response to music. Loved the natural way my body seemed to respond to the rhythm. I would dance around the house, in the garden, at school, at the studio, wherever and whenever I could. People would watch me, but it wasn't the praise and attention that motivated me. It was the feeling that dancing inspired in me that was the important thing, and I was swept away by it. As a child I had been willing to go to great lengths in order to pursue dance.

In 1935, my father was ordered overseas with the Mediterranean Fleet aboard his aircraft carrier. My mother did not want to stay in London alone, so she decided to accompany my father to Malta. We children, my brother and I, were parked in boarding schools. Actually, I was given the choice of traveling with my parents, or living in a boarding school in London. I had been attending a professional ballet school daily for the past year and if I chose the boarding school, I would be able continue my training. Amazing as it is to me now, I chose to stay behind in London, in the boarding school. I was horribly homesick and cried every night, I was only ten and every day seemed a month, but I could keep dancing, and that meant everything to me. I was pretty miserable though, and I'm amazed that I never asked to be allowed to change my mind and join my parents in Malta.

Boarding school in England was then, and still is, almost a matter of course for children of middle and upper-class families. Boys in particular were sent off routinely, sometimes as young as six or seven years old. It was considered an essential part of their development and character-building. Looking back, and to my way of thinking now, it bordered on child abuse. In fact, in many of the schools there was actual abuse, both from bullying students, and more sadly, some of the teachers. Blessedly, there was nothing like that at my school though, which was quite small and relatively mild. I went to boarding school for five years. I would finish my classes and go off to dance school every day and twice on Saturdays, as I worked my way through the demanding curriculum of the Royal Academy of Ballet.

I became very good. I was always given the solo roles in our performances. I was a star. Somehow, it didn't go to my head, there was always the next stage, the next level to master. Then disaster struck. I grew. And grew. I grew taller than everyone else in my class. At the age of fourteen I had gained almost my full height of five feet, eight-and-a-half inches. If you add in the four or five inches you gain in height *en pointe*, I was taller than most of the men who would partner me. I was too tall for ballet. I was devastated. Suddenly, my intended career was in ruins. My teachers did not despair, however. They told me I could still dance in musical comedy. All I had to do was learn to sing and I could be another Gertrude Lawrence, or more currently, Gwen Verdon.

Then, before I had a chance to adjust to my change in fate, a much greater disaster struck the whole world. It was 1939 and World War II began. Everyone expected the Germans to start bombing London immediately, we had to get out. My mother, because of a more personal disaster, had returned to England. My parents were divorcing. My mother took my brother and me, and we fled to Weymouth, a town by the sea in Dorset, the place where I was born, as a safe haven. My training was over. My world had disintegrated. I did not resume dancing until after my daughter was born, many years later.

My attention came back to the dinner party, which was breaking up. Mr. Baker was leaving on the six o'clock train in the morning and we did not linger over our goodbyes. We invited Charlie to visit us on the boat any time, and then ascended to our rooms in the hotel's golden elevator cage. The next morning, we drove Mr. Baker to the station. The three of us stood a little self-consciously on the platform, as the redcap loaded the bags into the Pullman car. Mr. Baker shook our hands very solemnly and told us we were doing a good job. "We took a bit of a chance on you," he said, waggishly. "You're both very young and haven't had much experience, but I'm glad to see you're doing so well." Then he turned and sedately mounted the steps, gave us a wave, and disappeared into the train. Peter and I waved our goodbyes and headed back through the station.

I'd have liked to stay around awhile and explore the town, but we were supposed to be getting back to Everglades and our job. We did take the time to find a camera store and enquire about equipment and prices. We had some rather grandiose ideas about photographing birds. Peter wanted to get a gunstock mount and a fancy Leica. We would also need a light meter and filters and goodness knows what else—nothing was automatic in those days. The fact that we knew nothing about photography didn't deter us in the least. We were sure we'd soon be producing wonderful pictures rivaling those found in the National Geographic.

After our camera splurges, it was time to leave, and we sped back along the Tamiami Trail. Way up ahead we could see a spectacular storm approaching. Dark gray-blue clouds were coming toward us, fast. As they passed over the green countryside, the color beneath the clouds washed out and it all turned a strange, incandescent silver. Distant trees appeared pure white. Within a few minutes we were enveloped in black rain pounding furiously onto the windshield. The canal immediately transformed into an evil-looking ditch filled with dark, forbidding water. Then as quickly as we had run into it, we were out again and into the sunshine. The surrounding country returning to its normally sunny aspect. Looking back, we could see the heavy blue-black clouds, their shadows sliding across the land, darkening it as they went, dramatically changing the landscape and then moving on, leaving behind all it had touched brightly sparkling in the sun.

As we neared the village of Ochopee, Peter suddenly braked, pulled over, and leapt from the car. He had seen a snake slithering across the road and had decided to try and collect it. It was a pigmy rattlesnake, a smallish brown snake with distinctive yellow markings. Peter, as any good naturalist would, always carried collecting jars in the car. Grabbing up a stick from beside the road, he managed to push the snake into one of the jars. I was terrified. It was small but nevertheless deadly. Peter, as in all such matters, was calm and competent. He'd learned well from his mentor, his famous Uncle Will Helmuth. Later, Peter chloroformed the snake and pickled it in alcohol. In those days, I didn't mind so much about collecting and killing creatures. Our attitude at the time was that it was all about science and you simply didn't question it. Now, I don't believe I'd be able to tolerate it.

Arriving in Everglades, we unloaded our new equipment. Art came over to check everything out, and he was surprisingly approving.

"Well, old Baker did all right by you," he grunted. "Let's get some of this stuff working."

He and Peter lost no time fixing the recalcitrant outboard motor and installing the generator in the *White Ibis*. I busied myself figuring out how to hang the used-tire fenders over the side of the boat to protect the boat from damage while it was tied up and bumping into the dock. It was nearly dark by the time we got everything done.

10

Tap. Tap. Tap. I was dreaming of a woodpecker tapping on our roof, a giant black-and-white-striped pileated woodpecker, his iron bill drilling a hole over the bunks. I awoke with a start. No, tap, tap—it was coming from the stern well door. Looking out over the galley stairs, I saw Rosamaria peering in through the screen door, her smile as wide and even more toothless than last time, her braids neatly hanging down her back.

"Hi," she called, "are you up yet?"

"Oh, sure, honey. Come on in. What's up?" I yawned.

Hearing voices, Peter rolled out of his bunk. "God, it's late, I'm supposed to help Art before we go back to Duck." It was the morning after our Miami jaunt and we were both a little off-kilter.

"Light the stove, would you, hon?" I asked him. I still hated the process of firing up the wretched thing.

I put the kettle on for tea. Rosamaria was playing with our two pet chameleons, Freud and Jung, in their makeshift herbarium—not that chameleons could be said to play exactly, but she liked to move her hands in front of them and make their eyes go in separate directions simultaneously.

"Have you had breakfast?" I asked her.

"Oh yes, thanks," she replied. "Can I feed the chameleons?" Usually we had to catch flies for them, but sometimes they'd eat a bit of banana.

"Here, try this." I handed her one. I had a big supply I'd brought from Mrs. Tooke's garden along with eggs, avocados and papayas.

After breakfast, Peter went off to help Art take the motor out of his old inboard, to see if they could rehabilitate it. I walked Rosamaria back to her house. The day was already warming up and the mud smell from the river rose around us. A boatload of scruffy-looking men chugged upstream. I guessed they were from Chokoloskee, coming in for a round of boozing. Their aspect sent a chill through me. I thought of them as "the enemy," I couldn't help it. They were the potential poachers, the erstwhile plume-hunters that we had been sent to guard against. I felt such a huge gulf separating us. Could such a distance ever be crossed? How did you go about changing anyone's views about their world, their assumed "rights," their entrenched habits?

As Rosamaria and I went into the house, Rosa came to greet us. I gave her the picture frame I'd bought her when we were in Miami. She was delighted.

"Oh, you shouldn't spend your money on me," she cried.

"Well, you've helped me out a lot," I said. I wanted her to understand how much I appreciated her kindness. "Well, we were there, just walking around in Miami shopping and there were so many fun places to look, it was fun." And I told her about our trip with Mr. Baker.

"Oh, Miami is such a big place. We go sometimes, I wish we could go more. Is very expensive," she added a little wistfully.

"I know," I agreed. "But, if you look around a bit, you can still find bargains."

While we were talking, I mentioned my plan of going to Sarasota to visit Donna and the circus. I wanted to know what she thought about this idea and how to get Peter on board with it. I was worried he might not feel comfortable about going away again so soon, leaving Duck Rock unprotected for several more days. Especially after Mr. Baker's pronunciamento, that we had to "stick close."

"You have friend in the circus?" exclaimed Rosa. "How exciting, what does she do?"

"Well, I don't know exactly, I think she's going to be one of the chorus girls. She's only doing it for a couple of months in the winter, just for the fun of it."

We discussed my misgivings about Peter, and then I rehearsed with her a little speech I was going to say, to try to persuade him to go. "Oh, hon," I would say, "we could just go up for the weekend. It wouldn't hurt anything. The nesting pairs haven't even come to Duck yet." Then, I'd tell him I'd seen the Chokoloskee people coming into town, probably to get drunk and lie about for a few days, so we wouldn't have to worry about them for awhile. I was really hoping I could persuade him.

Rosa, of course, encouraged me. She was always in favor of having fun. When Peter came back from helping Art, all greasy and dirty, Rosa said he could have a shower at her house, hoping it would help soften him up.

"Great," he grinned. "I really need it," he added this rather unnecessarily. "But afterwards, we've really got to get going back out to Duck."

Actually, this suited my plans. My hope was we could go back out for a few days, then, we could leave the big boat out at Duck Rock, and ride the smaller boat, *White Ibis,* into town, and then just keep on going to Sarasota for the weekend. The perfect plan. On the way out to Duck Rock I broached the idea to Peter.

"Well, for starters, we couldn't leave the big boat out there for three days unattended," he said, squelching my idea. "What would happen if a squall blew up?"

I hadn't thought of that. "Well, how about staying out here the rest of this week and then taking her back in to Everglades? We could ask Art to cover for us while we're gone?"

We went back and forth. I knew Peter really wanted to go, but he was being super-conscientious. Finally, after much pleading, he let me talk him into it.

A few days later, early in the morning, we left Duck Rock and got to Everglades in time for a mid-morning start on our five-hour drive up the Tamiami Trail to Sarasota. This was high season for tourists, so we were taking a chance going without a hotel reservation, but we just figured that if worse came to worse, we could always sleep on Donna's floor, so off we went.

In those days, Sarasota was a quaint place, sleepy and colonial. The circus had a permanent between-seasons home there and rehearsed under an enormous big top pitched on their grounds. We drove around and found a room at the Hotel Watrous. It was old-fashioned and expensive, $15 for a double room but what the hell, we were on vacation and it was better than the floor. Many of the circus performers, the lower ranks anyway, were staying at another old hotel not far from ours, the De Soto. Higher on the ritzy scale, it boasted ceiling fans in the lobby and a huge mahogany check-in desk. In the coffee shop, large autographed photos of past performers covered the walls—lion tamers and clowns, aerialists, and gaudily decorated horses. We took the elevator, with its folding see-through gates, up to the third floor where Donna and her roommate were staying.

My dear old friend, it was so great to see her. We fell on each other, hugging and exclaiming, delighted to be reunited. Donna was always so glamorous and theatrical. She looked a little like Tallulah Bankhead, an old-time movie vamp with a wonderful husky voice. She had the same deep-set bedroom eyes, a wide mouth, and a voluptuous figure that kept threatening to run to fat. But she had lost weight since I'd last seen her and she looked trim and in shape. Must be all the dance and exercise she's getting in rehearsal, I thought.

Peter gave her a great bear hug. He had known her almost as long as I had from the days that now seemed so long ago. Donna and I had lived together in an apartment off Central Park West while we made the casting rounds. Peter and I had just started "going together," whatever that meant at the time. We were more like sweethearts, really, and very innocent. We were only eighteen, after all. Peter, usually his brothers, and assorted friends would come to the city for weekend partying. Peter came from Andover, where he was in school, and the others came from East Hampton. With everyone camping on our floor, we had a lot of fun and some wonderful parties that often resulted in stupendous hangovers.

Besides having theatrical ambitions, Donna was very political. She was fiercely liberal, as for that matter, we all were at the time, but Donna went us one better and joined the Communist Party. In those innocent (or ignorant) days right after the war, Russia was still seen as our heroic ally. We didn't yet know the horrors Stalin was wreaking. Even so, to my mind, joining the Communist party was a bit extreme, and I had been concerned.

We needn't have worried. Donna's membership came to an abrupt end about six months later when she was kicked out. At some sort of Party shindig, she declined to dance with a young black man and was accused of being racist. This was patently absurd since, at the time, she was involved in a wild affair with a popular black folksinger.

As she explained to us later, "I didn't want to dance with him because he was drunk and disgusting. I don't care what color he is, I'm not dancing with a drunk jerk. Besides, he was a lousy dancer." And so, Donna's career as a card-carrying Communist was over.

Out of all the fifty-odd dancers and showgirls in the circus cast, she had luckily managed to find a very nice roommate, Judy. We took to her instantly. She was also from the East Coast and had an artist husband back in New York.

Donna and Judy had been rehearsing most of the day. "Wait till you see what we have to do up on the ropes," Donna told us. "I'm amazed at myself. You know me, not exactly the athletic type. I would never have believed I could do it." She was justifiably pleased with herself.

They changed out of their working clothes and Donna said, "Let's go out, I want to show you the M'toto Room. It's a famous place around here and all the circus people go there. We can dance, too—they have a pretty good band."

We'd parked our little blue Ford in front, and, as it was rainy and windy, we drove the short distance to the grand Ringling Hotel.

"You won't believe the decor in here," Donna said as we walked in. "It's incredibly kitsch, fake bamboo and jungle murals, but it's fun."

We spent the evening drinking, eating, and dancing, in that order, and we never stopped talking the whole time. There was so much to catch up on, all our friends and relatives. Who was doing what, where, and with whom? We talked on and on about everyone we knew, including our acting friends at Yale and our New York painter friends, like Robert Motherwell, who was on the verge of becoming famous. He and his beautiful wife, Maria, had befriended my mother, and she was staying with them in their cottage in East Hampton. Bob was building a house on a sandy lot on the edge of town, designed by renowned French architect,

Pierre Chareau. He and his wife had escaped from occupied France during World War II. The house was half underground, topped by a Quonset hut. Tres moderne. Although I'd only been away from New York for three months, it seemed ages longer and I was overcome with nostalgia for all the familiar people and places I was missing. I couldn't help but feel that our life in the everglades seemed sorely lacking in intellectual stimulation.

Just as I was about to feel sorry for myself, Donna said, "Your letters are marvelous, but what's it really like? I can't wait to see your boat."

"It's not too comfortable…" I started.

Peter would have none of it. "It's great," he said. "You'll love it. You and Judy can sleep up in the screened cabin. We'll take you for rides in the smaller boats and show you some absolutely amazing places. It's really an adventure out there." He went on, "And there are some people you simply have to meet. There's an old fisherman and his wife, the Tookes, who have been so kind and welcoming to us, they live on a shell mound in the middle of nowhere. They're quite the characters, you'd never meet anyone like them in the city."

"Well, there's no question, you're doing something incredibly important," Donna said. "I think it's just terrific."

I suddenly felt much better.

The next morning, the weather was still nasty, wet and chilly. A trifle hung-over, we dragged ourselves out of bed and went to see the circus and Donna in rehearsal. The huge big top seemed a madhouse, from the myriad ropes, swings, trapezes, and nets hanging down from the dim recesses sixty feet above us, all the way to the sawdust floor, which was covered with props and clutter of every imaginable sort, it was an overwhelming sight. People in various practice outfits, leotards, jumpsuits and overalls were milling around, waiting for their turn in the ring. Music blared forth from speakers, and the choreographer, the rope coach, and the show's director stood on a platform yelling through mikes.

Judy was in the number they were currently rehearsing. Peter and I sat on wooden bleachers and watched while the girls rushed around doing what seemed to be a semblance of a cancan. They wore full, frilly skirts which they were waving and shaking as they ran helter-skelter around in the huge space. They varied greatly in their dance skills and experience. Meeting some of the dancers later, I found they were an odd assortment indeed, from prim, technique obsessed ballerinas, to a charming French woman from the Follies Bergere. I wondered how I would have managed if I had joined up. The dance part looked easy enough, and I thought I was as good or better than most of them, but the rest of the life in the circus didn't seem too appealing. I also wondered what effect being off with the circus would have on one's career, assuming one was trying to have one? A person might miss an extraordinary opportunity in New York while swinging from the ropes in Florida.

While the dance practice was going on, Donna was up on the ropes practicing the aerial routine. I was very proud of her, hanging upside-down by one ankle from a loop in the rope and being twirled around by the rope-handler on the floor. Eventually this was to be performed thirty feet up in the air, but they learned everything much closer to the ground, at a safer level, and then, were gradually moved higher as they became more skilled. They still had a month to go so they were now only about fifteen feet up. Even at fifteen feet, we were duly impressed.

Over lunch, which was greasy hamburgers from the appropriately named Grease Top, an on-site diner for the cast and crew, Donna told us about the odd life of the circus performer. For instance, there was a strict hierarchy. The aerialists, trapeze artists, and tightrope walkers such as the Flying Wallendas were at the very top of the circus company pecking order. They were like circus royalty. Animal acts figured somewhere in the middle, and the clowns were in a class by themselves, special, but somewhat lowly.

Donna did not think the elephants were treated very well. "Most of the handlers are insensitive clods," she said. "They yell at them and hit them on the trunk for no good reason, and they use their hooks much too hard. I hate some of them. And the elephants are really good and so smart." She told us a sad, but funny story about one of the prop-men. He was supposed to keep a bucket of water next to his wagon where the elephants could slurp up a trunkful in passing on their way to the ring. "Well," she said, "this guy was a lazy slob and he couldn't be bothered to keep refilling the bucket, so he moved it out of reach and the elephants had to go thirsty on their walkaround. But then he got careless and a couple of days later he left the bucket out front again, and the first elephant who came by sucked up a trunkful and sprayed it all over the guy."

"Served him right," added Judy with her sly grin. They both began to bemoan the weather. "I swear," Judy was complaining, "if I have to sit on wet mud on Bessie's neck again, I'm going on strike." The elephants all had names, of course. Judy rode Bessie and Donna's was Eve. It seemed the elephants liked mud, and in rainy weather they would snurf it up and spray it all over their backs.

Even when they are well treated, there's something very demeaning about keeping a wild animal in captivity for entertainment. Nowadays many protests have made the practice less acceptable, and hopefully, despite its long-standing tradition, elephant acts are on their way out.

Actually, all these elephants had to do was parade around the ring, the handlers did most of the work. At a signal, the elephants knelt down on their front knees, a very cumbersome process, then the dancer stepped onto one of the folded front legs and up onto the creature's neck, swinging one leg over to ride astride the very wide neck. At another signal, the elephant stood back up with a huge lurch. This was the hardest part, explained Donna. You really had to hang on for dear life or be rocked off your perch. It was impossible to cling with your knees as you would on a horse, as their necks were too wide. Another unpleasant aspect of elephant riding was that there were no saddles of any kind and their rough skin scraped the inside of the rider's thighs, making them uncomfortably sore. After the girls had climbed on and off several times and ridden around the ring, the rehearsal was over.

It had been a strenuous day for Donna and Judy and I was sure they would just want to go to bed, but after a short rest, they were all ready to go out on the town again. They had the day off on Sunday, so we felt free to stay up and party on into the night, which we did. Our visit felt all too brief. I felt like we'd had just enough time to pick up the threads of our friendship and then it was time to go. On Sunday evening, with promises from Judy and Donna to come and visit us on the boat, we sadly said goodbye. The visit made me realize just how much I missed my friends and my life in New York. On the other hand, I also realized that our life here was temporary. Our time in the Everglades held great opportunity for both growth and discovery. We would get home soon enough.

The weather had been bad all weekend and now, driving back to Everglades, Peter began worrying about the boats. Perhaps he hadn't secured them properly, perhaps he hadn't left enough slack for high tides.

"But Art was going to be around, wasn't he?" I asked. I was sure he would have taken care of anything if there was a threat.

It was past midnight by the time we arrived at our berth in Everglades. But where was the boat? Our berth was empty. What had happened? We were frantic. There was a light showing at the Leightys' house and we went to their door. Ralph answered our knock and said he didn't know anything, but he had seen Art in town yesterday. Perhaps he'd moved the boat for some reason.

"We had really bad weather over the weekend. Maybe something happened to it. You can sleep here if you can't find it," he added. We thanked him, but although his words held some comfort, we were still very upset and worried.

Peter said, "Well, maybe Art took the boats to a different berth for some reason."

We started walking up the river looking for our boat. Although it was dark, the sky was clear and the moon shone down on the water, reflecting in the ripples of the current. Everything was silent and few lights shone anywhere. It being Sunday night, everyone was home in bed except for us, and we seemed to have lost our beds.

Finally, we came upon the *Audubon*, together with the small boats, tied to a piling about half a mile from where we'd started. What a relief! Thankfully we climbed aboard. All seemed to be well. The deck was dry, but every object we picked up in the upper cabin had a ring of water under it and the cot was soaking. The rain must have swept through the whole cabin. Luckily, the hatch above the bunks had been closed, or we'd have had wet bunks too. We still didn't know why Art had moved our boats, but we'd find out soon enough.

11

"Ah heard this real bad weather report, y' see. Said we were gonna get winds up over sixty-five miles per hour." Art was explaining why he'd moved our boats. "Yup, and they said we's gonna have a real high tide to boot. Upriver, they's less water action. Figured you'd be safer, anyway."

He'd driven in from the Tookes', moved the boats and gone back out again. He was pretty smug about it. He seemed to think he had "one-upped" Peter and that somehow now he had some kind of moral advantage.

"Well, thanks a lot, Art. That was good of you, no damage here, anyway. Everything okay at Duck Rock?" Peter asked.

"Oh yeah, we had some high water, but the winds never did get nowhere near to sixty-five. Tookes' dock got swamped, but that happens all the time."

We were sitting around in our cabin, having coffee. Art had come in to meet us. Privately, Peter thought there had really been no need to move the boats and Art had overreacted. But still, better to be safe then sorry, especially with boats and bad weather.

It was now less than two weeks before the boat was to be put up on the ways for the much-anticipated repairs and renovations. So, after stocking up on groceries, filling the water tanks, and getting gas, we unhitched the boat and chugged out to Duck Rock for a final stint before we had to go to Naples. I was looking forward to some time out on the water. I was still in the thrall of the incredible landscape with its mysterious beauty. When we were in among the keys, I felt both intoxicated by the lushness and intimidated by its secrets, I doubted I would ever lose my fascination for that aspect of the life here.

We got to Duck Rock and tied up the boat around noon. All seemed quiet in the mild sunshine. Duck Rock was at peace. A few cormorants were standing on the rocks at the edge, one with wings outspread to dry in the warmth of the sun. A Frigate bird flew sentinel overhead and a fish hawk sat at the top of one of the mangroves.

"Let's go see the Tookes," I suggested. I missed Mrs. Tooke and the comforts of her kitchen.

"Okay," said Peter. "First I want to go around the island and double check no one's been out here bothering it."

As we circled our special key in the outboard, the tide was up above the roots so we could get in close. Peering into the interior dimness I was struck once more by the primeval aspect of the mangroves. The murky water lapping around their roots, the small fish darting in and out amongst them, the pungent smell of the fertile brown mud wafting up so strongly all around us. Surely, I thought, this is the sort of place, with its rich mixture of fecund life-support systems, where life must have begun so many millennia ago. We surprised a cottonmouth and watched as it dropped off a low branch and swam away. Peter wanted to pursue and capture it, but fortunately he didn't have a collecting jar and the snake disappeared into the tangle of the roots. I shuddered. What if one were to fall on you? In general, I was not afraid of snakes, except when they were poisonous or threatening me, but there's something especially sinister about water moccasins with their wide white mouths and very poisonous bite.

I was at the tiller so that Peter could concentrate on bird watching. The osprey suddenly dove out of his treetop to grab an unsuspecting fish. Early migrants had begun to arrive and we saw a western palm warbler and a small flock of yellowthroats. Peter happily added them to his quickly growing list.

"Well, howdy, strangers," Mrs. Tooke welcomed us as we walked up the shell-strewn path to her door. "Come in and have some coffee."

We sat smoking and chatting. Mrs. Tooke seemed glad of the company. Her friendly open-heartedness let me think that she really had come to enjoy our visits, despite our "strange city ways."

Wanting to be accepted by the Tookes, this thought made me happy.

After a few minutes of chatting, we heard Mr. Tooke clumping across the porch in his big boots. "Got a bird for you," he said to1 Peter. "A new one on me. Ain't seen one like it afore." Peter was instantly interested.

Mr. Tooke did his best to describe it. "Pretty little thing. I didn't get a real good look. It was kinda yellow and speckled and had a reddish top to its head."

"Sounds like some kind of warbler," said Peter. "Maybe a yellow palm warbler. Had a reddish cap? Where'd you spot it?"

"Out in the back here,"

"Let's go look," said Peter, and off they went.

I told Mrs. Tooke about Mr. Baker and our trip to Miami. I told her about going to see Donna at the circus. She was immensely curious and wanted to hear all about it. Then, Mrs. Tooke wanted to tell me about Art moving the boats.

"Art got himself into a real swivet about your boats and the weather report," she told me. "Oh, he was fussin' up and down. Said he'd have to go into Everglades so's yer boat wouldn't get damaged. Bit of a mountain out of a molehill, if you ask me," concluded the redoubtable Mrs. Tooke. I tended to agree.

After a while Peter and Mr. Tooke came back. They had seen the elusive little bird, and it turned out, that it was a yellow palm warbler, just as Peter had predicted. "They are lovely little birds," Peter said to Mr. Tooke. "Good for you for spotting it. You've got a good eye."

We ended up staying for dinner, and then, loaded down with eggs, papayas, and coconuts, we had to say goodbye again, as we weren't going to see them for a few weeks. We drove back to the big boat in the dark, something that always made me a bit nervous. But tonight, the moon was full, reflecting on the water and shimmering in our rippling wake. By the time we got back to the *Audubon*, all the birds were back in for the night.

As we approached, we could hear their guttural gurglings and chucklings as they settled down onto their roosts.

I was tired from our long day and thought the birds had the right idea, so, climbing aboard, we turned in early.

For the next few days it rained. The boat rocked and rolled and we had to keep the shutters up constantly. When the wind blew the rain against them, they leaked and I spent a lot of time mopping. I also spent a lot of time in bed reading. I had ploughed through most of Proust and now I was determined to finish the final chapters of "The Past Recaptured." Peter worked on his notes and smoked restlessly. Luckily, the sun returned in time to keep us from going completely stir-crazy.

On our last evening before we were scheduled to go to Naples, we sat up on top of the cabin to watch the birds. Some of the egrets were beginning to develop their display plumage with all the filmy, showy feathers and plumes that made them so desirable to the feather merchants.

"They'll be pairing up and nesting before long. I hate to be leaving right now," Peter said regretfully.

"Well, let's hope it won't be for too long." I tried to sound encouraging. I didn't want to be stuck up on those ways for too long, either. I was actually rather dreading the whole operation. It sounded inconvenient and uncomfortable to say the least.

As we cruised back to Everglades the next morning, the day warmed up considerably. I decided to take a bath and wash my hair so that I would arrive in town looking presentable at least. I was standing on the stern where I could pour water over my head, splashing freely. The water ran over my bare skin and I closed my eyes as it trickled down my face. Suddenly Peter gave a yell.

"Chloe, get inside, there's a boat coming."

Before I could move, a small fishing boat appeared from behind, overtaking us. I scuttled in and wrapped a towel around me. Oh, hell, I thought, you can't even get naked around here without some stranger appearing and spoiling it all.

We stayed overnight in Everglades. The next day Art came in to help us get the *Audubon* to Naples. He drove the boat because Peter wasn't experienced enough yet to navigate the unfamiliar channels up the coast. When we came up in the car later, we found the boat moored in Naples Bay, close to the ways where she could be easily reached by the crane that would lift us out. It was midday and the boat yard was slowed down even more from its usual leisurely pace as people wandered off for lunch break. We had already met the foreman, Mr. Greathouse, who came over to us now and said the team was almost ready to hoist the Audubon up onto the cradle.

Two beefy young men appeared with coils of ropes over their shoulders. One of them climbed into the cabin of the huge crane, close to the water's edge and started up the motor. A sling was lowered just behind our boat and Peter very slowly reversed until he had positioned the boat over the sling. He climbed off and I held my breath as inch by inch the old *Audubon* was winched up out of the water, dripping slime and seaweed. Then she was slowly, slowly swung over to the waiting cradle and lowered to rest in its wooden arms.

Once it was safely ensconced, our two workmen (George, the skinny one, and Junior, younger and jollier) constructed a scaffold around the boat with a ladder for climbing on and off. By nightfall there we were, six feet off the ground, in the middle of a boatyard. I climbed up the shaky little ladder rather apprehensively and scrambled aboard. I fully expected the boat to rock, or even tip over. Being up in the air took some getting used to. We had been told we were quite safe to move about, sleep in the cabin, cook and wash, but we were forbidden to use the head and were thus condemned to use the filthy, smelly, inadequate toilet in the boatyard. I spent most of our first day with a bottle of Lysol and another of Clorox. I scrubbed and cleaned until that small, dark closet stopped smelling so awful. Then, I went and found George, and asked him to please fix the door. I was the only woman in the place and the least they could do was provide a toilet that closed and locked. The door was quickly repaired. Conducting our lives so publicly, we were like a forerunner of "reality TV." We generated a lot of curiosity. I suppose human beings can't help being curious about each other's hidden lives. A lighted, uncurtained window is an invitation almost impossible to resist; hints of the lives exposed appeal to the voyeur in all of us. However, I didn't appreciate being exposed in that way, so my natural sense of privacy felt continually violated. Our sleeping quarters were below decks, with only the small portholes and the glass hatch above for openings, so no one could "accidently" peer in, but up on the main cabin deck only the screens were between us and anyone who glanced over. Even though we were perched up in the air, we were still highly visible as we went about our daily routines.

I felt very self-conscious about the way the men looked at me. I quickly learned not to go up and down the ladder in short shorts or a skirt. Every time I went to the horrible toilet, I ran the gauntlet of the stares of a dozen workmen. I don't think they meant to be rude—it was just such an anomaly to have a woman among them, and a young pretty one at that—but even friendly stares can be uncomfortable. As the repairs got going, George and Junior were on the boat a lot of the time too, and I often found myself hiding out in the sleeping cabin, reading or writing, while they banged and hammered away.

The first thing they did was rip the roof off, but then they went away and left us for four days. There was a hot spell and I had to wear a hat even in the galley. The mosquitoes and sand flies were merciless and we were at their mercy. We sprayed DDT around liberally, not knowing at that time how lethal the stuff was, but at least it worked and kept the insects somewhat at bay. The excuse we were handed, quite unapologetically, for the inaction on the roof, was that they didn't have the right materials yet. So why, I thought to myself, did they take the roof off so prematurely? I didn't have the nerve at that point to say it to anyone. I decided to give them the benefit of the doubt, they had expected a shipment that hadn't arrived, fine. Little did we know that this was just a foretaste of what was to come. Day after day the job dragged on due to numerous and various excuses. I've since come to the conclusion that all repairs, renovations, and remodels always take longer than predicted. Why this should be I don't understand, but it seems to be a law of nature, and we were suffering for it.

Being so uncomfortable aboard the boat, we stayed off as much as we could. Nearby the boatyard was a pristine white sand beach, lapped by aquamarine waves and covered with an amazing array of shells. We spent a lot of our time consoling ourselves there—swimming, picnicking, collecting shells, or just lying under an umbrella that we'd acquired from the used furniture shop in Naples. Peter was getting terribly frustrated over not being able to check out the bird migration around Everglades and Duck Rock. It was now nearly the end of March and the spring migration would soon be in full swing.

One early morning, up on the cradle, we awoke to yet another scorching, cloudless day. The workmen hadn't arrived yet and I stood there washing and dressing without concern about anyone observing me. I climbed down the rickety ladder and picked my way across the untidy boatyard, avoiding piles of lumber and debris to get to the miserable toilet. This really isn't much fun, I thought. Back at the boat, Peter had made tea and we sat at our unprotected table, sun beating down on our heads, while we ate breakfast.

"Let's go into town and look around a bit," I suggested. "I have to get groceries and stuff anyway."

"Okay," he agreed, rather glumly. Grocery shopping wasn't his favorite activity, but getting off the boat was becoming imperative.

The village wasn't much bigger than Everglades, but it was more spacious and its location, right on the Gulf, was more picturesque. The usual palm trees lined the streets of "downtown." There were just a few shops and stores, and a cafe or two, but what was really exciting to us, there was a movie theater. The marquee announced "In Old Sacramento"—a B Western, but anything would have been welcome in our entertainment-deprived lives.

"Let's go to the flicks tonight," said Peter, and I happily agreed.

"I'm going to take the car while you shop," he continued. "Baker told me there was a great birding place down the shore here, Rookery Bay or something. I'm going to see if I can find it."

"Okay, but don't be too long, I don't have that much to get." I knew he could go off and easily lose all track of time.

He was back in a little while, having found the place, but disappointed as it was almost empty of birds

"I don't know why there were so few birds there," he said. "Perhaps they all went somewhere else for the day."

Rookery Bay, was a beautiful mangrove-lined bay with cypress, palms, live oaks, and other hardwoods growing all around it. At the time we were there it was pristine wilderness, now it is a huge preserve with tours, hikes, and wooden bridges crisscrossing all over it for the tourists.

That night we went to the movies, but they'd changed the show and now it was "Murder in the Music Hall," a schlocky mystery. But we really didn't care. We went home and literally climbed into our beds. The mosquitoes were nagging and we had to spray the cabin and ourselves.

"This is wretched," I complained. "When are those darn guys going to do something about our roof?"

"I'll talk to them in the morning," Peter replied, trying to mollify my mood, "Why don't you come over here and cuddle me?"

I was too uncomfortable and miserable to feel like cuddling, and we went to sleep in our separate bunks. In the morning Peter talked to Mr. Greathouse about the roof, but to no avail. They were waiting for the materials, he was told.

Peter returned to the boat disgruntled and frustrated. "Let's get out of here." he said, swatting a mosquito. "This is really lousy."

I agreed wholeheartedly. "Where shall we go?"

"Well, we could take the Eiflers to Key West," he suggested.

"What a terrific idea!" My mood lifting, "Of course, that's just what we should do. Sometimes darling, you are just brilliant." Peter grinned his wide grin at me and agreed.

"So, when shall we go?" I asked. "We could drive down to Everglades today and tell them we're ready. We have no way to phone them."

"We can't stay away too long," Peter cautioned. "Not since Baker issued his edict about our being here to keep an eye on things, but seems like there's nothing to keep an eye on at the moment, anyway—they aren't doing a bloody thing."

"Yes, and poor old Frieda would have a wretched time on the bus, as Art said. Not to mention we've both always wanted to see Key West."

"We'll get to drive that famous highway. It's supposed to be absolutely fantastic." Now we were getting excited about the trip.

"We'd better stow as much as we can in the cabin in case it rains," said Peter, so we gathered up all our covers and pillows, the table cloth and boxes of belongings we'd hidden under the tables, folded the cots, and piled the whole jumble onto our bunks. It sat looking like the result of some disaster. With that done, we told the foreman we were leaving, packed the car and were on good old Route 41 back to Everglades within a half hour.

The Eiflers were glad to see us and more than happy to make the trip, although Frieda complained loudly (as usual) about it being very short notice. This was true, but she didn't really have anything else to do. It took a couple of hours, with Art chivvying her along, before she was ready, complaining and fussing. We bundled her into the car and set off again along the Trail headed for Miami and points south. Art sat in back with Frieda, holding forth about their plans for retirement to their lot in Tavenier, on Plantation Key. Plantation Key is the second-largest key in the middle of a chain of keys that curves outward from Florida's southern coast like a vestigial tail.

"Yup," he said, "we got some good friends there, me and the Missus. We gonna build us a real home there some day."

Reaching Miami, we turned south and drove along the eastern edge of the Everglades. "This here's still wild enough," said Art, indicating with his thumb the thick mass of cypress, palms, swamp oaks and opening to the plains of sawgrass beyond. "But I betcha it'll be changin' soon. Even with this national park and tryin' to protect it an' all. They cain't seem to leave the place alone. Imagine, they even wanted to drain it once. Can you believe anything so dumb?" he snorted scornfully.

Little did he know how prophetic his speech was. Nor that "they" were still planning to drain this incredibly perfect ecosystem, wrecking it for all future generations forever.

Crossing the toll bridge at Card Sound, we drove onto Key Largo and the beginning of our 125-mile trip across the keys to Key West. Art and Frieda wanted to stop in Tavenier for the night to check on their lot and see their friends. We continued on the narrow highway, crossing bridges between keys, the Gulf water unbelievably blue, now aqua, now sapphire, now jade green, stretching away on either side of us. The sun was setting as we came into the little village of Tavenier and drove to the sole hotel in the place.

The Lowes Hotel was rather ramshackle and run down, but it was only $3.00 a night. To our disappointment, our room had single beds. When we asked for a double, we were informed they didn't have any. I found that hard to believe, but I had no recourse. The only bathrooms in the hotel were down the hall, one for men and one for women. Fortunately, there were no other guests, but it was a far cry from the plush Columbus where we had stayed in Miami. At least it was clean and pleasant. The old proprietors were kindly folk who were glad to have us. It wasn't too hot and a big ceiling fan moved the air slowly around. Outside our windows the Gulf sparkled and beckoned.

The Eiflers stayed with their friends, an expatriate couple from Pennsylvania who, when they heard I'd lived in Philly, as they referred to it, were happy to talk to me. When they learned I'd lived in Haverford, on the Main Line, they were less enthusiastic. The Main Line was too snooty for their taste, but I tried to seem as lowfalutin' as possible and seemed to win them over. Peter was acceptable as Art's junior helper (as Art characterized him).

Word spread that Art and Frieda were visiting, and several other folks from that small outpost began dropping in. Most of them were like the Eiflers' hosts, retired farmers and small business people and one ex-vaudeville performer named Happy. His act, he told us, had been with two little dogs, Mutt and Jeff.

"Of course, in those days, I wasn't drinking. Well, not so's you'd notice. I had to have steady hands, don't you know," he said. "I'd balance the dogs on my hands and on my head and them little dogs, they jumped through hoops of fire, and I had to have timing. Timing's everything in vaudeville. In life too, I reckon," he added.

"What was the hardest part about it?" Peter asked.

"Oh, it was the music," he replied. "I had music that had to be timed to the act. You know, some of the orchestras you'd get in the sticks, they weren't up to much. But in the cities, o' course, like Philly or Boston or even here in Miami, then you'd get your real musicians. I had good loud music, you know? Sousa, Bizet."

He invited us over in the morning to see his house. He'd built it single-handed, using cement bricks he'd made himself. Inside, he'd painted brightly colored murals all over all the walls, depicting circus and vaudeville scenes, with animals, clowns, magicians, and balloons.

It was really quite amazing, primitive art that, even to my untrained eyes, went beyond corny amateur, into the bizarre and surreal. I admired it, but I wouldn't want to live with it.

Another member of that odd assortment of people was John, a young man who worked for Marineland collecting sea life for their display aquariums. Since the end of the war he'd lived in a small house in Tavenier with his wife and child. He had a degree in engineering from MIT, but seemed to have switched to marine biology at some point. He offered to take us out to his barge in the bay where he kept his specimens before shipping them to Marineland. So, the next morning, after we had sufficiently admired Happy's astonishing domicile, we rowed out with John to his barge. The boat's main deck had dozens of different-sized tanks full of colorful marine life. A canvas canopy was rigged above as protection from the fierce Gulf sun. In one of the tanks, an octopus had laid a batch of eggs in an empty conch shell.

As we leaned over the tank, peering down through the water, John said, "By golly, those babies are almost ready," and so saying, he reached into the water and took one of the eggs out, cut it open, gave the baby octopus inside a helping squeeze, then dropped it in a bucket of water near-by. The little thing, not more than a quarter of an inch long, was a perfect miniature octopus, and I watched in amazement as it took only a few seconds to struggle out of the rest of its constricting shell and started swimming around and around as fast as it could. I know Peter could have spent a lot more time than we had, examining all the tanks and discussing with John the details of his many captures, but we had to get going.

Taking leave of all our new acquaintances, we set forth on the road again. The drive became more and more spectacular. Long white curving bridges crossing brilliant, unbelievably clear aqua water, they then merged into highway that took us over narrow green keys that were mostly uninhabited, and some indeed were too small for habitation. Crossing the bridges, you could look down into the water and it was so clear, it was like looking into one of Johns aquariums, you could see the sandy bottom and fish swimming around. The road was living up to its reputation as one of the most beautiful drives in the country. We hadn't gone far when Frieda, who'd been sitting silently (uncharacteristic for her) in the back, suddenly started rummaging in her voluminous black leather purse, muttering.

"What's up, Missus?" asked Art.

"Ach, Gott," she exclaimed. "I've left ze deed to ze lot at home. Ach himmel und blitzen." And she wailed on.

"Oh, Lord, Frieda, what you go and do that for?" Art was annoyed.

"Do I have to think of everything around here?"

"You know," Peter interjected hastily, "I expect they'll have records of the deed and everything at the tax office." And we all agreed he was probably right. I certainly hoped so, this was a long way to come for nothing.

Arriving in Key West, the first thing we did was walk around looking for the tax collector's office. The morning sunshine was already hot. We wandered down narrow dirt streets lined with one-story wooden buildings, somewhat rundown, but with a rakish air of tropical casualness. Our footsteps made hollow clunks as we trod across wooden sidewalks and peered into a few shops full of dusty gewgaws and knickknacks made of shells and rope. Corner bars were open and doing brisk business under the ubiquitous slow-moving ceiling fans. At last we found the tax man and, as Peter had predicted, the clerk had records of their deed, so all was not in vain. The capper was hilarious, it turned out the taxes we'd come all this way to pay amounted to *one dollar*!

Walking along by the water, we watched some fishermen unloading their catch on the dock. A huge slippery mass of yellow jack and catfish, pompano and snapper. We exchanged pleasantries and one of the fishermen, a squat, fellow with only one arm, asked if we were hungry. Pointing with his only arm, he said, "That's the best place for seafood, iffen you like it. Cooks it to order, they does, and only the freshest. Mostly from us." He grinned.

"Thanks for the tip," said Art. We headed farther along the dock where he had pointed to "The Jolly Roger," which had a painted sign above it like an English pub, with a picture of a grinning one-eyed pirate. Delicious smells wafted out across the air and hunger grabbed me.

"Let's take that fisherman's advice and eat here," I said.

"Sounds good to me," Art replied, the others nodded agreement.

We chose a table outside. Light from the sun shone and shimmered all around us, reflecting and dancing off the water, dappling the building, flickering over our faces. We sat watching the gulls and pelicans swarming around the fishing boats, diving and squabbling over the throwaways.

Sailing vessels, power boats, barges, launches, fishing boats of all sizes, plied back and forth across the small harbor, but there was no sense of haste. All was leisurely in this sleepy tropical atmosphere. Cold beer, hot chowder, and pompano. A feast for a king or a commoner.

"Guess you ain't too happy up there in Naples," Art remarked. "Well, shouldn't take 'em too long once they get goin' on it. Trouble is, you can't count on 'em. They likes to take their own good time," he added, not altogether sympathetically, I thought. Art was always a little jealous of Peter and having us out of the way for a while suited him.

"I just hate missing the migration," Peter said. "I'm worried about being away from Duck Rock."

"Oh, I'll go out there, never you fear. The birds'll be okay for a couple of weeks." Art thought Peter was overly conscientious.

"Let's hope so," Peter replied.

I could have idled there indefinitely, just looking at everything. I hadn't explored the town nearly enough, but Peter was firm. It was a long drive home and we planned to do it without stopping. Regretfully, I climbed into the car, declaring that we must return soon. Back up the beautiful highway we went, halting in Everglades only long enough to drop the Eiflers. Then we sped on to Naples. Arriving at the ways, we found the boat still a shambles and the bugs worse than ever. It all seemed quite unbearable and I burst into tears "I can't sleep here," I wailed. "I'm too tired, I hate it and I'm getting my period. Please," I begged Peter, "please let's go to the motel."

He looked at me worriedly.

"We really shouldn't spend any more money," he began. But looking at my woebegone appearance and the wretched mess everywhere, he relented.

"Oh, what the hell. Okay. Let's hope this will all look better in the morning." We climbed down the ladder, got back in the car, and drove to the Ocean View Motel for a good night's sleep.

12

As it often happens, things do improve after they've hit rock bottom. When we arrived early the next morning, the boatyard was already humming along. George and Junior were aboard our boat, and they were starting on the new roof, Hallelujah! I was elated. Action at last, perhaps we would be freed before too long. Of course, as it turned out, my optimism was premature. It took the rest of the week to complete the roof because of one important detail, there was no canvas to finish it. Until they could apply that, the roof would leak.

"Well, at least it will keep the bugs out," I said to Peter. "We must just pray for the sun to keep shining."

"And the canvas to arrive soon," he answered dourly.

Unfortunately, as luck would have it, the rains started early that year, and a couple of days later a storm blew in. At first it wasn't so bad. We put the shutters up and placed pots and pans around to catch drips, and the roof leaked only a little. In the afternoon the storm intensified and it began to pour in earnest. Peter rushed off to the beach to take a bath (swim, wash in the sea, then rinse off in the rain), something we'd both done a few times and it was really fun. Since there was no one ever around in the rain, there was no need for a swimsuit.

I was lying on the bunk down in the cabin swatting mosquitoes and trying to read, and I wasn't paying too much attention to the storm. Then I became aware it was raining harder, drumming on the new roof, hissing on the decks, and splashing all around outside. I began to worry. Coming up onto the cabin deck, I was horrified to find it awash in at least three inches of water. The boat was slightly aslant so the water, instead of running out the scuppers as it was supposed to, was piling up on the opposite side and running into the bilge.

My always overactive imagination went into high gear. I had visions of the bilge filling up with water and tipping us off the ways. This may have been a ridiculous idea, but it didn't seem so at the time, with the torrents of rain leaking through the roof, coming in around all the shutters and pouring across the floor. I was hysterical as this idea took hold, so, snatching up the broom, I started furiously sweeping the water into the scuppers and out towards the stern well. When for a few moments this seemed to be under control, I grabbed pots and pans to bail out the bilge, which was actually beginning to fill up. When that problem was momentarily contained, it was time to empty the various other pots and pans set about to catch the worst of the leaks, then to start sweeping again, over and over. I worked for at least an hour, frantic, and cursing Peter for not coming back. All the dock workers were gone since it was Sunday. I was alone with the threatened disaster.

Finally, the rain began to let up, the leaks diminished, and in another short while the storm had moved off and a watery sun emerged on the edge of the horizon. When Peter showed up a little later, all cheerful and clean and pleased with himself, I was wet and exhausted and furious. My immediate reaction was to lash out and yell at him.

"Where the hell have you been? Why didn't you come back and help? I've been killing myself here trying to save the boat…it was awful…I was sure we'd fall off the ways…," I raved on, and then to my annoyance, I began to cry.

Peter hugged me and soothed me and made me feel better by praising me for saving the boat. After I began to calm down, it even started to seem pretty funny and we laughed about it. I got cleaned up, and we went out for beer and a fish dinner. We went to the movies again at our musty little theater, which we had learned opened only on weekends and Tuesdays. This time for some mysterious reason they had brought back "In Old Sacramento." There was also a Mickey Mouse cartoon, a "March of Time" short, and a trailer for "King of Kings," a huge religious epic with H. B. Warner as Jesus and Joseph Schildkraut as Judas.

In 1943, when I was eighteen, Donna and I were making the rounds in New York looking for our big break and we had both had encounters with "Pepe" Schildkraut. He was a famous character actor of the time and he was also addicted to aspiring young actresses. Donna and I didn't know this at the time, and we went backstage to meet him after we'd seen a performance of his hit Broadway play "Uncle Harry," thinking he could be a valuable contact to help us get acting jobs. When we were ushered into his dressing room, no less, it should have given us a clue, but we were starstruck. After he had looked us over, he said he wanted to see us each again privately and made dates with us. I was naive enough to think it had to do with casting, but it turned out these "meetings" were about the "casting couch." He tried to seduce me, but I was too virginal and scared. When he said he liked redheads because he liked the color scheme of red pubic hair, I fled the theater. He had better luck with Donna, who was more adventurous sexually than I, and they had a short-lived romance. Not surprisingly, he never made any effort to get either one of us a reading, let alone a part.

We decided that we would come back to see the movie when it was playing, and headed home. When we got there, at least the boat was dry and had a "very clean deck."

Unfortunately, that week our situation didn't improve much. Work was started, only to stop again. We sat for days while nothing was being done, marooned in misery. There was always the "good" excuse, first, no materials, then, wrong materials had been delivered, other jobs taking precedence, on and on. To be fair, there weren't enough workers, and furthermore, since they were all paid by the hour, it didn't make much difference to anyone which job they worked on. Peter would remonstrate from time to time, but to little avail. At last, George showed up and started tearing out the planking of the deck in order to remove the tanks from the bilge. We had to pile everything at the other end of the deck or take it down into the cabin, and it was a mess.

We decided to leave for the day and drive to Everglades. Half an hour later, in Everglades, we were met by Art on his way back from the drug store. We gave him a lift to his boat and he gave us a big packet of mail.

We had letters from my mother, Uncle Will and various friends, a veritable treasure trove. Mail was all-important to us, our only link to our former selves, phones being almost non-existent here. While Art and Peter talked business, I sat in the car and read my letters. I read them through once fast and then a second time to savor their voices, all those beloved people I missed so much. It seemed everyone was planning to visit us at some time or another and so I had that to look forward to.

Peter and Art were still gabbing.

"So, how're they treating' you up there?" he said to me as I emerged from the car. He didn't really expect an answer, he already knew of our discomfort.

"Oh. You know. I'm getting used to it," I lied gamely.

"Well, you keep after 'em. Should be done by the Fourth of July. Haw, haw." I ignored him.

"I'm going over to Rosa's," I said to Peter.

"Good. I'll be over in a little while."

I headed over to the Leightys' little house. I wanted to complain and moan to Rosa about our miserable plight. I knew she'd be understanding and sympathetic.

"Is funny," she concluded. "Sometimes we go camping, we sleep on the ground, we have the bugs, we are so uncomfortable, but we choose it, so it is all right. Is funny, no?"

To cheer me up, Rosa now said, "I have good idea. How would you like to go to see one of the Indian villages this afternoon? I have seen the deaconess yesterday and she is saying she would be happy to take us to the chickee up the Trail."

I jumped at the suggestion. One afternoon a while back, Rosa had taken me to the deaconess's house. She had shown us some of the Seminoles' handcrafts. When I had expressed an interest in going to visit a chickee, she had enthusiastically invited us to go whenever we liked. I had also seen Rosa's collection of beautiful Indian crafts, which I admired and coveted.

Deaconess Bedell was a local character. This doughty lady was a Christian missionary, now in her seventies, who had come to Everglades some fifteen years ago to convert the Indians to Christianity. She had revived something called the Glade Cross Mission, which had been defunct since 1898. In all her time there, she hadn't made any converts, but she was undaunted and did her best to help the tribe in many practical ways, which they sorely needed. The tribe lived on the margins, keeping proudly aloof from the white settlers who had pushed them there. They farmed, fished and lived undisturbed in the swamps and mangroves, and had been basically self-sufficient for more than a hundred years. Then in 1928 the Tamiami Trail was built, and the federal conservation and flood control agencies put up fences and built canals that lowered the water table. By 1950 the situation had deteriorated to the point that it was no longer possible for the tribe to live off the land.

At the time we were there, they were still struggling to keep their way of life. The deaconess helped them to develop their handicrafts, which they sold to tourists from their chickees. In time they added alligator wrestling to their repertoire of tourist attractions, but she disapproved of this activity and discouraged its practice.

This afternoon seemed to be a good time to take her up on her offer of a visit, and as soon as Rosamaria came home from school we got ready. She came flying up the path and raced into the house to give her mother a hug. We told her our plan and she immediately became one big "yes," dancing around the living room crying "Let's go, let's go." I didn't have to worry about Peter as he was busy with Art.

We set off on foot for the short walk to the eastern edge of town where the deaconess lived in a small house amidst a tangle of palms and bougainvillea. We had walked only a few yards down the dirt street when, passing under a date palm, we were suddenly enveloped in a cloud of butterflies whirling upward from where they'd been feeding on a fallen cluster of dates. They were monarchs, part of the annual migration to Mexico. We stood stock-still in enchantment and let them swirl around us, though Rosamaria couldn't resist trying to catch one.

When we reached the deaconess's house, she came immediately at our knock and invited us in.

"Welcome, welcome to my humble dwelling," she greeted us cheerily.

"I hope we are not coming at an inconvenient time…" began Rosa.

"No, no, no. I'm most happy to see you," she replied. "I expect you want to visit a chickee. Well, it just so happens I was planning to go out to one of them this afternoon, so your timing is just right."

The interior of her house was cluttered and dark. Walking in the front door, we were met by lurid technicolor pictures of Christ with thorns and blood, and one with an exposed heart bearing a flame in it. Crucifixes were hung on every wall, and all the books had religious themes. There were at least a dozen named "The Life of Christ," all by different authors. Newspapers with names like "Church News" and "Christian Sun" were piled everywhere. The cumulative effect was overwhelming.

The deaconess herself moved with energy and an agility that belied her age, and her lively face and cheerful disposition were in distinct contrast to her gloomy house. She wasn't wearing a habit, but a sort of uniform, that consisted of a white shirt, a short navy blue skirt, and on her head she wore a coif, a modified version of a nun's head-covering.

"Come along, my dears," she said, ushering us outside the back door to where her old rattletrap car was parked. As we set off up the Trail, she told us the Seminoles had been having trouble with local poachers raiding their tomato fields.

"The sheriff knows who's doing it, but he pretends he doesn't. There's a lot of corruption, I'm afraid, at many levels in our little part of the world." She sighed. "I'm bringing some medicine to one of the old women in the chickee. They usually only want their own herbs, but sometimes they'll take white man's remedies." She went on, "I bought Grandmother Birdfoot some Golden Eye ointment for her sty. She has continual eye problems."

The mention of Golden Eye ointment gave me a momentary stab of nostalgia. It was a staple in my mother's arsenal of curatives for both my brother and me when as children we suffered frequently from sties. While so many remedies from those times seemed to hurt, we didn't mind Golden Eye because it didn't sting. You can't buy it any more because it had mercury in it, but it was very effective.

In a few more minutes we came to a stockade, with a sign above a large gate that read "Ochopee Indian Village." A little bridge crossed the canal and led us through the gate and into the middle of the stockaded area, half of which was shaded by a palm-thatch roof. On the other side, a couple of small cabins squatted along the edge of the sheltering stockade. The whole village was occupied by one extended family as was their custom. The shaded area appeared to be a communal space where the family cooked and ate. It was also the area where the women sewed and the men carved small animal sculptures. The floor was dirt. Several treadle sewing machines stood at one side. Piles of brilliantly colored fabric lay about in profusion. The space was dusty and smelled of cooking oil and swamp.

The deaconess was greeted with warm friendliness and a certain deference, as befitted an elder. Unfortunately, we were told that almost everyone was away picking tomatoes. Grandmother Birdfoot was lying on a pallet under the thatch, keeping an eye on numerous children, as they ran around or played near her in the shade.

The deaconess introduced us to Billy Tiger, the only man in the compound that day. He turned out to be the chief, but because no one was supposed to know the chief's real name, I assumed it to be an alias. I knew this detail because Mr. Tooke had told us that the Seminole chief's identity had been kept a secret since the 1800s. Apparently, a chief had been lured to Washington to talk about a treaty, but had been imprisoned, presumably because he wouldn't cooperate, and had died there. From that time on the identity of the chief had been kept secret.

Billy Tiger was large and dark, he seemed somewhat dour, though he was probably just shy. He did not seem particularly interested in talking to us, but why would he be? We represented everything that was wrong with his situation. At a later date we saw Billy Tiger again, at the Tookes'. He and some of the other men from the chickee were fishing up the Chatham River and had stopped by. The Tookes always made the Seminoles welcome, and we all sat around drinking coffee and smoking their hand-rolled cigarettes. Although none of them was ever talkative or forthcoming, we managed to break the ice a little on that occasion. We found Billy Tiger a very gentle and dignified person, and to me he appeared as though he had the weight of the world on his shoulders, I guess he did in a way.

At the chickee, after we'd been introduced, he left us and went off to fix his fishing gear. His wife, a motherly woman named Mary, offered to show us around while the deaconess was tending to Grandmother Birdfoot. "You friends of the deaconess?" she asked me. Before I could explain, Rosa jumped in. "Oh, yes" she said referring to me. "She is my friend and friend of the deaconess too, not tourista. She is living here on a boat with her husband. They are saving the birds," she added, boasting a little about her new friends. Mary's face lit up. "You are working for the Audubons?" she inquired. "Oh, them people, they are good people. They are helping us too." It was flattering to be so appreciated, even though Peter and I hadn't had a chance to do much "saving" and I smiled at Mary and Rosa. While we were being shown around, Rosamaria went over to the children and made friends at once. They were playing a skipping-rope game, and she joined in with her usual gusto. Rosa, the deaconess and I looked at the skirts and capes, some still half-finished, lying on the old sewing machine table.

They were cleverly fashioned out of cotton fabric cut up into hundreds of tiny pieces sewn together in intricate patterns. The patterns represented various forms found in nature, such as lightning or feathers or snakes. The forms were quite abstract, reappearing over and over again, sewn together in rows. The result was colorful and harmonious, and each garment was one-of-a-kind. The skirts were voluminous and floor-length, and the capes hung in a half circle to the waist in one solid color with a design along the hem. In addition, there were shirts for the men, full-sleeved and loose-fitting, worn outside the pants and made out of the same patterned fabric. I bought a skirt and a carving of an alligator. The wood carvings, we later learned, were not traditional at all and were just made for the tourist trade. I liked them anyway and thought they were quite beautiful.

After we had paid for our purchases, Mary offered us coffee and we sat on the few hardback chairs around the worktable. Grandmother Birdfoot gathered herself together and joined us. Her body was bent with age and hard work, but her big dark eyes, despite the sty, missed nothing.

She didn't speak much English, Mary told us. I was sorry because I thought she must have many tales to tell. Her late husband, Tall Tiger, also a chief, had lost a hand to an alligator in his later years. Just like Captain Hook, I couldn't help thinking.

Mary said, "Oh yes. I was only a child, but I remember all the men in the family and from the chickee down the Trail, they all came out and they caught that old alligator and killed him. When they cut him up to skin him, they found grandfather's hand in his belly. We got his skin pinned up in our cabin." She pointed to the largest cabin along the wall of the compound.

Rosamarie, who'd joined us when the skipping-rope game ended, wanted to see it. "Oh, please, could you show us, could you please?" she implored.

Mary smiled at her. "Sure, little Rosa, you can look."

I wanted to see it too, so we all got up and walked to the cabin. I was curious to see not only the alligator skin, but also the interior of the cabin. Through the open door we looked at the back wall where the truly huge skin stretched clear across it, some fifteen feet. I shuddered. Truly, a dinosaur for the modern age, I would not want to encounter such a monster. The room was dim, but we could see sleeping pallets covered with deer skins on the floor along the walls, for Mary and Billy Tiger and one of their unmarried sons, Jackcatcher. The wooden boards of the floor were covered with hand-woven rugs, some apparently handed down from former generations. On another wall was a black panther skin.

"We didn't kill that panther." Mary explained. "That one was just left in the swamp by some of them swamp poachers. They was after the pelt, but they musta got scared off by something. Grandfather came across it before they could come back and get it."

It was getting late and so, thanking Mary for her hospitality, we said goodbye and took our leave. Back outside in the brightness of the afternoon sun, we climbed back into the deaconess's rattletrap and drove back to Everglades.

There I found Peter and Art talking agitatedly on Art's boat. A rumor was buzzing that the notorious Gomez boys (not their real name) and some of the nefarious pals on Chockoloskee Island had heard we were up on the ways in Naples and were planning a raid on Duck Rock. To them, it would be an afternoon's diversion, go shoot it up, maybe collect a few carcasses to eat, and go home again. Those guys really felt it was their right. Hadn't they and their fathers and perhaps even their grandfathers been doing it all their lives? Who were all these outsiders and interfering foreigners to come here and tell them what to do? They were the remnants of a very tough and independent group who had survived here in this wilderness for generations, ignoring the law and going their own way. In todays world they would have been closely akin to "survivalists." Most of their forbears had come from up north, running from the law, to find a kind of rough haven here in the Ten Thousand Islands that makes up the Everglades. We had been told they were usually armed, often drunk, and were considered dangerous by the locals. Naturally, I was afraid of them.

The Gomez boys, everyone knew, were the craziest and most reckless of all. Everyone, including the law, had heard the rumors that they had at least two stills hidden away amid the countless creeks in the mangroves, but no one wanted to take the chance of getting shot trying to shut them down. I'd been hearing scary tales about them from Art and the Tookes ever since we'd arrived. The reputation of the inhabitants of Chokoloskee Island made them seem especially scary and alarming to me.

Occasionally we'd seen one of their families in town, a mother trailed by half a dozen children, some clinging to her skirts, others looking shyly or furtively around, while she negotiated the purchase of a few necessities in the grocery store. While the man accompanying her would usually head straight to the dry goods store and start drinking beer, whatever time of day it happened to be. I watched them with a mixture of fear of the men, and concern for the women and children. Their lives seemed so hard, and it all seemed so difficult. There were no social services anywhere in the area, but they would probably have been too proud to "accept charity" and avail themselves of such help, even if there had been any. They kept strictly to themselves.

I wasn't comfortable with my feelings towards these women. I felt alienated and shy around them, and never knew what to say. I felt we were representatives of the Audubon Society, and as such, should be able to communicate and establish good relations, at least on some level. Looking back, I was very young and inexperienced. I had never encountered people in such circumstances before, lacking the basics that we all took for granted, and with very little chance that things might improve. Mrs. Tooke told me they were superstitious and very leery of strangers or anyone they saw as authority figures. So we, being representatives of Audubon, represented the very things that they seemed to feel threatened by.

In some respects, their fears were justified. Their lives were about to be dramatically changed forever with the coming of the Everglades National Park. Within a few years everyone living on the various small keys and islands, including many who had been there for generations, would be relocated to someplace completely foreign to them. Their situation seemed ironically akin to that of the Native Americans whom their ancestors had helped run off their homelands.

Now we had to decide what to do, if anything, about this rumor. Art was up in arms. His paranoia, always simmering just beneath the surface, had burst out full force. The problem was that our hands were somewhat tied and we had few options. Our big boat was obviously out of commission. Art's was apparently not running either, having broken down the day before. We could go out and patrol around in the small boats, but that would be quite ineffectual as a deterrent. The Gomez's' boats were faster, for one thing. They could easily outrun us if we came upon them in the midst of shooting up the birds, and they could just as easily avoid us altogether and wait for us to go back in again, which we'd have to do as we couldn't stay out all night.

Peter was inclined to think the rumors were exaggerated. There were always rumors, he said, about the Gomez boys, and this was true. Still, the rumors could not be completely discounted. Round and round we went. The discussion was interrupted by the sudden arrival of Mr. Tooke. He appeared, ruddy and good-humored, on the embankment above the Eiflers' boat and came aboard. After the usual greetings and pleasantries, Art blurted out our dilemma. Mr. Tooke laughed.

"Oh," said he with a chuckle, "you don't have to worry about them for a while. Them Gomez boys went past my place this mornin' headed up for the cricks. They'll be layin' out drunk, I reckon, for the next three days at least."

"What about the rest of 'em?" Art questioned nervously.

"Nah," Mr. Tooke reassured him, "without them Gomez people, they ain't got the initiative. Anyway, they'll just be waiting for the Gomezes to come back out with some moonshine for 'em is my guess."

Thus reassured, everyone took a breath and the meeting broke up. We went with Mr. Tooke to the grocery store for a few staples. I complained to him about our wretched situation, and he commiserated. I tried to tell him how much we missed him and Mrs. Tooke, and how I longed to be back there, tied up to his dock, in the peace of the Chatham River.

"Well, you'll get there afore long," he said calmly.

I wasn't so sure. Our next move would be to get to Duck Rock and the real heart of our mission: to stay there, tied up to those three mangrove stakes, and guard the birds day and night for the rest of the summer.

13

One morning, a few days later, I sat at the table in the cabin. I was trying to have a peaceful breakfast. Peter had gone off in a grumpy mood to look for birds, and I was alone, or as alone as one can be in a boat with no curtains surrounded by a boatyard full of workmen. It was especially noisy. The banging and hammering, the whine of chain saws, the crashes and clanging of large metal objects being dropped and stacked, seemed louder and more continuous than usual. The day was going to be another hot one as the Florida climate began heating up towards the end of spring.

By now it was April 8 and we'd been up on the ways for two miserable weeks. It looked as if we'd have to be there for as long again. Peter and I were both going crazy. The gas tanks had been removed from the bilge three days before and nothing, not one thing, had been done since. We were left with a gaping hole in the deck where the planking had been taken up in order to get down into the bilge. Consequently, our living space was cut in half, as our cabin was directly above the bilge. Everything from the cabin had to be piled up forward, by the steering wheel, on our camp-bed couches, and in every spare corner. I did my best to ignore the mess and eat my egg in peace.

Not a chance. A few moments later, Peter came stomping back onto the boat in a terrible mood of anger and frustration. "Goddammit all to hell. I've just seen a flock of chimney swifts over on the telegraph wires getting ready to leave and you know what that means, don't you?" he fumed.

I didn't, but without waiting for me to answer, he went on.

"It means, goddammit all to hell, that the spring migration is about finished and I've missed it all, sitting up here on this frigging boat waiting

for some action from these half-witted, incompetent, frigging idiots…,"
he ranted on.

I felt very bad for him. I knew how important the migration was, not
only to him personally, but also for the records he was compiling for the
National Audubon Society.

"Well, we should get out of here in a few days and maybe there'll still
be something left to see," I said, rather feebly.

"Goddammit, we'd better get out of here, and soon. I'm going to see
George again and find out what the hell is going on." And he stormed off.

Whatever he said to Mr. Greathouse and George finally had an effect,
or perhaps they just took pity on us. Whatever the reason, the next day
our new fuel tanks were hoisted aboard and installed below deck. It turned
out the old tanks they had removed were in even worse condition than
Art had warned us they were and it was indeed a miracle we hadn't been
blown to Kingdom Come. I was more than thankful to have the new ones
installed, and when the new deck was laid I was ecstatic.

Moving all our belongings back into place was a great relief. Our
usually cramped quarters seemed positively palatial. Peter's mood lifted,
too, which helped the situation greatly. He'd been quite
uncharacteristically difficult to live with recently, drinking more beer than
was good for him and losing his temper over relatively minor frustrations.
We didn't fight much, usually, and the unaccustomed friction was wearing.
Not that I blamed him really, but still it was a welcome change when his
state of mind improved.

There was still plenty of work in store for us before we could be re-
floated. The whole boat had to be painted, inside and out, and the bottom
first, of course, while still up on the ways. To this end, the next morning,
Peter and I were standing on the scaffold, electric sanders in hand, to
begin the huge, and thankless task, of preparing the hull for painting. Even
though it was still early, the sun was already hot. We had tied masks over
our faces for protection, as the sanders blew clouds of old paint dust at
us.

It was hot, nasty work, and after a while I couldn't take anymore grit
in my eyes and up my nose and decided I'd had enough, so I climbed up

the ladder and went back aboard. Thankfully, George came over to help Peter, so I didn't feel guilty about quitting. Anyway, I was supposed to be painting the interior. I remembered my earlier vision of how I'd paint the cabin, with white windows, blue ceiling, and buff for the deck, and now I could make that vision a reality. I set to work. As tedious as all the preparing and painting was, it only took a few days for all of it to be done.

We now had a new roof, new shutters for the screen windows, new tanks, and a cleaned-out bilge. The interior with its new color scheme looked cool and airy. Peter had added a sporty green stripe at the water line of the newly white hull. When he mounted the big brass letters we'd bought in Miami, A U D U B O N, across the stern, I thought she indeed looked a credit to the Society. The painting was the final stage of the refitting and now, after twenty-three miserable days in this boatyard, we were ready to be launched.

George's head appeared at the top of the ladder.

"Ready to go when you are," he announced.

We've been ready for two weeks, I wanted to say, but instead we both smiled and followed him down the ladder. We stood watching a little apprehensively as the scaffold was removed, the cradle lowered, and rollers placed in front of the keel for the Audubon to slide down the few yards back to the water. Slowly she began to inch forward. Then, gathering momentum, with a heavy swoosh and a slithering splash, she lurched into the water, bobbed gently a few moments, and floated free. The white of her new paint shone brightly against the dark water murky with harbor flotsam. I turned to Peter as we stood on the bank. I was ecstatic.

"Hooray. I can't believe we've done it, honey, we're on our way," and I gave him a big kiss. He hugged me back, as elated as I was.

Many of the workers had come over to watch the launching. We shook hands with everyone we knew and bade them farewell.

"Good bye and good luck," said Mr. Greathouse sincerely. "I respect what you-all's tryin' to do and I'm sorry it took so long to get you back on the job, but that's how it is sometimes. Anyway, at least you got a safe boat now."

Peter thanked him and praised everybody for the job they'd done.

Now that everything was finished, all our frustrations faded into the distance.

Underlying my delight at our deliverance, I was feeling a nagging disquiet that had arisen because I had been delegated to drive our little blue Ford back to Everglades while Peter brought the boat down. It sounded so simple, but I was in a nervous dither about the drive. The truth was, driving actually petrified me. I had never had a drivers' license and all I had right now was a learner's permit. In the thirties, growing up in England, my family had seldom had a car. We traveled around by bus and train, it was simpler and cheaper. My mother had finally gotten her license in her middle age, but she rarely drove. She was very anxious when she did, and I was nervous in the car with her.

My father on the other hand, being a naval aviator, was completely at ease driving machines of all kinds and he loved cars. To me, as a child, he always appeared dashing and glamorous. His gloved hands on the wheel, he drove us around with skill and panache, and I always felt comfortable and safe. Unfortunately, this didn't help to give me confidence in my own abilities. Now I was actually faced with this task, and I quailed. Peter had been giving me sporadic lessons driving up and down the local streets, and I'd managed to get to the store and the post office a few times, but I was still very fearful behind the wheel. The idea of driving thirty miles down the Tamiami Trail to Everglades, even though the road was usually empty, filled me with dread.

Added into the mix of feelings was the fact that Art, who had come up to Naples on the bus to get a part for his hothead motor, wanted to drive back with me. I would have preferred he go back on the boat with Peter, but he needed to get back to Everglades as soon as possible and the car was quicker. We waited long enough to see Peter start up the newly refurbished engines and chug out towards the Gulf. Waving goodbye, we climbed into the car. I didn't know whether having Art's company made my nerves worse or not, but at least he was a distraction.

"That hubby of yours, he's one eager beaver," he began. "He was tellin' me he's been writing reports regular to the Audubon people in New York." He made it sound as if this was some sort of high heresy.

"Well, sure," I replied, wanting to appear casual. "It's part of the job, I guess. Don't you ever write reports?" I added innocently.

"Well now, I've sent in something occasionally, when there was something to report, but not regular-like. What's he say in them?" he wanted to know.

I was wary of this conversation. Something in Art's manner raised a signal flag of caution in me.

"Oh I don't know," I said truthfully. "I think he just tells about the birds he's seen and the numbers. Stuff like that."

"Seems like he's got a lot more education than this job calls fer," Art said darkly.

I wasn't about to go into the whole confusing story of how Peter didn't actually have even a high school diploma yet, let alone a college degree, with Art. Peter viewed being here, working for Audubon, as a time for him to figure out what he wanted to do with the rest of his life. He was hoping it would be something in the field of environmental studies, and being on this boat in the everglades gave him the chance to experience field work first hand. But I couldn't explain all this to Art right now.

I merely said, "He wants to study the environment and he's going to be some sort of naturalist, so this is a wonderful chance get some experience. It's really a perfect opportunity for him."

I didn't know if this would satisfy Art's concerns, but it was the best I could do. I changed the subject and got him off on his plans for building his house in Tavernier, which kept him going till we reached Everglades. Because Art had been so long-winded, I'd been distracted the whole way home and I realized as we drove into town that I'd forgotten to be nervous about driving. All the same, I was relieved to have made it in one piece.

We were way ahead of Peter and the boat. It would take him at least two hours to get here. I went over to see Rosa. She greeted me warmly and offered me a sandwich. I'd forgotten about lunch and accepted gladly. We chatted awhile, and then she asked me if I'd like to take a shower. Would I! What a splendid offer. What a wonderful woman.

Luxuriating in the rare sensation of hot water pouring over me, I stood in the shower thinking about the next stage of our lives here, actually going out to Duck Rock and spending some real time. Peter, I knew, was eager to get there. My feelings were somewhat mixed. Not having the scientist's fervor to explore and discover, I would have to find my own interests in our unusual situation. It was so entirely different from the life I was used to. As a dancer and an intensely physical person, I was beginning to wonder how I would fare, cooped up on our small boat day after day. Up to now, I'd been able to get off onto dry land often enough that I hadn't felt too confined. Although, now and then, I did feel as if the whole situation was confining in more than merely physical ways. I was coming to realize, that no matter how much you loved someone, rubbing up against them day and night, with few outside distractions and little other social life, put a serious strain on a relationship. As our favorite mentor, Peter's Uncle Will, had said, "Even Tristan and Isolde would have gotten fed up with each other under these circumstances." He'd been trying to warn us what to expect, but of course we didn't believe it then. Now, we'd just have to figure it out.

Rosamaria was very excited and kept dashing out of the back door to watch for the arrival of Peter and the *Audubon*. Finally, we heard a shriek, and Rosamaria calling, "It's here! It's here! Come on, everyone!" The Leightys, the Eiflers, a few neighbors, and I all gathered as the boat docked by the bank. Art and I caught the lines and tethered them to the pilings. It was quite a triumphant return for the old boat, and everyone shared in the moment, admiring the paint job and saying how much better the "old girl" looked.

"This calls for a celebration," said Peter. "Let's all go up to Ochopee and have dinner." The Eiflers declined, but the Leightys joined us and we drove up to our sweet, though bit of a greasy spoon, little local cafe. We ate hamburgers, drank a little too much beer, and danced to the juke box. Even Rosamaria got to dance with her dad. I put my concerns aside for the time being, and let the beer go to my head and the music to my feet.

In the morning, we got ready to take off for Duck Rock. While in Naples we had acquired a new (used) icebox, larger and more efficient than the old one, and now it was filled with supplies. The water tanks were filled, the new gas tanks were filled—we were ready to go. I checked the two smaller boats to make sure they were secure, cast off the lines, and pushed off from the bank. Peter stood holding the wheel as he drove the boat confidently downstream and out to the Gulf. The water was calm, changing color from green in the channel to lighter blue, then slipping into dark blue as we moved into the main channel by Chokoloskee Island. I was perched on the pilot's stool next to Peter, and I marveled at how much we had both learned since we'd arrived here a mere four months earlier.

Hardly had we got outside the mouth of the river, when we came upon a Greek sponge boat, that had run aground on the side of the channel. We knew it was a sponge boat because we'd seen them a couple of times before. Once, out at Turkey Key, getting water, and once just passing by, their rigging festooned with sponges scooped up off the floor of the Gulf and hanging out to dry. The boat was large and black, decorated with red, green, and white designs along the bow and the sides of the deck. Usually they just stayed out in the Gulf and didn't come in, unless there was bad weather or something was needed.

The crew hollered to us as we passed. Peter stopped and we turned around, rather awkwardly, to see what we could do. None of the men seemed to be able to speak English, but one large mustachioed fellow threw us a line and indicated by sign language that they wanted to be pulled sideways back into the channel. We secured their line and began trying to pull them off the bar. The poor old *Audubon* strained and struggled, but their big boat didn't move an inch. Finally we had to give up, for fear of damaging our engine. We threw back their line and waved goodbye, shouting our regrets that were no doubt understood in some sort of universal language.

We had hardly gone on much farther when it became evident we had indeed done some sort of harm to our boat. It started vibrating and shaking so badly we had to stop. Peter took up the floor boards over the engine to see what the trouble could be. The water pump was leaking and the stuffing box was dripping badly. What a disaster! And just after we'd had everything put into such good shape. With great ingenuity, Peter managed to find a way to stem the leaking, at least temporarily, but it meant we'd probably have to go back to town again soon.

As we came nearer to Duck Rock, we could see a terrific squall blowing up ahead, swiftly approaching across the water. We were still in the sunshine, but where the clouds formed a heavy wall of dark gray, pouring rain, the water changed to an amazing combination of silver-gray and bright green. It looked like taffeta or shot silk creating a quite extraordinary effect. We didn't have time to linger, however. We wanted to make it to Duck Rock before we were engulfed by the storm.

Just as we reached the stakes at Duck Rock, the squall hit us. For a few moments it blew us around like a cork, and rained like a monsoon. Then, as quickly as it had materialized, it moved on past and by the time we were safely tied up, the sun was peeking through once more. In its wake, it had left a rainbow which before long became double, the second one being larger, but fainter, two perfect arches curving over the dark green of the mangroves. As we watched, the birds were coming in, some with nesting materials dangling from their long bills. Flying around and through the rainbows, came a steady stream of blue and white. I was filled with awe at the soaring spectacle. It struck me, as it had before when observing this amazing formation, why this small key, out of all the many hundreds of Florida keys, why had this one been chosen as the special perfect key, to which the birds always return? To make it even more puzzling, the birds come to Duck Rock to nest, but then ignore the nesting material that abounds on the key and continue to fetch it all the way from the mainland. So many mysteries yet to be solved.

The double rainbow slowly dimmed and faded, making way for a grand sunset to develop. The banks of clouds stretching out along the horizon were rimmed in gold and tinted purple and orange in a stunning profusion of color over the dark purple and gold water. The birds continued to come in, line after line, as the roosting birds, coming from their day jobs, flew in to join their nesting neighbors. A flock of roseate spoonbills was feeding on the flats at the western edge of the key, and as the sun went lower, they too flew in for the night, adding to what was already a truly magnificent spectacle.

"So here we are at last, honey. I feel like now this job is really beginning." Peter was exultant. "I'm finally going to get the chance to see what I can do as a field researcher. Put my money where my mouth is. There is so much to learn and be discovered here. The possibilities seem endless."

Peter was always an optimist, but I was sure he was right. We were each drinking a beer while our chili was cooking on the little gas stove in the galley. The delicious smell of dinner covered up the new paint smell that was still hanging over the boat, but the Gulf breeze would soon blow it all away. I was happy to see Peter feeling so much more cheerful about everything, and we went off to bed and made love in a spirit of celebration, a celebration of both each other, and of our extraordinary life adventure as it was unfolding here.

Part II

14

I awoke with a start. The *Audubon* was at an odd angle and I was lying pressed against the bulkhead. Low tide. The boat had settled into the muck on the bottom. She was slightly tilted and would stay like that until the tide came in again and floated us off. I smelled coffee, and the radio was telling us about President Truman addressing Congress. Peter was standing naked in the galley. I admired his strong brown body and thought happily of making love the night before in my narrow, hard bunk. The set-up was so uncomfortable it was not conducive to conjugal couplings and our sex life had suffered, but so far, we'd managed to overcome the difficulties often enough.

"Hi," I said. "Make me some tea, will you, darling?" He grinned over at me, "Sure, the water's almost hot."

The galley was only two steps from the cabin. He came over and gave me a kiss. "I'm going up to watch the birds leave. You coming?" "No, I'm too sleepy."

He made me my tea, dressed quickly, and went out and sat on the cabin roof with his coffee. The sun was barely over the horizon when the birds erupted into their spectacular morning takeoff. I could hear the thrum and whirring of their wings as they flew up and away from the key, headed for their day in the Everglades. Duck Rock sat across the water from us, squatting on its mangrove roots, humming with life, seen and unseen, and oblivious to us in our role of protectors and caretakers. A constant burble of sound issued from its murky interior. Movement agitated its branches, as birds went about their lives, flying in and out, splashing in the shallows, and tending their nests.

The downside to this cauldron of activity was that it smelled worse than the crowded bird house at the zoo, a gross combination of dead fish, rotted vegetation, muck, and bird excrement. It was a primordial soup, life as it must have been at the beginning of time, forming itself out of the fertile compost of Earth's basic elements. It smelled of the careless over-abundance of nature, creating, growing, and destroying in an everlasting cycle. Unfortunately, despite its relationship to our ancient beginnings, on a hot day at low tide, when the wind blew across the key in our direction, the stench was overpowering.

I'd never been closer to the key than a boat's length away when we'd rowed around it once or twice. Peter didn't go over there often because he didn't want to disturb the nesting birds. I felt that sooner or later, like it or not, I would probably have to go. I was not looking forward to it. To me, the interior was definitely a forbidding, scary place. Not only was it dark, dank, and bad smelling, but all sorts of nasty creepy creatures lived there besides the birds. Cottonmouth moccasins, for one, swam in the brackish water or coiled above on higher branches, just waiting to drop on you. Millions of mosquitoes, no-see-ums and other biting, stinging insects swarmed in the damp under the trees. Snapping turtles, which could easily lop off a finger or a toe, swam around among the tree roots. At least there were no alligators out here, but that didn't give me much comfort. I knew enough about the other hazards to be plenty apprehensive about venturing into our own little "heart of darkness."

The screen door banged and Peter came back in.

"Well, the birds seem to be okay," he said. "I counted about fifty thousand. There'll be more later and there were at least one hundred spoonbills. I need to go over there and check out the nesting birds," he added.

The morning light danced on the water, reflecting all over the screens and the ceiling of the cabin. I felt a twinge of nerves.

"You mean this morning?" I asked. "Do you need me to come?" I tried to sound as if I didn't care one way or another.

"Don't you want to?" He seemed surprised.

"Yes, of course. It's just there's a lot to do around here," I answered lamely. "I was going to clean out the turtles' bowl and stuff." I was reluctant to admit my fears.

"You can do that later," he dismissed my excuses. "I'll need you to help with the camera equipment. I'm determined to try to get some pictures this time, and maybe with the new gun-stock mount and the telephoto lens we'll have better luck."

Well, I thought, a photo shoot might be fun. May as well give it a go and get it over with.

"Okay, let's have breakfast and then I'll get ready." I said gamely.

"Just as long as we can get there and back on the tide. I have to get the boat running, and the goddamn motor is acting up again. Why those idiots at the ways can't get it to stay fixed, I don't understand."

A little later, I got into my jeans and sneakers for the expedition. I wouldn't need my boots, they were for the rattler-infested Everglades and sawgrass savannahs. Sneakers were better for scrambling around on the slippery, tangled roots of the mangroves. I did hope I wouldn't fall in. It was easy enough to slip off into the water and the slimy mud below. I came up on deck ready for the fray. I had sprayed myself copiously with bug spray, and I tossed the bottle to Peter as I climbed into the skiff. We were going to need buckets of it. I wished I had some sort of total body screen I could wear, the kind beekeepers have.

"Come on. Let's go," said Peter. He had the small boat up and running, his equipment organized. We had a fancy Leica camera, a separate light meter, and the aforementioned gun-stock-mounted telephoto lens. We were way over-equipped. We had absolutely no experience and very little expertise on how to use our 1940s high tech gear. So far, our attempts at photographing birds had been a dismal failure. In all fairness, we did face some formidable obstacles. The birds were almost always in motion, their nests were way up in the highest branches, and whenever we got close they flew away.

We pushed off from the *Audubon* and putted across the short expanse of sparkly water, dazzling to the eyes, into the dark recesses of Duck Rock. Peter cut the motor and we drifted into touching distance of the mangroves. As my eyes adjusted to the lower light, I could see into the dim, dense interior and hear the birds cackling and gurgling. The smell intensified. For a moment I felt a little dizzy. I was sitting in the bow, and grabbing the first root I could reach, I swung us alongside and grappled the boat to it with a rope. The next hurdle was to get out of the boat and scramble up onto the roots. This without falling into the water or capsizing the boat. We both managed to get a footing and finally stood on a precarious skinny red root, clinging to the trunk for balance. Because, as with all the mangrove keys, there was no solid ground between the trees to walk on, one just had to clamber from root to root, I wondered if this was how a tightrope walker in the circus felt. The nesting birds acted disturbed and flapped around a bit with a few protesting squawks, though they weren't upset enough to leave. The air was fetid and still. I felt a heaviness pressing down on me, oppressive, almost paralyzing. I didn't want to move from my unstable perch on the tree root.

Looking down past my feet into the tannin-colored water, I saw small fish darting in and out between the roots. A stingray was lying motionless in a deeper pool, his bat wings flat on the muck, his spiny tail lying out behind. I wouldn't want to slip and land on *him*, I thought, he could give you a nasty sting.

Cautiously we started to move toward the interior of the key. We couldn't see beyond a few feet ahead, so dense and thick were the mangroves. I felt like I was hardly breathing, both from the stink and my anxiety. Duck Rock covered a scant two acres, and as we moved further into the mangroves, the light became ever dimmer and the air danker. Fifteen feet above us, the tops of the trees were lit by bright sunshine, but the thickness of their fleshy, dark green leaves kept the light from penetrating any lower. In that thick humidity I was sweating profusely just standing still. Peter started inching forward and I reluctantly followed, slithering and scrambling as quietly as I could. A couple of turtles plopped off their perches on a fallen log next to us, I was relieved to see they weren't the ugly scraggy-necked snappers.

Up in the higher branches, we could see the nests of the herons and ibis, untidy clumps of sticks, casually piled on top of each other, it seemed amazing to me that they held together. All we could see from below, was the underneath and occasionally a skinny head on a long snaky neck, its bill pointing down, observing us warily.

"How are we ever going to get a shot of anything that looks like anything?" I wondered aloud.

"Shh!" hissed Peter. "Just whisper."

We continued along, painfully slowly, stepping from root to root, and clutching the trunks for balance. Peter was carrying the heavy gun-mount with the camera and its zoom lens hanging around his neck, making him even more unsteady. I had the camera bags with the light meter and some filters. Looking up I saw a herons' nest that appeared just like the rest of the tree except for the feathered mass sitting on it. At the same moment, Peter spotted it too. He braced himself on a couple of roots as I awkwardly handed him the light meter and he took a reading. Meanwhile the heron had become aware of us and she reached her long neck down, regarding us with one beady black eye. Peter slowly raised the camera and tried to focus, which meant he had to let go with both hands and maintain his balance. At almost the same moment the heron decided we were a threat. With a squawk she flapped away through the branches, totally frustrating Peter's opportunity. Peter almost toppled into the water, but just managed to hang on by grabbing a root at the last minute.

And so it went. After an hour of this, Peter had managed to shoot about five pictures of the bottoms of nests. We were sweaty, buggy, and muddy. The bug spray only worked seventy-five percent and we were being attacked by swarms of gigantic mosquitoes. Even Peter had had enough, and as for me, I'd been ready to leave five minutes after we got there. All this time, the tide had been coming in and the water was beginning to cover the roots. It was time to return to the boat. We made our way back to the waiting skiff. I clambered down into it thankfully and turned to help Peter. Balanced on a root, he began to disencumber himself of his unwieldy equipment. As he handed over the heavy gun-stock and lens to me, the boat gave a lurch and I was thrown off balance. Grabbing for the equipment, I pulled him off balance too and he tipped forward, slipped off his treacherous perch, and with a grunt and a splash sat heavily and wetly, bottom first, in the shallow water between the roots.

It was a miracle it hadn't happened before, but he looked so surprised and outraged it struck me funny and I couldn't help laughing. Fortunately he wasn't hurt and managed a rueful smile at his mishap. The camera was water-damaged, though, and we had to take it to Miami for repairs. The rest of the equipment escaped unscathed, although the film was ruined. It was some time before I ventured back onto Duck Rock.

Long after we were gone, in the great hurricane of 1963, Duck Rock was completely destroyed, reduced to a few stumps sticking out of the water. By then the birds had begun to decrease in number and they moved their nesting places to other keys.

15

Not only were we expected to guard Duck rock, Peter also had to patrol many other places up the Chatham River. In and out of the numerous creeks and bays, and around the many small islands and keys that surrounded us. We hadn't seen the Tookes for several weeks, consequently, our laundry was piling up again, so it was time for a visit. The morning after our excursion onto Duck Rock I said to Peter: "Let's go up the river and see the Tookes. I've got a ton of laundry and I've missed them, too."

"Yeah," agreed Peter, "and I should check around Gopher Key and Watson's Prairie. If there's anything left of the spring migration, we should find some birds in that area."

"We can ask Mr. Tooke as well," I offered. "He usually notices what birds are around."

"Yeah. He's pretty on-the-ball about birds. We can go up later."

The sun was just coming up. It was going to be a good day by the look of things. We climbed into our midsized runaround boat, the *White Ibis*, and started up the Chatham River. The ride in the warm morning air, slightly damp, always smelling of tangy mangrove mud, brought us to the Tookes' in about half an hour. As I scrambled out onto the rickety dock, Mr. Tooke appeared from another boat tied up ahead of ours. His son Hamp, a mullet and mackerel fisherman, was visiting. We'd met him once or twice before. A larger, younger version of Mr. Tooke, he had the same kindly nature, but his shyness kept him from being quite as gregarious as his parents. Still, he was friendly and welcoming to us as we greeted each other on the dock.

The sand flies had increased as the day warmed up, and we all hastened inside the sanctuary of the farmhouse. Mrs. Tooke, large, motherly, and barefoot, was happy to see us and immediately invited us to dinner, which in these parts meant lunch. We accepted gladly, but I insisted I was to be allowed to help with the cooking and preparations. It was a sign of acceptance that I was permitted to help now. I had graduated from "company" to "friend."

During a bit of chit-chat, Mr. Tooke told Peter he was sure Duck Rock and the surrounding area had been shot up while we were gone on the ways. This was disturbing news. It wasn't as bad as if they'd waited till the nesting birds all had families, but it meant we had to be even more vigilant. While absorbing this unpleasant news, I heard Peter mention that he wanted to check on Watson's Prairie, a key located a few miles further up-river and deeper into the mangroves. This key had an open area where many species of birds came to feed, and he wanted to be sure they hadn't been disturbed.

"Don't go up the wrong creek," said Mr. Tooke. "You might run into them Gomez boys. They've got a still up there somewheres. They'd shoot you soon as look at you. Unless they thought you was a customer, o' course," he joked.

This made me nervous, but Peter didn't seem worried. Even though our maps were somewhat incomplete, he assured me Watson's Prairie was easily identified. He waved good-bye and set off. Mrs. Tooke and I went inside again and sat down at her well-worn kitchen table, to settle in for a good gossip. I could tell she was bursting to tell me some news.

"Art's been carrying on about you-all again," she started. "He's thinking you came here to spy on him for the Society. He and the Missus have got themselves really riled up about it. He's saying he's gonna quit and retire to Tavenier. Course he's been saying that for years." I remembered the conversation between Art and I in the car driving down from Naples.

"Oh," I said, "that explains why he was asking me all that stuff about Peter. I thought there was something strange about it." I told her what Art had said.

"But," I continued, "what would make him think we're here to spy on him? Why would we want to do something like that? It's silly really."

"I know that, honey," she reassured me. "He's just that way. He thinks you must be here for more 'n just the job, with the pokey salary they're paying you."

I had to agree with the pokey salary part, but Peter had repeatedly emphasized his interest in the environment and his particular desire to do field work. This was apparently incomprehensible to Art (or perhaps he just didn't believe it).

"Don't you worry about it," she said. "Don't make no nevermind. He's just got a real suspicious nature. He'll get over it."

Whatever had precipitated it, I was disturbed by it. We had to deal with the Eiflers all the time. It would be extremely awkward if our relationship became clouded by suspicion and mistrust. I hoped we'd find a way to calm Art's fears and get back on a friendly footing. Meanwhile, I assured myself, Mrs. Tooke definitely didn't believe such nonsense and took us at face value. On the other hand, the Tookes had known the Eiflers a lot longer than they'd known us, and, after all, we were the outsiders. If they started to believe weird things about us too, it would become much more difficult and uncomfortable to do our job.

There was another aspect of it, too. There were hints and indications that Art was a little intimidated by Peter, and might even be annoyed by the fact that Peter worked hard and was so gung-ho. With Peter sending in his reports regularly, and Art only haphazardly, the contrast would have been evident between how much work (i.e. counting and guarding birds and local propagandizing) Peter got done and Art did not. But that wouldn't be Peter's fault, and Art seemed to have forgotten how we went expressly against Mr. Baker's edict and drove them to Key West. Peter was always very careful to say only positive things about Art when he reported in, but of course Art didn't know that. Perhaps Art's reaction was in part generated by a slightly guilty conscience. Besides, he was supposed to be retiring, wasn't he?

Our little tête-à-tête was interrupted by Mr. Tooke and Hamp, who came clomping in for coffee. Mrs. T and I went outside to the garden to gather greens for dinner. Even though it was still only spring, she had rows of greens —collards, kale, spinach, chard, and mustard—all coming on. In her herb garden there was sage, sorrel, borage, parsley, dill and many others I didn't know. Onions and garlic, chives, and spring onions were coming up too, some ready to harvest. We cut leaves of chard, collards, and kale and brought it all into the house. Mrs. Tooke was planning to have a loin of pork (which they'd butchered and smoked themselves), plus biscuits, corn bread made with cracklings right in it, fried eggs, and the greens. Once back inside, she gave me an apron and I became her sous-chef.

I was happy cooking and preparing alongside Mrs. Tooke as she showed me how to make biscuits and corn bread and how to fix the greens, a little overcooked by today's standards, but still delicious. The stove had to be stoked from time to time with wood which I fetched from the woodpile. I kept a wary eye out for scorpions, I'd learned that lesson. As the day heated up and the stove heated the kitchen, we began to heat up too. Sweat was rolling down my back and under my arms and forehead. By the time the meal was cooked, so was I.

It was after two when we heard Peter's boat returning, just in time for dinner. He came in, field glasses slung around his neck, boots muddy from the swamp, a little tired and very hungry.

"Not many birds," he informed us. "I bet it was shot up last year." Mr. Tooke confirmed this depressing thought.

Then we all sat down and ate huge platefuls of the grand meal Mrs. T and I had prepared. After coffee and pie, we were getting ready to leave, when we heard the soft putting of an outboard coming from upriver. Around the bend we saw a skiff approaching with three Seminole men seated in it.

"Looks like Billy Tiger and his brothers," said Mr. Tooke. He walked to the end of the dock, caught the rope Billy threw him, and made the boat fast to a piling. I was disappointed they weren't in their spectacular dugout canoe.

"Welcome," Mr. Tooke greeted the men as they climbed onto the dock.

They had come for water and carried their various jugs and bottles with them, and Mrs. Tooke invited them for coffee. Peter and I were much too curious to leave at this point. We followed everyone back up to the house in a small procession and stood around under the banana palms while the Indians filled their water containers from the big well in front of the house. Mr. Tooke took out a pack of cigarettes and we all solemnly lit up. It was like a modern-day version of a peace pipe, and the clouds of smoke kept the insects somewhat at bay while we talked.

I'd met Billy Tiger when I visited the chickee with the deaconess. His two brothers, Joe and Charlie, were large, serious, and very dark. All three wore the traditional wide headbands and colorful shirts, which made them look amazingly exotic and like something out of an epic movie. Joe and Charlie stood, silently smoking, but Billy told Mr. Tooke they were going fishing.

"Got to get some jack to smoke," he told us, and I remembered the Seminoles were partial to their own smoked fish. Then he said, "You want some?" and Mrs. Tooke spoke up and said she'd be glad to trade some of their smoked pork for Billy's fish.

Mr. Tooke now introduced Peter and me, explaining our presence there. We were in a slightly awkward position because, even though the Audubon Society was completely on the side of preservation and conservation, and had good relations with the local tribes, we still carried a faint aura of officialdom and were a reminder of all that represented to the Seminoles. Peter was wearing his khaki shirt with its shoulder patch saying "Audubon," which made him look like a warden or some sort of cop.

Mr. Tooke eased the potential discomfort by saying, "This young fella's a scientist. He's workin' on the animal life around here. Gonna make them sit up and take notice back up north. Make people see the importance of preserving the swamps. Ain't that true, Scotty?" he said.

"Well, that'd be nice," Peter answered. "Haven't had much time to do anything about it so far. There's an awful lot to cover."

Billy Tiger and his brothers looked at him.

"You think anyone's going to listen?" said Billy, flatly. "There's people

I know who are really interested in trying to keep this place the way it is. Trouble is, there's just as many who only see it as real estate and a way to make money, and they usually speak the loudest."

The Seminoles had survived incredible hardships since they fled to the Everglades in the early 1800s to escape persecution in the north. The swamps gave them some protection, as many people feared the dark and dangerous region and gave the place a wide berth. Andrew Jackson though, made it his particular business to try to eradicate the Seminoles, and he ordered his soldiers into the Everglades and the Ten Thousand Islands to hunt down and kill the "heathen" Indians. It was a dark time in our history, and their population was cut from several thousand, down to a mere five hundred, but then, luckily for the Seminoles, the Civil War broke out and saved them. The whites turned to fighting each other and no longer had time to hunt the Seminoles.

The survivors had continued to make their home in these harshly inimical swamps, fishing and subsistence-farming on the higher ground. As time went by, a market for alligator skins developed. Both the Indians and the white "outlaws," who had also sought refuge in the Everglades, took to hunting them. Fierce competition developed between the two groups, until this means of livelihood became more hazardous than it was worth. The tribe went back to farming. In later days, the Indians found it was more lucrative and less dangerous to entertain tourists by wrestling with alligators instead of hunting them.

Mr. Tooke spoke up. "If they go ahead with this here National Park 'n all, you wonder what's gonna happen to all the people squatting on keys around here," he began. "Lots of folks lived here since their granddaddies settled. Don't reckon they's gonna get the same consideration as the critters. Not that most of 'ems worth a plugged nickel, shiftless lot that they are," he added.

Billy Tiger grunted. "Huh. Lots of folks' living gonna be taken away. Hard for a man to stay independent."

"I reckon they's two sides to everthing," Mrs. Tooke concluded. "We just got to do the best we can."

The coffee was drunk and the cigarettes stomped out on the ground.

Everyone took their departure. Although I was completely in favor of having the protection of the National Park for this magnificent place, I was also becoming aware of the delicate balance between the humans and the wildlife here and how difficult it was to manage things so that all could coexist in peace and harmony.

On our way back to Duck Rock, I told Peter about Art Eifler's mistrust of us. Naturally, he was furious.

"How could he think we'd sink so low as to spy on anyone? It's insulting. And how come he thinks he's so important the NAS would actually send a spy to watch him? It's preposterous. Silly old goat." He was spluttering.

"Oh well," I tried to be mollifying, "he's old and feeling vulnerable or something. I expect he'll get over it."

"He'd better. I just won't say a single word about him any more in my reports, even though I've only said good stuff about him. I guess it could be misinterpreted or something."

And we let it go at that.

Later, over our evening meal under the swinging lantern, Peter told me he'd seen hundreds of glossy ibis, a beautiful purplish-black marsh bird with a long curved bill that is now very rare. He said he didn't want to tell anyone else about seeing them, even the Tookes. The fewer people who knew the better, he said.

"Don't want to give anyone ideas about shooting up the Prairie," was his comment. We were tired from our long day, and after cleaning up the dishes we started getting ready for bed. A rising wind and high tide were causing the boat to rock more than was quite comfortable. Before we turned in, we stood in the stern cockpit and looked at the sky. The wind had blown away the no-see-ums and the mosquitoes for the time being, and we could be outside without their nagging attentions. As we looked up at the dark bowl of the sky, clear and filled with stars, we could see clouds forming over to the west and distant lightning flashing in giant sheets, sometimes white or yellow and even pink.

"We'll get rain tonight, I bet," Peter said.

"Good, I said, we're low on water so I hope it rains hard and fills up our tanks."

We turned in for the night. Hardly had I closed my eyes when there came a huge clap of thunder. The storm hit suddenly, lightning and thunder began flashing and crashing almost directly above our heads. If I could have, I'd have dived right under my bunk. The sound was deafening and took me back immediately to England and the air raids during the war. Although I'd left before the Battle of Britain and the London blitz, the Germans earlier had bombed the navy port where I was living with my mother, and we had endured nightly raids for a while. Not having a proper shelter then, we used to huddle in the broom closet under the stairs, though looking back, I don't think it was much protection. We'd go to bed with our clothes piled next to the bed along with our flashlights and gasmasks, and when the sirens sounded, we'd jump up, put on our clothes, and dash down to the closet. When the bombs fell close by, the noise was terrifying.

Ordinarily I'm not afraid of thunderstorms, but this one seemed to be directly overhead, and so loud I was sure we'd be struck by lightening. Torrents of rain streamed through the screens. I got my wish for rain and then some. Just as I was sure I couldn't stand it another minute, the storm started to move off, growling and flashing as it continued on over the land, diminishing until it became merely a distant grumbling. The rain let up to a mild patter. Peter got up.

"I'd better check on the small boats," he said, and I heard the screen door bang as he went out. Then I heard him call urgently, "Hey, Chloe, come and look at this."

I couldn't imagine what he had seen, and I scrambled out of my bunk not knowing whether to be alarmed or merely curious. The sky was almost clear with a big silver moon rising, and high above us, arching across the mangroves, was a luminous white bow, a moonbow, Peter told me, hanging pearly and serene, shining against the indigo sky. I could scarcely believe my eyes. A moonbow? I'd never heard of such a thing. It glowed there for what seemed a long time, peaceful and pure, in deep contrast to the recent disturbance of the storm. As it shone down on us, an ethereal and ghostly arc reflecting silver in the choppy waves of the Gulf, I was reminded of how the first rainbow after the Flood was supposed to be God's promise never to flood the world again. Is a moonbow a promise too, I wondered? A promise, perhaps, that calm will follow the storm, there will be peace after the struggle, and ultimately a restoration of balance in the world. Wouldn't it be nice to think so?

16

As the days lengthened towards summer, the weather grew hotter and our lives began to settle into something like regularity. Our work was not clearly defined. Apart from protecting the birds and keeping the boats running, there were no directives as to how we were supposed to spend our time. We had to figure it out as we went along. In many ways our situation was much like an extended, floating, camping trip, where simply dealing with the basics took up a major part of our lives.

Peter now had time to investigate some of the innumerable keys and shell mounds out in the Gulf or hidden up the rivers and creeks around us. All of them held secrets and surprises and only one or two were inhabited. Most had been untouched by man and were a scientific treasure trove just waiting to be discovered.

Peter began exploring regularly. He kept careful notes and recorded everything in his cramped handwriting in his tiny notebooks. (A few of these notebooks survive, but why he chose such little ones I don't know. Probably because they were easy to fit into his shirt pocket.) This whole vast region was so far off the beaten track, no one really knew much about the flora and fauna or if it differed from key to key. Peter's observations were of real value to the burgeoning environmental movement. Not far north of Duck Rock, a short way out into the Gulf, lay Pavilion Key, one of the larger keys, we saw it regularly in the distance as we went about our victual runs. We had noticed what appeared to be a sandy beach on the lee side, and Peter was curious about the place.

"I'll bet there's solid ground in the interior," he said one day, looking intently through his binoculars as we came back from a trip to Turkey Key for ice." I think I'll go over there this afternoon. Want to come?"

"Sure," I answered. "Let's take a picnic."

Water, sandwiches, beer, hat, dark glasses, binoculars, collection jars, bug spray, bag for shells, notebooks, pens—we were ready to go. A short while later, approaching the sandy, lee side of the key, we stared in disbelief as the entire surface of the beach appeared to be moving away. Dragging the skiff up onto the sand, we could see the cause of the illusion, many thousands of small crabs, all scurrying sideways down the sand on their spindly little legs. Closer inspection showed them to be some sort of fiddler crab with one front claw that was bigger than the other. Stamped on their red-and-purple shells was a white design that looked like a Japanese brush stroke.

Unfortunately, on this inviting tropical island there was little shade, even in the interior where a few skimpy trees shared the built-up area with the mangroves. Away from the beach there were a million bugs. We found a slightly sheltered spot for lunch, but we didn't dawdle over it. Then Peter braved the interior to look for birds while I walked along the beach collecting shells. It was a spectacular treasure trove of shells, probably no one had ever picked up a shell here before. My bag was full too quickly and I realized I needed to become more discriminating, throwing back the lesser specimens and keeping only the most perfect. I found beautiful, perfect coquina, big conches (conks, as they were called locally), sea urchins, starfish, scallops, and even an occasional rare spotted juinoia.

The fine white sand reflected the sun and heat, glaring into my eyes despite my sun glasses and shady hat. We should have come earlier, I thought. I was beginning to feel uncomfortable in the heat, but I was too enthralled by the amazing shells to quit. As I walked farther afield, I came across an even more exotic find, tree snail shells. These were quite rare and a real collector's item. No one was sure if these beautiful snails inhabited any of the outer keys, or if they washed up from Cuba. Tree snail shells are about three inches long, pointed and gracefully twisted into a spiral. They come in a wide variety of colors and markings, some orange or yellow with white spiral stripes, and others with red and purple bands around them.

As I continued walking down the beach, I made another discovery, a shallow, ragged hole with the remains of what looked like egg shells scattered around. I hollered, "Look what I've found," and Peter and he emerged from the bushes. I showed him the nest.

"I'll be damned, it's a sea turtle's nest," he exclaimed. "Let's see if there're any eggs left." He dug around with his hands and finally discovered three ping pong-sized eggs still unhatched.

"Judging by the tracks round here, it looks like coons got most of 'em," he said.

"You mean they didn't just hatch and go back to the water?" I was disturbed.

"No, I can see bits of egg left in the shells. They weren't ready to hatch yet. We'll take these three and see if maybe they'll hatch and we can protect them until they get a bit bigger."

It was still awfully hot, so by the time we'd gathered all these treasures, I was beginning to feel woozy from the sun.

"I've got to get out of this sun," I said. "I'm feeling a bit weird."

"You do look awfully flushed." Peter sounded a little worried. "I'd better get you back to the boat, I think you may have gotten a bit overexposed to the sun." We sped toward home, but I kept feeling progressively worse until I threw up over the side. As soon as we climbed aboard the *Audubon* I lay down in my bunk. Peter made me drink lots of water with a little salt and I recovered quickly. It was just a mild case of heat stroke, but I was more careful on future outings, because it can be dangerous.

Peter fixed up an aquarium for the turtles. While waiting for them to hatch, we kept them in a bucket of sand. They struggled out in a few days and started swimming around in their little dishpan right away, three perfect mini-turtles, delicate and vulnerable. They were greatly entertaining and I grew very fond of the tiny creatures. After they'd grown up somewhat and we released them back into the sea, I quite missed them.

We now had a growing menagerie that along with the turtles, included two chameleons and a small snake. The chameleons didn't do much, most of the time they just stayed immobile on their branches and I never saw them change color, they just rolled their eyes this way and that. They were wizards at catching flies though, flicking their long tongues out with amazing speed and accuracy, to capture and pull in their unsuspecting prey. When they eventually escaped and made their way back into the wild, I didn't miss them like I did the turtles. The turtles were cute and slightly humorous, while the chameleons were coldly prehistoric in a miniature way.

I realized I wanted a pet of some sort, and when Mrs. Tooke told me one of her cats was pregnant, I asked if we could have a kitten. I knew I'd have to work to persuade Peter, who wasn't too keen on the idea. I just figured I'd wait to bring it up until the kittens arrived and grown to that adorable, irresistible stage, and hope he'd weaken.

One day, coming back from an expedition to Gopher Key, where Peter had been counting pelicans and herons, he said, "I want to see if we can find this Mr. Darwin that Art and the Tookes have been telling us about. I bet there's some great stuff on his shell mound for me to check out." Meaning of course, creatures of one kind or another.

What we'd heard about Mr. Darwin sounded quite amazing. He lived all alone in the mangroves, sort of like a latter-day Robinson Crusoe. We didn't know much about him and had no idea where he came from or how long he'd been living on his shell mound. We'd met him once at Turkey Key, getting ice. He'd invited us to visit any time, so we felt it would be all right to drop in unannounced. Since there was absolutely no way of contacting him except to go there, we could hardly give him any warning anyway.

Finding him proved to be more difficult than expected. He lived up one of the innumerable creeks, somewhere near Gopher Key. All Peter had was an X on a rough map Art had given him with the instruction: "Look for the two creeks that come out across from each other by the hairpin bend before Gopher Key creek entrance." These directions did not make me happy. I was sure we'd get lost and end up fodder for the alligators.

"Well, I can find the hairpin bend easily enough," said my intrepid explorer husband, "but I'm not too sure about the two creeks. We'll just have a looksee and if there're any doubts, we won't go today and we'll get better directions."

What could I say? He always sounded so reasonable and he had proved quite talented at navigating through these treacherous waters. We circled around, went up and down a couple of creeks and finally came to the entrance to a creek that seemed to answer the maps description. So, we set off in what we hoped would be the probable direction of Mr. Darwin's camp. As we putted up the narrow water way, it began to widen and we could smell smoke. We came around a bend and there on the bank was old man Darwin himself. He was bending over a campfire cooking what turned out to be palm cabbage in an old blackened pot. He looked up and hailed us, and as we approached the landing spot, he came to help us tie up our boat.

"Well, if it ain't the warden and his missus." He smiled his toothless smile. "Come on up." He handed me out of the skiff with old-world aplomb and led us across a sandy stretch to where he had his tent rigged up. There was only a top to it, no sides, but I noticed he had a mosquito net hanging over his cot in the corner. The camp was neat and orderly, supplies were piled in crates and boxes, while utensils and tools were placed on makeshift shelves. No trash or garbage littered the ground, which looked lately swept. The usual mixture of palms, swamp cypresses, mangroves, and even a large poinciana, grew thickly behind his living space.

He reminded me of Walter Brennan, spare and leathery, in his ragged pants and cracked leather boots without laces. His deeply tanned and wrinkled face was lively and expressive, making him seem much younger than his seventy odd years. He moved around like a young man in his thirties, agile and competent, as he arranged makeshift seats out of boxes for us.

"Here. Try some of this hearts of palm. Real delicious. Good fer you, too," he offered, ladling some of the stewed vegetable into a couple of tin bowls. I nibbled it gingerly at first, but the taste was pleasing, mildly reminiscent of a chestnut combined faintly with cabbage. We praised his cooking.

"If you like it, I'll cut you out one before you leave," he promised.

He showed us around his domain, which had a kind of shipwreck charm. He was almost completely self-sufficient and was starting to farm the place. He'd already planted rows of beans and lettuce, a few tomatoes, and some different squashes. We wandered all over, hoping to see the Indian shell mounds we'd heard about, but the paths leading to them were impassable. They were covered with the trees he had been clearing to make way for the future farm. He told us he used to be a commercial fisherman, but now he fished only for his own needs. He was hoping to sell his produce, once it materialized, to make a little cash for the few things he had to buy such as gas for the boats, salt, and flour.

He had somehow managed to procure a large cistern for water, and while we were poking around, Peter discovered some white-footed mice in the crevices underneath it. He got quite excited and said that, to his knowledge, they had never been recorded in this part of the country before. He tried, but couldn't catch them, they were too shy to be enticed out of their niches. Peter asked if he could come back and try to trap them another time, which seemed fine with Mr. Darwin, who was interested in everything. In talking to him, it didn't seem that he knew much about the wildlife that surrounded him, which was too bad. As Peter pointed out later, his living situation provided a great opportunity to keep records of whatever he came across, observations that might have been quite original discoveries.

It was clear to us he had a tremendous amount of work to do and we didn't want to outstay our welcome, so we started to leave.

"Hold on there," he said. "I want to get you some of this hearts o' palm," and taking up his well honed and oiled machete, he chopped away at a small palm tree and extracted the "heart," the growing center, and gave it to us to take home.

Art had told us Mr. Darwin was fond of beer and liked to read newspapers, so we promised we'd bring him some in exchange the next time we visited. We did end up going back to visit several times and Mr.

Darwin became a friend. We'd bring him his beer and the papers, and he'd give us hearts of palm.

While Peter had his "bird business" and his scientific interest in the wildlife everywhere, I was often thrown on my own devices. Apart from housekeeping, which obviously was limited in such a small space, there wasn't much for me to do that was built in, as it were. Luckily, as I said, I had always been an ardent reader. I kept a list of books I read that summer. I'd long forgotten about it, and when I looked at it again after so many years, I have to say I was impressed. Here it is:

Remembrance of Things Past (7 Books), Proust; *Howard's End*, E. M. Forster; *Room With a View*, E. M. Forster; *Where Angel's Fear To Tread*, E. M. Forster; *Passage to India*, E. M. Forster; *The Odyssey*, new translation by E. V. Rieu; *Really the Blues*, Mezz Mezrow; *Sanctuary*, William Faulkner; *The Counterfeiters*, Andre Gide; *Leonardo Da Vinci*, Freud; *Modern Woman*, Ferdinand Lundberg and Marynia F. Farnham; *Zuleika Dobson*, Max Beerbohm; *Green Mansions*, W. H. Hudson; *Origin of Things*, Julius E. Lips; *Walden*, Thoreau; *Butterfield 8*, John O'Hara; *Orlando*, Virginia Woolf; *The Heart Is a Lonely Hunter*, Carson McCullers; *Robinson Crusoe*, Daniel Defoe; *Man Against Myth*, Burrows Dunham; *Heavenly Discourse*, Charles Erskine Scott Wood; *Young Man With a Horn*, Dorothy Baker; *How To Like an Englishman*, C.V.R. Thompson; *E. M. Forster*, Lionel Trilling; *Long, Long Ago*, Alexander Woollcott; *Now Listen, Warden*, Ray P. Holland. This is not counting numerous murder mysteries, magazines and other miscellany.

However satisfying reading proved, movement has always been too important to me to ignore. Since I was six years old, I had danced in various milieu. At the age of nine, I was enrolled in a professional ballet school in London where I went six days a week (and twice on Saturday). Every afternoon I took the No. 70 bus from St. John's Wood to the Kathleen de Voss Studio in George Street, a 20-minute ride. I would climb up to the top of a red double-decker bus, there I'd try to get the front seat with the wide window, so I could ride in style above the traffic and dream about being a great ballerina. This continued for five years until, in 1939, we had to leave London because of the outbreak of WW II. Even after that, I always managed to find ways to dance wherever I happened to be, both in England and in the United States.

So, to be confined to a 30-foot boat was like being caged. At first it hadn't seemed to be a problem. I was too distracted by the demands of our new way of life, and the adjustments I had to make. But as we settled into a more routine existence, I began to feel the familiar restlessness I encountered if I stopped getting enough exercise.

I tried to find activities to keep me occupied aboard the *Audubon*. I wrote daily in my journal on my ancient Olivetti. For a while, I tried my hand at water colors, but became discouraged by my total lack of talent. There was always painting of the more practical kind to be done. In that climate, paint didn't last long, either exterior or interior, and I found myself all too often, paintbrush in hand, redoing the floor or the ceiling or the shutters. But none of these things satisfied my need for movement. I began to suffer for it and so did my moods and my relationship with Peter.

17

Thunder rolled, the boat rocked, and I could hear the wind starting up. Peter and I lay there in the dark, waiting. How bad would this blow get? I just wanted to go back to sleep, but the rocking and the noise of the oncoming storm was making it impossible. Then the rain started, at first a scattered pattering on the roof of our cabin, then stronger and stronger until it was just pelting down. There was no help for it; we'd have to get up and put the shutters over the screens if we didn't want to find a flood in the morning.

"I'll go, honey," said Peter, but I knew how much easier it would be with two, and I joined him. Struggling in the dark, the wind tearing through the screens, we wrestled the shutters into place.

"I'd better check on the small boats," he said, and he went out the back door. "They're okay for now," he reported, as he came back in dripping.

"Good. Let's go back to bed."

I hoped at least we'd get enough rain to fill the water tanks. We were getting low, and if we couldn't catch enough rainwater, we'd have to make the long run into Everglades just to fill up the tanks.

The thunder rumbled on, lightning flashed around us, and the wind whistled above while we continued to rock. The strength of the squall was diminishing, I could tell. Soon, it would pass on towards the mainland, where it would die out in the mangroves. A few minutes later the rain stopped abruptly. Now we had to get up again and take the wretched shutters off the windows, it was too hot to leave them up. By that time the wind had almost died away, the skies had cleared and the moon was out.

I scurried thankfully back to my bunk. Peter wanted to get in with me, but I was too hot and too grumpy. He got up again and went to smoke a cigarette. I knew he was miffed, but he'd get over it. I slept.

Fortunately for both of us, Peter had a forgiving and resilient nature. He was perfectly cheerful in the morning and my affection for him welled up as I cooked our favorite breakfast, scrambled eggs (the way his mother did them, very slowly, stir lightly, no salt till set), the last of the bacon, and lots of toast and marmalade.

As the storm had not brought enough water to fill the tanks, we decided to take the big boat and go in to Everglades. Actually, I couldn't wait to get to town. Even a middle-of-nowhere little town like Everglades City seemed like civilization, after a week at Duck Rock. I was anxious to get the mail. Mail was such a high point in our lives, isolated and without other methods of communication as we were. It's hard to describe the importance of mail in those days. Now, in our digital age with its variety of instant communications, World-Wide Web and cell phones, the glacial pace of connections fifty years ago seems unimaginable. But for us, the mail, once you had it in your hand—tangible, palpable—was a treasure to be savored for days. Reading and rereading the pages, even though the feelings, thoughts, and reported doings were probably quite out of date, nevertheless there was the illusion of immediacy, of someone speaking to you off the page.

People wrote more back then, too. Writing a good long letter, say three or four pages, could take an hour, but people did it without thinking too much about it, because that was how you stayed in touch with friends and family, it was what you did. My spirits rose at the thought of walking over to the little shack that was our Post Office. There were no post office boxes—you just went in and asked for your mail and the post mistress, Mrs. Little (a very large lady) knew who everyone was. Taking my packet of letters from her, I would be filled with a tingling sense of anticipation, hoping especially for letters from my friend Donna, who always had great gossip to tell, or from my mother, who told me all the latest doings (not quite gossip) about all the folks in East Hampton. Missing my family and friends was a constant internal struggle and these letters helped to keep me going.

"Tide'll be up soon." Peter spoke through a mouthful of toast. "We'd better get ready to go."

The storm had left the air cooler, and the horizon was a shining line between sea and sky, the distant keys standing out sharp and clear against the blueness of the Gulf. I gazed across the smooth expanse of water, dazzled by the early morning clarity, breathing in the still cool air that for once was not smelling of mangrove mud. Even though most of the birds had left for their day of foraging, there was still plenty of bird action going on around the mangroves. Gulls and terns swooped back and forth, some landing in the exposed mud picking up crustaceans and other tasty morsels, while the nesting birds fussed about, straightening, tidying and staying vigilant against any outside threat.

By this time, Peter's experience driving the boats had given him confidence in his ability to navigate the twisting, narrow channels and shoals along our route. The sea was as calm as the proverbial millpond as he sat on the high stool steering easily, while I sat at the table, reading *Robinson Crusoe* out loud as we chugged along. I had to yell above the pounding of the engines. Even though I tried to put into practice the skills I had learned at the American Academy of Dramatic Arts, the year I spent trying to be an actress in New York, I couldn't keep it up for long. Projecting your voice, even with breath control and relaxation was no match for the *Audubon's* noisy racket. I soon gave up, and we rode along looking out over our watery domain. As we moved further out into the Gulf, we passed Rabbit Key and Turtle Key, skirted along the very edges of the Ten Thousand Islands and on by Demijohn Key and Dismal Key. We slipped unnoticed by the notorious Chokoloskee Island and Chokoloskee Pass, on to Indian Key, which was a beautiful long green island with large white herons dotted in its trees. Then finally, on up through Indian Key Pass to the Barron River and Everglades City. The whole ride we saw very little boat traffic, it felt like we were the last humans on earth. We saw a trawler way out in the Gulf, and as we got closer to civilization a small boatload of fisher folk from Russell Key waved to us as they preceded us up the Barron, but that was it. It was easy to get lonely and feel isolated out here.

Peter cut back the motor and we glided smoothly towards our usual berth in front of the Leightys' house.

"Gee, the tide's awful strong today," Peter said suddenly. He was trying to turn the boat around, making a U-turn so we could berth facing down stream as we were supposed to. The boat kept shearing off and ending up in mid-stream, far from the bank. The motorboat and skiff, which were tied on behind us all the time like a caudal limb, made the maneuvering all the more difficult. The Leightys had come out of their house and were watching, looking worried.

Art emerged from the *Spoonbill* where he was tied up further along the bank. After a minute he scratched his head and called out, "Throw me a line, maybe I can pull 'er in."

I flung a rope from the stern well and then Art and Ralph hauled. With the extra resistance, Peter was able to head the boat into her berth and we finally tied up safely. I was relieved to get off the boat and onto something solid, glad for a reprieve from the constant rocking and rolling. It's true what they tell you about getting your land legs or your sea legs, it always takes a few days to make the transition. As I headed for the post office, everything continued going gently up and down, it was such a strange sensation. Even this early in the morning, the sun was beating down on us. I'd forgotten my hat and my scalp felt scorched. By the time I got to the post office, I was dripping sweat. Mrs. Little gathered up a small bundle of mail and handed it to me.

"You look hot, missus," she said concernedly. "Better sit in the shade a while. Here, I'll get you a drink."

She disappeared into the back and returned with a glass of water, which I downed thankfully. There was an old metal bench, just outside the post office, in the shade of a big jacaranda tree. I made a beeline for it. I wanted a place to sit in privacy and comfort, taking my time to relish my precious mail. To my delight there was a letter from my mother. She was planning on visiting us and now she confirmed she could come in three weeks. She could stay a month. Would that suit?

I was thrilled. She'd be here for my twenty-second birthday in May. My mother and I had been separated for the five long years of World War II while she remained in London. She had been in America only a brief year, and now I'd gone off again on this mad adventure to Florida. I missed her. I seemed to have spent a large part of my life missing her, and I longed to be with her again, to catch up on our lost times and life experiences. I so looked forward to showing her everything, she would love it. "Mummy" (as my brother and I had always called her), had an enormous zest for life. She was undaunted by the many hardships she had faced. First the war, with air raids, buzz bombs and rationing. Then there was the worry of having a beloved son out on the high seas, on dangerous convoy duty with the Royal Navy. Finally, she had come through a completely devastating and unwanted divorce suit brought by my father. Her ability to keep up her good spirits through it all was amazing and inspirational to me.

Three weeks. That would give us time to organize a bit. I would have to get some bedding for the cot in the cabin, make sure we had some good tea, and try to make things as comfy as possible. We would meet her at the Miami train station and she could have a glimpse of the city before we came back to the boat. My mind ran on, planning details. I hoped Peter would be as pleased as I was with the prospect of a visit from his mother-in-law. They got on perfectly well, but even so, I realized it might be rather close quarters for a whole month. I wondered if perhaps my mother could stay with the Tookes for part of the time.

By now, I had cooled off, and I walked slowly back to the boat. No sign of Peter and Art. Perhaps they were talking to the Leightys. I went in their open back door. Inside it was cooler and Rosa had the big overhead fan going. Everyone was sitting in the living room drinking coffee and smoking, so I joined them. I can't believe I ever smoked. I quit thirty-five years ago, but in those far off days of my youth, even though we called cigarettes "coffin nails," and our elders assured us it would stunt our growth, we simply didn't really believe there was any reason for serious concern.

Rosamaria was allowed a soda and she came and sat on my lap. She was an adorable child and we had become firm pals. Her big brown eyes gazing up at me, she implored me to take her for a ride on the boat.

"Oh, Rosamaria," I said, "I'd love to take you for a ride, but right now we can't do it. We're on business, you see. I tell you what, you can come out to see us by boat when the tours start." When would that be, she wanted to know. "Pretty soon." I said. Rosa wanted to know more.

"These tours are starting soon, no?" she asked.

Peter answered, "Yeah, Charlie Brookfield in Miami is supposed to be organizing them right now. We're waiting to hear from him."

"Who is going to be coming on the tours?" Rosa was curious.

"I guess anyone who's interested in the region and conservation, or it could just be nature lovers. The tours are going to be really cheap, because the NAS wants to make it easy and affordable for anyone who wants to go. The tour will include, coming to Everglades, staying at the Rod and Gun Club, and then going out on the boat to Duck Rock. The boat will take you all around the keys near Duck Rock, and the high point will be watching the birds fly in to roost, while eating a picnic dinner. All for ten bucks," he elaborated. It was a good deal, even for those times. I spoke up, "We've heard that maybe next weekend there's going to be a special inaugural tour. Mr. Baker himself is supposed to come. He's bringing some bigwigs or something."

I still wasn't sure how I felt about the tours, but we didn't have much of a choice. I think I was just worried about hosting groups of people I didn't know. The subject of preservation and its promotion locally was considered to be part of our job here. There were plenty of folks living in these parts, who didn't hold with the idea at all. To change their entrenched notions about the regional bioecology would not be an easy task. There was also a deeply held suspicion and distrust of the government, not entirely without reason, and by extension, of anything even vaguely smacking of Authority. Anything "the government" said was greeted charily. Rosa read my mind.

"This conservation is such an important idea. Ralph is wanting to introduce this idea to his classes. Maybe you, Peter, could come and talk to the PTA sometime? Tell them how they could help?"

"Maybe," said Peter dubiously. "I'm not much of a public speaker." We finished our coffees.

"Well, we'd better be off," said Peter, standing up. "Got to get gas and fill the water tanks."

"I'll give you a hand," said Art. I could see he wanted to talk to Peter privately, so we said our farewells, and headed back to the boat.

Art was in the throes of his continuing paranoid misconception of his relationship with the Society. For some reason, he had it in his head that he was about to be fired. There was not a shred of evidence for this dark thought, but he kept on about it anyway. Peter was doing his best to mollify him, so I left them to it and went off to the grocery store.

The grocery owners, Mr. and Mrs. Monroe, were a very friendly couple and always made me feel that they were glad to see me.

"Well, how's the bird business?" asked Mr. Monroe with a smile.

Everyone repeated this to us—it was a source of much self-amused chuckling at the cleverness of the phrase.

"Oh, we're doing fine," I said. "We really love it out there."

No one seemed able to believe that we could possibly, actually enjoy our job.

"Lots of birds, are there? No one been bothering you?"

This last was an allusion to the Chokoloskee folks and the Gomez boys in particular, I guessed.

"No, we haven't seen any troublemakers out there," I answered. "Why, has anyone said anything?"

"Oh, no, not so as you'd pay them any mind. They's always braggin' they's goin' to go out there and shoot it up as soon as you-all leave."

I found this far from reassuring, but I put on my usual brave face and brushed it off. "Oh, well, they're big talkers, we know that." I said, and got out my grocery list. Mrs. Monroe pumped me a little about the Tookes, but I was determinedly bland and non-committal. Not that I knew any interesting gossip anyway, I just felt I needed to be extra cautious saying anything about anyone, to anyone else around here.

"I hear them Audubon Society people's going to start tours out there," said Mr. Monroe, raising his eyebrows, "Can't imagine who'd want to go out there with all them bugs and all, just to look at them birds." He sounded quite scornful. The Monroes weren't the greatest on conservation and natural wonders.

"Well," I answered, "We're going to give it a try. If the tours go well, it might bring you some customers at any rate."

Apparently, this was an aspect he hadn't thought of. He changed his tune a little. "Yes, well, maybe it might bring a few new tourists around, and that's always to the good. Business been fallin' off lately."

I paid for my groceries and headed back to the boat. Peter had gassed up and filled the water tanks and was impatient to be off while we still had the tide. He'd been in the drug store where the Gomez boys were getting drunk on gin with beer chasers. They had made cracks about shooting the birds and had told Peter that, since the tide was a little low, he'd better go out the long way around by Indian Key. Peter was worried they were planning to run out ahead of us and get to Duck Rock before we did and shoot it up.

The weather was holding and it looked as if we'd have an easy ride home. I cast off and we started down the smooth green waters of the Barron River, now so familiar. A few gulls flew along with us on their way to the Gulf. Once out of the mouth of the river we headed for Sand fly Pass, the faster way home, albeit shallower. Peter figured the tide was perfectly adequate to get us through.

We were nearly home to Duck Rock when suddenly, looking out the stern, I saw that the skiff, the smaller of our two auxiliary boats, had come untied and was floating with the tide, about three hundred yards back. We turned around and as we came up to it, we slowed down, and I managed to jump in, landing with a thump in the bottom. After some maneuvering, I was able to reach the other boat and secure the skiff once more to its stern. Then I had to scramble from one boat to another, until I could get myself back onto the big boat.

We started off again, but now Peter was getting worried we were taking too long to get back. A few miles further on, once more we stopped.

"God, this is ridiculous. Those Gomezes could've gone around the other way and raced out there ahead of us easily by now. I can't delay any longer, I'll take the skiff, and you can bring the *Audubon* the rest of the way back."

"What are you talking about? I've never driven the big boat," I wailed.

"Yes, you have. Just take the wheel, honey. It's not far so don't worry, I know you can do it easily," and with that, he climbed into the speed boat and raced off, hell-bent for election. Suddenly here I was alone in our big boat, out on the blue waters chugging along between innumerable mangrove islets. Peter was right and it wasn't very far, but I wasn't convinced I could navigate the shallows and channels safely. But after all, I reasoned, Peter must have believed I could do it or he wouldn't have gone off so cavalierly and left me. Or would he?

After a while, my nerves dissipated and I began to enjoy myself. Standing there at the wheel, looking out over the bow as the boat cruised steadily along, I began to gain confidence. Faint echoes of my nautical background came to my mind and I imagined that, if I'd been born a male, I would certainly have headed for a career in the navy, as had all my forbears. Obviously, this was hardly a naval situation, just an old tub putting along in a backwater, but it was fun fantasizing—I was the captain of a vessel on a mission. Somewhat to my surprise, I managed a competent job and brought the boat safely through the waterways, to arrive at our three stakes sticking up out of the muck. A pair of frigate birds were circling majestically overhead to welcome me home, as I tied up.

Peter came back from a short patrol he'd taken around the keys. I was very relieved when he reported there was no sign of the Gomezes.

"I guess they got too drunk to make it, this time," he said rather grimly. We knew the threat never went away entirely. They would almost certainly try again.

18

For the tenth time I opened the screen door to the stern well and looked out toward the mainland. No sign of any boats.

"Where are they?" I fussed to Peter. He was sitting up on the high stool by the steering wheel, cigarette in hand.

"Relax," he answered with irritating calm, "they'll be here soon. You know how it is with boats, anything could have happened."

Nervously I checked everything over. The boat was tidy and as clean as could be under the circumstances. There was a fresh block of ice in the icebox. The head was clean. I'd given it an extra dose of Lysol, plus we had a bottle of chlorophyll open beside the toilet, as there was a leak Peter had not been able to fix and it was apt to smell unpleasant.

"You're sure Art knows to bring beer?" I said, although even if he forgot, there wasn't much I could do about it at this point.

"That's one thing he will remember," Peter answered, smiling. He got up, stretched and stubbed out his cigarette. "Stop worrying honey. Anyway, it's Charlie's responsibility to get all the food and stuff together. He's sharp. He won't forget anything as important as beer." My husband was right, of course, but it didn't help my nerves much.

I had butterflies in my stomach about the start of these summer tours. Mr. Baker in New York, in coordination with our pal, Charlie Brookfield, in Miami, had been planning them for months and finally the inaugural tour was about to happen. I was unsure of myself as a hostess and couldn't quite imagine how the event would unfold. I went out to the stern well again and thought I could see a white dot, way off, coming from the direction of Everglades. "Get the glasses," I told Peter. "I think I see the boat."

He came and stood by me, binoculars in hand.

"Yeah," he agreed, holding them to his eyes. "That looks like the *Snowy Egret*. Wait a minute," he exclaimed, "I think there's another boat. Yes, by golly, there're two. That must be Art's *Spoonbill* as well. Baker must be bringing a bunch of friends for the first tour." Great, I thought sarcastically, but did not say.

The boats came bumping towards us across the dark blue water of the Gulf, the white spume of the bow waves neatly unfurling on either side of their prows. As they neared us, the drivers cut their motors, coasted to a stop, and secured a line around our mooring stakes. Art climbed aboard first, all decked out with a red kerchief knotted around his leathery throat.

"Here's the grub," he said, as he handed Peter a huge hamper of food from the Rod & Gun Club hotel.

Then Mr. Baker debarked, and after heaving his rather large bulk over the side, he greeted us with dignified warmth.

"I want you to meet my friends from New York. This is Mr. and Mrs. Adams, long-time supporters of the NAS."

We shook hands. They appeared to me, to be the type of people who would hang out with my father-in-law, George Scott, at his snobby Maidstone Club in East Hampton. Mrs. Adams seemed particularly up-tight. Her face was so stiff, she seemed afraid it might crack and fall off if she smiled. Still, I wanted to give them the benefit of the doubt. Afterall, they had made the effort to come to this far off wilderness, so they must have some redeeming qualities.

"This is Mr. Davis," continued Mr. Baker. "He is also from back East, but he's visited us out here before on several occasions. An old hand, you might say," he added in his overly jocular manner.

Mr. Davis, gray-haired, wearing shorts and sandals, looked rather under the weather, and pleading a hangover, made a beeline for the cabin, where, without so much as a by-your-leave, he stretched out on a bunk for a rest. Apparently, he knew his way around the boat.

Before I had time to react, Charlie Brookfield, who had piloted the *Snowy Egret*, now appeared leading his troop of visitors. He was all dressed up in nautical rig with a yachting cap and blue blazer, looking very natty.

He called out as he came through the screen door, "Ahoy there, shipmates. Good to see you again. Looks like we've got a good night for this, anyway."

He had brought Mr. and Mrs. Andrews from Miami with their two young sons in tow. They appeared much more affable and I felt relieved. She was small and dark with a gentle face. He was on the staff of the Miami Herald. He was planning on taking pictures for an article he was writing about what Audubon was trying to do out here. There were twelve of us in all and I was a little overwhelmed as they crowded into our cabin. The two little boys, tanned and barefoot, ran all over the boat, banging in and out of the screen door. I was rather alarmed at first, but their parents didn't seem concerned, so I stopped worrying.

At first, it was all rather stiff and stilted small talk, and the conversation felt awkward. *How was your trip out here? Those boats are rather small. Yes, it is an amazing place, we are just beginning to realize how lucky we are to be here. You can put your jacket here if you like. The bathroom is just down the steps there, I'm afraid it's rather primitive. Do you need 612? The mosquitoes are really awful. Would you like a drink or anything? We have Coke or beer and there's hot coffee.*

Peter's role was naturalist/tour guide, pointing out the birds and the different keys, and in general explaining things. That got him out of the "host" chores, which meant they were left to me. The children in particular were full of questions. *What's that bird? When can we go over to Duck Rock? Are there alligators over there?* They liked the baby turtles, which we let them pick up.

"What will you do when they get too big for their bowl?" asked Joe, the older brother.

"Oh, we'll let them go long before that," I assured him.

Soon after the preliminaries, Mr. Baker pointed over to Duck Rock. "Well, ladies and gentlemen, shall we take a closer look at this amazing island? I can see a lot of birds over there, even though they haven't started to come in yet." "Boys"—this to the children—"ready to go for another boat ride?" Then to Charlie, Art and Peter, "Let's get going. We'll take the boats around Duck Rock and maybe up the Chatham a ways. Peter, you can lead us."

With that, he swept the party (except for poor hung-over Mr. Davis) back into the small boats, and off they went for the "sightseeing" part of the tour.

Happy to have a few moments alone, I eagerly read the mail Art had brought us from Everglades. I knew Peter's two younger brothers, Henry and Tom, and their cousin, Walter Helmuth, wanted to come and visit on their way to a Mexican adventure. Now I had a letter from Henry, the middle brother, stating that they were in the midst of refurbishing an old World War II weapons-carrier truck. Apparently, they'd acquired it from some army surplus store, and as soon as it was ship shape, they planned to set forth on their odyssey, which included a visit to us. Weapons-carrier? What on earth were those boys up to? I sort of hoped their visit wouldn't overlap with my mother's, as we'd be awfully cramped for sleeping space with everyone there at once. Maybe they could stay with the Tookes for some of the time. We'd manage somehow. I couldn't wait to see everybody. I longed for a real old-fashioned, stay-up-all-night drinking and talking gab fest. One of those sessions of sharing and joking, where you could say anything without censoring yourself and trust you would be completely understood, the kind of time which was only possible to have with old, tried and true friends and family.

Peter and I seemed to have run out of that kind of conversation. Our communication, though easy enough, tended to be mostly on a practical, more day to day life level. Peter was uncomfortable with the sort of youthful delving and questioning that most of our friends enjoyed. We were busy dismantling middlebrow American ideals and in revolt against the conformity of that priggish conservative era. Peter agreed in principle with our liberal leanings, he just didn't like talking about them. Maybe he just had a hard time articulating his feelings. I was too young then to grasp this difference between us or the importance of it for me. I just felt something was missing.

I had almost forgotten Mr. Davis, still languishing in the cabin when

I went down into the galley to wash up some cups and glasses. He looked so miserable I offered him an aspirin, which he refused with a wan smile. In about an hour, the tour folks returned, delighted with their explorations and exclaiming excitedly about the variety and number of birds they'd seen.

"Just wait till you see the real show," said Peter. "You'll truly be amazed." He was full of enthusiasm. The sightseeing trip had gone well and all the tourists were properly awed. The Adamses seemed to be more relaxed and a little less reserved. Peter told me later they had been impressed because they'd found out his parents were the *St. Louis* Scotts and were in the Social Register.

As the birds began to come in Mr. Baker said, "I'm sure everyone could use a drink at this point. We've got gin and tonic, beer, and some sodas, I think."

Peter and Art chipped ice and helped serve everyone. Mr. Davis reappeared from the cabin, cheered by the prospect of a drink. The birds made a particularly beautiful showing as they returned, with the sun lowering on the horizon, sending streaks of golden light into a few low clouds to the west and reflecting on the water all around us, illuminating the brilliant plumage of the birds. The magic moment stretched out as the long lines of herons, egrets, cranes, and spoonbills, with a few attendant cormorants and anhingas, came streaming in. Duck Rock sat comfortably on its long-legged roots as the thousands of birds descended into the dark green foliage of its treetops, and settled themselves down for the night with their usual squawks and gurgles. With only a few late stragglers still flying home, Mr. Baker said, "That's quite a show isn't it? Not many places in the world you can see something like that. More than worth the bit of trouble to get here, don't you think?"

Charlie raised his glass, "Here's to the Duck Rock tours, it looks like we're off to a good start."

Everyone murmured "Hear, hear" and raised their glasses in return, and then we all fell to on the excellent sandwiches and salads, cake and cookies, provided by the Rod & Gun Club in Everglades, where the group would be returning to spend the night. It seemed everyone had a good time, even the uptight Adamses. The Andrews family especially had enjoyed themselves. Mr. Andrews promised to come back.

"Need some more pictures," he said. "I'm going to do a special about this place and you folks and the job you're doing. Make a great story."

After the picnic, everyone piled back into the boats to head home. As they were leaving, Mr. Baker told us privately he was very pleased with this inaugural tour and felt it had been an unqualified success. Peter and I were gratified that our efforts had paid off. Exhausted, we collapsed into our bunks.

But it was not quite over. The next morning being Sunday, Peter and I were sleeping in, when to our horror we saw a boat approaching fast across the water. It was the *Snowy Egret* and they, whoever they were, were obviously coming to see us. Our boat was a mess and I wasn't even dressed. We flew around tidying up and I retired to the cabin to throw on my jeans. I heard male voices, mainly Mr. Baker's, and when I emerged, he, Art and two strange men were standing in the cabin. Mr. Baker introduced them as Mr. Barron Collier Jr. and Mr. White. It seemed they were supposed to have come to Duck Rock on yesterday's tour but had missed the boat (as it were).

Collier was a very big name around Florida then and still is. According to Art, the Colliers "run everything in southern Florida." No matter how unreliable Art's information might be, I did know the family was big in major real estate developments and politics. There seemed to be something ulterior in the purpose of this visit, something I couldn't put my finger on. I decided it must be connected to the coming of the Everglades National Park. I did not believe Mr. Collier would be much interested in conservation, so I suspected that there were deals being made. Perhaps Mr. Baker, acting in his capacity as president of the National Audubon Society, was a go-between for the National Park Service and the powerful interests represented by the Collier family. The whole National Park project was a major issue, generating much argument, not only among the locals, who, granted, had a lot at stake, but also among the Army Corps of Engineers, the real-estate developers, fishermen, and of course the Seminoles. I must say, I didn't have a very good feeling about Mr. Barron Collier. He was a glib, fast-talking character, who went on and on about his experiences in the war in New Guinea. To hear him tell it, he was some kind of big naval hero. Mr. White, who seemed to be his flunky, had nothing much to say and mostly stood there silently agreeing with whatever Collier said. All in all, we weren't very sorry when they headed back to Everglades.

As the weeks passed and the tour groups became more part of our routine, it developed that they came in many different flavors. Some were chatty and lively, which made our job easier, while others were shy or unresponsive, making it more arduous for us. Luckily, most were enthusiastic or at least interested. I always felt responsible for everyone's experience and took it personally when people seemed disappointed. Peter wasn't burdened with this attitude. If they didn't enjoy themselves that was their problem. This, I told myself, was a much more sensible approach, but no matter what the particular characteristics of any group, I couldn't help feeling it was up to us to make the tours as enjoyable as possible. Consequently, we made every effort to make the tours successful. We hadn't bargained on being tour guides when we signed on for this job, and nobody had asked us if we wanted to do it. Audubon had just simply assumed we'd be happy to oblige. While I agreed that the idea behind the tours was certainly commendable, and I was all for educating the public, I wasn't so sure I was the one for the job. But ready or not, here came the tours, every weekend all summer. On top of it all, it turned out that 1946 was one of the rainiest years ever recorded. Of course, we didn't know this at the time. All we knew was that it rained a lot.

Usually the tours were canceled when rain threatened, but sometimes the tourists got caught, like one boatload that arrived in a driving rainstorm. Charlie was navigating, and everyone aboard was soaked. We were able to come up with enough spare clothes to share around so no one would freeze. Fortunately, it stopped raining after a while and everyone managed to have a good time in spite of being damp.

One tour consisted of two almost identical old ladies, their classic blue hairstyles neatly held in hair nets, who announced they should be called Aunt Lil and Aunt Marge. Longtime birders, they came with their life lists in hand and were thrilled to be able to add glossy ibises to their roster.

Once a large group of twelve showed up late. They'd been stuck on a newly emerged sandbar for two hours. Our facilities were instantly overwhelmed as everyone had to go to the bathroom, which meant pumping the poor faulty pump to the point of destruction!

We had our share of near and actual catastrophes. On one outing Mrs. Sherman, a doughty lady dressed in seersucker and pearls, dropped one of her tennis shoes into the water as she stepped from the *Ibis* onto our boat. Fortunately, she thought it was funny.

"Oh," she said, shaking with laughter, "I'm glad I wore my old sneakers. I'd have hated to lose my new pumps." And she took off the other sneaker, adding, "I like being barefoot better, anyway."

Seasickness was hardly ever a problem, surprisingly. But one group arrived with a tour participant pale green and heaving over the side. The poor woman wanted nothing more than to lie down and die. We put her on one of the bunks and gave her ginger ale, an old-fashioned remedy. It was calm at our mooring and she began to recover, but she never left the cabin, and she worried the whole time about the trip back.

One of our most amusing incidents was during a high school outing when young Jim Fitzgerald fell overboard. I thought it served him right. He was showing off for one of the girls and he slipped off the stern and splashed into the warm Gulf water.

At first, he flailed around shouting, "Help, help! I can't swim!"

No one took him seriously because we knew it was so shallow, he could easily stand, so to his dismay we just laughed. When he discovered he could put his feet down, he looked so sheepish, it was quite endearing and I got over being annoyed with him. We pulled him out dripping and muddy. Fortunately, it was at the end of the day, but he still ended up having to drive home uncomfortably wet.

We got quite used to the tours. Once or twice we had repeats. Mr. Andrews of the Miami Herald came several times and wrote a piece about the tours and us, which pleased the powers that be in New York. Audubon headquarters often sent out directives on ways to increase our public involvement, not political exactly, but educational. Mr. Baker thought it would be a great idea for Peter to visit local schools and talk to the kids. This idea had already occurred to Rosa and we'd discussed it. Peter was willing, but there was the matter of time, our days were full just trying to keep everything together, boats running, supplies in hand, plus staying out at Duck Rock consistently enough to discourage poachers.

Peter's greatest interest was in exploring. He would have been happy to spend all his time poking around and studying the nearby keys. In particular, Pavilion Key, with its thin sandy accumulation of land, turned out to hold many surprises for the investigating naturalist. Peter went back there frequently after our initial foray. Overall, he sighted 164 different species of birds there. In addition to the bird nests and turtle nests he found, he collected one poor little mouse that turned out to be a hitherto unknown subspecies of white-footed mouse. He trapped a couple more on Mr. Darwin's key as well. They reposed in jars of formaldehyde until Will Helmuth took them back to the New York Natural History Museum, where they were duly cataloged. Peter reported his investigations to Mr. Baker, who seemed to approve as long as it didn't interfere with our main tasks.   I really felt Peter should have gotten more encouragement and support for his pioneering work.

19

From across the river, the brilliant red blossoms that covered the towering crown of the Tookes' huge Poinciana tree, flamed in the morning light. Stepping from the *White Ibis* onto the rickety wooden dock, I was right under the branches as they reached out over the water, their radiant reflection rippling in the gentle current. A few of the blossoms, fallen into the water, floated slowly downstream.

Peter carried the bag of laundry I'd brought along and followed me up the crusty, shell-strewn path, to the Tookes' always-open front door. Through the screen we could hear Mrs. Tooke scolding one of the dogs, and a moment later she shooed him out. Her face creased up into a welcoming smile as she saw us standing there on the porch.

"Well, haven't seen you for a month of Sundays," she cried. "Come in and have some coffee. Got some laundry, have you? Well, bless you, you've got a good day for it."

We sat around her vast kitchen table catching up on local news and gossip. I told her about the tours and all the people who'd come. When I mentioned Barron Collier Jr. her eyes popped.

"Why, he's a real important fella," she told me. "His daddy owns the Collier Company, you know. He built the canal and the Tamiami Trail. You might say he's a kinda pioneer in these parts."

"Oh yes." I remembered now, "and aren't they the ones who want to dig a lot more canals and drain the swamp?"

"That's right. They're the ones. Them and the Government. They want to build lots of houses and I don't know what all. I don't hold with it. We don't need lots more people here. I don't know what he's doin' comin' out lookin' fer birds." I had no answer to that. I could only guess that what I'd already surmised was true, that he was some sort of player in the deals going down around the new park.

"Hear tell he's a wild one," Mrs. Tooke continued. "Never settled down after the war. Those folks got altogether too much money. Ain't good for a person, makes gettin' what you want too easy."

I agreed with this in principle, but I thought briefly that I wouldn't mind the opportunity to find out first hand. I didn't want to talk about the Colliers and all the politics, it made me uneasy. Peter and I were on the periphery of it all, and even that was too close for comfort. Our roles as warden and helpmeet included certain aspects of ambassadorship. We felt we had to watch our P's and Q's. Although I hadn't particularly taken to Mr. Barron Collier Jr., I didn't feel free to say critical things about him to anyone either. Now I merely said, "Yeah, you're right. Too much money isn't good for anybody." Peter added, "The war messed up a lot of people."

Mr. Tooke now appeared from the bedroom, where he'd been sleeping late after fishing all night. He looked tired, but his smile was welcoming. "How's the tourist business?" he asked, rather dubiously. Mr. Tooke thought the tours were a bit of a fraud.

"They had that Barron Collier out on the first one," Mrs. Tooke jumped in.

"You don't say. What was he doin' out lookin' at birds?" Mr. Tooke was also skeptical. Peter quickly said, "Oh, he was a guest of Mr. Baker. I suppose he just wanted Collier to see what we're doing out here."

"There were a lot of other people," I chimed in. "Mr. Andrews from the Miami Herald came to take pictures. He says he wants to do an article about us."

This did not impress Mr. Tooke. "Huh," he grunted. "That'll just bring a whole lot more of them people around to mess things up."

I think he imagined hordes of people, in fleets of boats, streaming up the river and tromping all over everything.

"Well," said Peter mildly, "at least they're the kind of folks who want to preserve the place instead of exploiting it."

Just as we were about to get into one of those endless discussions, pro and con, about the coming of the National Park, the dogs started barking wildly outside.

"Now who's that?" wondered Mrs. Tooke. "Hope it ain't the Gomezes."

We went outside, and happily, it was not the Gomezes, it was Billy Tiger again, and a couple of other men from the chickee on their way to fishing. Mrs. Tooke brought out more coffee for everyone and we stood around the big brick cistern under the palm trees. I wondered if the Tookes' hospitality extended only to the outdoors, and whether perhaps they didn't want to invite the Indians inside. It was uncommon enough that the Tookes had befriended them at all. Mr. Tooke, I knew, respected the Seminoles as a people and as superb fishermen and farmers of this unfriendly terrain. Cigarettes were passed around and everyone except Mrs. Tooke lit up. The air became wreathed in blue tobacco smoke as we all puffed and exhaled, chasing away a few little dancing balls of sand flies.

Billy Tiger confirmed that the Gomezes were up in the backwaters beyond Gopher Key, running a couple of stills. The Seminoles, though largely invisible, knew everything that went on in this part of the world, and Billy Tiger, as chief, had forbidden his people to have anything to do with moonshine.

"It ain't no good for no one, but it's death to us," he said. He could enforce this edict around his own chickee, but it was hard to control all the others.

Peter asked, "How come the sheriff doesn't try to close them down?"

"Too hard to find 'em," was the answer.

"Well, you know where they are, don't you?" Peter pressed a bit.

"If you mean, young fella, why don't I show the sheriff where they are—well, think about it. We all got to get along. I don't hold with what they're doin', but I sure as hell ain't gonna rat on 'em. Make things real hard on all of us if I did. No, as long as they stay out of our way, we'll stay outta theirs."

Billy Tiger stamped out his cigarette, then asked Mr. Tooke if they could fill their water bottles from the cistern before they set off fishing again. Once the odd collection of stone and glass bottles and jars (no plastic back then) were refilled, they climbed into their boat and putted off down stream.

Peter and Mr. Tooke went onto Mr. T's boat to unload some nets. Mrs. Tooke and I went over to the gasoline-powered washing machine. We filled it from the well and I piled my dirty clothes into it. While the little contraption chugged away, Mrs. T and I sat on the sandy ground in the shade of the palms and papayas, the poinciana blazing away overhead. Warblers and finches were singing in the bushes, a lone great blue heron flapped regally down the river.

Mosquitoes weren't bad at this time of day, and altogether it was one of those rare moments of contentment.

We sat and watched her three new Mallard ducklings, with their fuzzy yellow heads and downy backs, splashing happily in a makeshift pond, really no more than a large puddle, but they were so small it didn't matter. Mr. Tooke had taken them from a nest he'd found up the river. I suppose, technically, he should have left them alone, but they seemed quite happy in their new home, and duck eggs are wonderfully rich and good eating. I told Mrs. Tooke about all our family coming to visit, and she said she would be more than happy to put any of them up if need be. I had to argue quite firmly to get her to agree to accept any payment in exchange, but eventually she relented and let it be a business arrangement as well as a gesture of friendship.

Her old pregnant mother cat, distended and awkward now, waddled up to us and rubbed her head on Mrs. T's knee to be petted, purring loudly.

"When's she going to have the kittens?" I asked.

"Oh, in a week or so, I'd say," was the reply. "Has Peter changed his mind, then?" she asked me.

"Well, no, not exactly, but I'm sure he'll come around when he sees how cute they are." The laundry was done, so we hung it up on the line between the banana palms.

A short time later, Peter and Mr. Tooke finished laying out the nets on the bank to dry. They joined us under the trees, lighting up their ever-ready cigarettes.

"How about a beer?" suggested Mr. Tooke. We were happy to take him up on his offer, the day was warming up. Nothing like a cool, sudsy beer on a hot morning. Mrs. Tooke pressed us to stay for dinner (their lunch), but we refused this time, and in a little while, we set off for home and Duck Rock. But not before Mrs. Tooke had loaded us down with avocados, papayas, and greens from the garden, as well as eggs galore, for which she refused adamantly to be paid anything. On the way home, I trolled off the stern and caught a couple of fine snook for dinner (our supper). I'd go back to get the wash the next day when it had dried.

Unfortunately, the next day the weather had turned foul and the rain beat down on us in torrents. The wind rocked the boat unmercifully, except for when the tide went out and we settled into the mud, but then I worried we'd be blown over. Being on the boat in the wind and rain for a day was quite a miserable experience. I wrote in my journal, read my book and tried not to be depressed. Peter was working on his field notes for Mr. Baker and writing his bird lists. We were grumpy and snappish. Our relationship was not helped by our physical circumstances. The continual close proximity, plus the lack of much satisfactory social life was beginning to grate on both of us.

I turned on the radio. I'd forgotten it was Saturday, we very easily lost track of days and dates. The soothing voice of the announcer for Texaco, introducing "Tristan and Isolde," came crackling out of our little portable radio, and the full glory of the Metropolitan Opera with Kirsten Flagstad singing, engulfed us in nostalgia and homesickness. Peter and I had often listened to Wagner's operas in the days while we were courting, and Tristan was the first opera I ever saw. In that brief, heady time when we were engaged, Peter's Uncle Will had taken us to a performance at the Metropolitan Opera House in New York for a special celebration.

The opera house, with its ornately decorated walls, its gilded boxes, plush seats, enormous chandeliers, and that heavy gold curtain, enveloped us in a sensual overload. Going for a drink in the bar in the interval seemed the height of sophistication to me in my youthful unworldliness. I was glad I was so familiar with the music. Four hours of Wagner, even when being performed by Kirsten Flagstad and Lauritz Melchior, is a lot. Looking back, I'm a little surprised at how much we were both under the spell of Wagner. My feelings towards that heavy German music have undergone such a change, that now I can't listen to much of it for long. But on this wet, miserable morning, the music moved me to tears and I was flooded with sadness mixed with familiar feelings of alienation and displacement.

Peter tried to comfort me and made us some coffee. I was grateful for his sympathy, but I remained sad until the final chords of the tragic, heart-wrenching "Liebestod" brought the opera to an end. After a good cry, I started to feel better. The wind and the rain had let up, and Peter said, Let's go over to Turkey Key and see if we can get some ice. We're about out. We need to get off this boat, too."

He was right on both counts. We were down to a last little stub of ice and were in danger of losing a lot of food, not to mention drinking warm beer! The water was still choppy and there were intermittent gusts of wind and rain, but we didn't care if we got wet.

Wrapped up in our oilskins, we set off. The journey of twenty minutes or so was uneventful, if a bit bumpy and windy, but the effect was exhilarating more than uncomfortable. Up on the dock, we ran into a couple of fishermen we knew, including Dutch Futch, who greeted us with his usual unintelligible mumble. It took us a while to decipher what he was saying, but it seemed he'd come in to buy fish, as he hadn't been able to go out for a week because his nets were in need of repair. We picked up some ice and set off back to Duck Rock feeling much better. Unfortunately, our relief was premature. Hardly had we gotten beyond the ice house, when the motor died with a strangled snort, and no matter how Peter pulled the string on the outboard and cursed and fiddled with the choke, nothing would avail. We had to turn around and row back to the ice house.

Then, fortunately, luck was with us. Dutch Futch was still there and he kindly offered us a tow back to Duck Rock. Within a few minutes we were once again on our way, this time bumping along in the other boat's wake. We invited our savior to come on board and have a beer, which he did. He offered to look at the outboard to see if he could help Peter fix it. The two men climbed over onto the smaller boat and after a good bit of tinkering, they decided a major part would need to be replaced. Our new friend took his leave, and we were faced with trying to figure out the fastest way to go about getting the new part.

The next day being Sunday, we didn't have many options. We'd have to wait until Monday and try to find out what was needed, then see if they had the part at the Everglades boatyard, or we might have to go up to Naples? Communication again. No one growing up now can possibly imagine what life was like "in the old days," when even long-distance telephone calls were considered miraculous, all those cables and wires, even crossing under the ocean! Our experience was limited to crackling radios and limited walkie-talkies. Such inventions as cordless phones, cell phones, pagers, e-mail, and the whole wireless revolution we take for granted today were quite inconceivable. At the time, Peter and I sure could have used a cell phone or even e-mail. We would have been saved endless time and hassle driving all over the place for information if we'd had access to a modern communication system. Take this day, for instance, we could have called Everglades, then Naples, and found out about the part without ever having to leave Duck Rock. But we couldn't. That was how the world was in those days, and we didn't know any different anyway.

20

"If you and Peter are really nuts enough to let me come and stay with you for a week or so, I'm nuts enough to accept and I'll try not to disgrace myself by falling overboard or otherwise making a fool of myself. Need to get out of here before the full summer madness hits our picturesque village, and the tourist hordes descend and clutter up the place. Plan to be there mid-July, but will let you know more definitely when things gel. Mardi sends her love and can't wait to be rid of me. Monty sends a tail-wag and wishes they let dogs on boats. Love, Will."

Another visitor. Well, let 'em all come. I'd been complaining about not enough good company, and our Uncle Will Helmuth was certainly one of our favorite people. Peter's uncle had always been an important influence on him, and in fact, Will was the reason we were in the Everglades at all. He had known all the right people and steered us towards them when Peter was trying to figure out what to do with himself after the war. Not only was Will a well known and highly respected ornithologist, he was also a bit of a self-made botanist and was in the midst of documenting all the grasses, sedges, vetches, mosses, and lichens in Suffolk County, on the southeastern end of Long Island. Aside from all that, he was a funny, irreverent, and charismatic eccentric figure, and we loved him dearly. He'd arrive before the end of summer and before the hurricane season. I could handle that, now that I'd talked to Mrs. Tooke about putting people up in her house, I felt better about the whole subject of visitors.

In the shade of the jacaranda, there was still some coolness left in the air. I was sitting on the old iron bench, outside the little Everglades post office, reading the mail. First thing in the morning, Peter and I had zipped into town in the *Snowy Egret*, bringing the outboard from the *White Ibis* to be repaired. Unfortunately, the guy at the local boatyard didn't have the part we needed and advised us to try up in Naples—where we'd been on the ways for all those agonizing weeks. Peter was telephoning them now, from the drugstore, and I was awaiting the outcome. A moment later, Peter came out of the drugstore looking pleased. Yes, they had the part. Suddenly I was seized with the spirit of holiday and I thought of the beautiful beaches around Naples and nearby Marco Island. What if we made it into a little break and took a picnic and went for a swim? And what if we invited the Leightys to come along? Rosamaria had been dying to go somewhere, and we had promised her a trip. I told Peter of my brilliant idea. At first, he was doubtful and thought we should just go and pick up the part and come back.

"Come on. We hardly ever leave Duck Rock. We've been very good. We deserve a day off," I cajoled him.

It didn't take much to talk him into it, and we climbed up the bank and walked over to the Leightys' little house.

Rosa was welcoming but not her usual ebullient self.

"I'm just a little homesick, is all," she confessed. Her sister, husband and their two children had been visiting, but now had gone back to Puerto Rico.

"I'm wanting to go with them," she said. I understood. Rosa and I were both displaced persons. I was doubly so, from my prewar English childhood and now from the surrogate American family in Philadelphia, and Rosa from her large extended family in Puerto Rico. Now both of us had landed in this strange, fascinating, but isolated, backwoods hinterland, trying to create a life for ourselves despite the difficulties. At least Peter and I had the comfort of knowing the situation was temporary and that we'd be returning to our own natural habitats before too long.

"Rosa," I said, "how about going up to Marco Island with us? We've talked about it and now might be a good time. Peter and I have to go up to Naples anyway to get a part for the outboard, and we could all go have a picnic on the beach at Marco Island."

Marco Island, just thirty miles up the coast from Everglades City, has one of the great beaches of the world. Collectors from all over come to gather shells from its wide, white sandy stretch, where the blue Gulf laps gently, bringing treasure from as far as Cuba. We were the lucky ones who had the opportunity to experience its magic while it was still undeveloped and virtually uninhabited.

Rosamaria was immediately jumping around with excitement. "Oh yes, yes, let's go," she shrilled. "Let's go *today*. I want to go to the beach."

"Yes, why not?" said Rosa. "It will be fun to have a picnic, I will make conch sandwiches. Ralph can come too because school is closed today."

"I'll bring something too. I've got all those avocados from the Tookes, and we have to have beer of course," I added.

"I want a Coke." Rosamaria was only permitted Cokes for special occasions and she was betting this was one. "And let's bring cookies, too," she added, feeling she was on a roll.

"Okay," said Rosa. Rosamaria's day was made. She ran off and started collecting all her beach gear, her sand toys, her shovel, and her bucket for collecting shells.

Peter went to get gas for the Ford, while Rosa and I made sandwiches and filled a picnic basket. Then we all piled in and set off up the Trail. We were somewhat crowded, but we didn't care. We rushed along with all the windows open, the warm damp air blowing across our faces, nearly deafened by the loudness of the frog chorus. By now we were becoming used to their roundelay as they sang from the canal running beside the Trail. On the wide, grassy verge we passed two wood storks standing hunched, their large bills tucked down on their chests, looking for all the world like two old monks deep in meditation. Egrets, herons, and ibises were crowded in the trees, their filmy white plumage standing out in shining contrast against the green, while giant cypress trees covered with air ferns and Spanish moss stood guard over them all.

Rosamaria was dying to see an alligator up close, and she was not disappointed. We had barely gone ten miles when we came upon a full-grown bull alligator, grave and prehistoric. He was lying in the middle of the road, sunning himself in complete confidence that no one would dare run over him. He roused himself reluctantly and glittered his yellow eyes at us when we stopped in front him. Then he waddled off, his long thick tail wagging behind him, like "the serpentine dance of a dragon" as he slithered down under the water hyacinths in his ditch. We were riveted. He was not the only one we saw, several others of various sizes basked on the verge as we drove past, but he was the biggest. Each one elicited squeals of excitement from Rosamaria and pleas for us to stop. However, the adults thought it wiser to let sleeping 'gators lie, and we continued on our way.

Once in Naples we all got out at the boatyard. While Peter concluded the business of getting the part for the motorboat, the rest of us poked around, looking at everything. I showed Rosamaria how we'd been suspended up on the scaffold while we were being refitted. Another boat sat up there now and she wanted to climb up and look in. The kindly boatyard manager, George, let her up the ladder to peek into the roofless cabin. In those days, things tended to be more laissez faire regarding individual safety liability. It was not such a litigious society and people didn't worry about lawsuits every time they turned around. Cars didn't have seat belts, fireworks were legal, no one had to wear a helmet when they rode their bicycles or roller-skated. Not that this was better, it's just how things were, and in this case, it meant that Rosamaria was allowed the thrill of climbing up onto the slightly precarious ladder to look into the suspended boat.

With the precious part safely stowed in the trunk, we drove the few miles south to Marco Island. Crossing a narrow bridge over the causeway, we were greeted by clouds of gulls and terns rising up from the nearby beach, flying around and squawking before looping back down to their resting places on the sand. The sunlight reflecting from the sand was intensified, shining brilliantly on our faces.

"Let's explore a bit before we have our picnic," said Peter.

We set off on the only main road round the island. It turned out to be quite large and surprisingly hilly, but we still toured the entire place in less than an hour.

Marco Island is the only one of the Ten Thousand Islands still inhabited today. Both the town of Naples and Marco have become developed as upscale resorts, complete with big hotels and condos, swimming pools, and golf courses. Every square foot of it is built on. When we were there, it was inhabited by a few families living in marginal conditions in a tiny community called Caxambas. The families were employed by the Collier Company and they were living in company housing. A recent hurricane had rendered their homes all but unlivable, and some of the inhabitants had resorted to putting up tents inside their houses for shelter. None of the tenants could afford the repairs themselves, and for some reason the company refused to pay for them. To add insult to injury, they were still being charged the same rent as they had paid before the devastation of their homes. It was disgraceful.

On the top of one of the hills, looking out over a magnificent view of the gulf, was a famous mansion with a sad and romantic history. It had been built in the early part of the twentieth century by a local tycoon for his bride-to-be, who died of unknown causes on her wedding day. The house had been built of natural hardwoods and pounded seashell cement, replete with marble fireplaces, mahogany staircases, cedar paneling, and a large completely stocked library. With its elaborate Italianate red-tiled roof and thick white walls, it looked as if it should have been out West in California or in Cuba. The bereft fiancé never went near his beautiful, melancholy mansion again and left it as it was, without even locking the doors. Needless to say, as time passed, the house was looted of anything that could be moved—especially the books, which were scattered among many homes and local schools. We peered into this moldy shell, now boarded up and quite uninviting.

Down the road, we passed through a small community with a dilapidated sign proclaiming it to be Collier City. Once this collection of shanties and lean-tos had been a favorite refuge for rum-runners and smugglers. Even now it remained a lawless enclave of outsiders and renegades. We had been told stories by the locals of three generations living in the same shack with "grandfathers who never sober up and think nothing of going to bed with their granddaughters." Not much law 'n' order around here—it was like Chokoloskee in many respects.

"I'm hungry," said Rosamaria, who was beginning to squirm a bit. "Let's go to the beach."

"Good idea," agreed Peter. "I'm ready for a beer. What about you, Ralph?"

We were all ready for a break and a swim. Back on the west side of the island, we drove out onto the hard white sand of Marco Beach. It was a relief to get out of the car on this empty and pristine stretch, with a few palm trees fringing the landward side. We set up our picnic under the umbrellas we had brought, as the day was turning out to be a scorcher. We had put our suits on under our clothes and it was only a matter of moments before we all dashed into the sea and fell into the clear, sparkling blue-green water, the waves so gentle as to be hardly more than ripples. Swimming in the soft, warm water was pure bliss. I felt as if I were flying, I wanted to frolic like a porpoise. Such freedom of movement was close to dancing, and as I splashed on my back and twirled doing pirouettes, my body remembered that joy. I could even leap in slow motion, arching my back and stretching my legs. But everyone was hungry and it wasn't long before we all came out again to have our picnic.

Munching our conch sandwiches and washing them down with beer, we watched a small flock of terns winging and dipping in their characteristic aerobatics. Peter had his field glasses out and was watching the shore birds running as fast as their tiny stick legs could carry them. There were dozens moving together in their breathless water ballet, in and out of the waves, stopping just long enough to probe the sand with their long bills for some morsel of sea food. Suddenly Peter jumped up and set off briskly to the water's edge where he crouched, following through the binoculars with great intensity the gyrations of a flock of small grayish birds. Then he stood up, brushing sand off his pants as he came back.

"Cuban snowy plovers," he announced. "Haven't seen them around before this year. There were some in California when we were out there last year. Great little birds. Hard to identify, though; they look so much like piping plovers."

Now Rosamaria wanted to look through the glasses too. Peter held her hand and led her down to the water where he patiently helped her to focus them, pointing out different shore birds. He was obviously happy to have a small pupil.

Rosa said idly, "He'll make a nice dad some day." And I thought a little sadly about the miscarriage I'd had last year and wondered if I'd ever manage to have a baby. This certainly wasn't the time or place to try, but I deeply hoped to have a family in time.

The birding lesson over, Rosamaria picked up her bucket and said she was going shell collecting.

"Come too, Mama" she entreated, "and you too please, Chloe." She didn't have to persuade me. I was eager to walk around and stretch my legs a bit more. We strolled off, leaving Ralph with his little portable radio listening to a ball game. Peter wandered away again, looking for birds.

Rosa was feeling more cheerful now, and she told me how much she missed her brothers (two) and sisters (three), all of whom still lived in Puerto Rico. Their lives were hard, no one had much money, but they lived near the sea and the men all fished for a living. One of them had a fish market that supplied local restaurants.

"Ralph is really more of an indoor sort of person," Rosa continued. "He is liking to go to the outdoors, but he has to have his things with him."

"How did you two meet?" I asked her.

"Oh, is very romantico," she laughed. "He is coming for vacation to Puerto Rico and he went to the dancing studio where I am teaching Latin dance. We meet and fall in love right away. But he has to go back home, to Florida. Then we write and then I come to Florida for a visit and decide to marry. He is good dancer." She laughed again.

"We'll all have to go dancing up at Ochopee one of these days," I said. I loved the idea of another couple to go out with. The cafe at Ochopee was not much, but they had a good juke box and a tiny dance floor. If Peter and I had companions, I'd feel more secure, as sometimes the crowd could be a little rough.

While we were chatting, we were also collecting shells. There was a treasure trove of them lying at our feet. Rosamaria kept running up to exclaim over her latest discovery. We found sunrise tellins, turkey wings, starfish, cockles, olives, tulip conches, turnip whelks, moon snails, and

Florida fighting conches. While from a distance the beach looks pure white, on closer inspection the shells themselves are colorfully flecked with red, orange, tan, or sometimes lemon and green. The high-tide line today was marked by lines of red and green algae and wind-drift of mangrove leaves, feathers, shark egg sacs, and other bits of detritus.

A few cumulus clouds had gathered in a lofty pile in the western sky. The sun was lowering, and a grandiose sunset was promised. Time to be collecting ourselves and taking leave of our beautiful beach and heading home. Rosamaria objected strenuously, but her kindly dad assured her we'd come back again.

"When, when, when?" she wanted to know. As we drove back down the Trail, the promised sunset developed, setting the sky alight with pink and orange fire, with turquoise slashes of sky visible between huge, darkening purple clouds. It lasted almost all the way home, reflecting in the water in the ditch beside the highway. There were no alligators to be seen now, just a black-crowned night heron that flapped across the road in front of the car.

I felt sandy and salty and my skin felt the tight beginning of a sunburn. Rosamaria went to sleep across her mother's lap. The rest of us fell silent out of that pleasantly tired feeling that comes from exposure to the elements. We journeyed home swiftly in the gathering dark and made it back in time for supper.

Peter and I now had to face a night journey back to the boat out at Duck Rock. But Rosa wouldn't hear of it. "You can sleep on the sofa bed. Is too late to go now out to that Rock. You stay here with us. We like to have you. Tomorrow you go." Peter agreed, somewhat reluctantly, but I was happy—I could take a shower and get the salt off.

Shortly after we were settled down in Rosa's house, Art came knocking at the door. He was bursting with some news he had to share.

"Them Chokoloskee boys got themselves thrown in the clink," he announced with relish. "Yup, Red and Virgil Gomez got drunk up to the Almar Cafe. Got in a fight with some fellers from over Pelican Key. Red pulled a knife and cut that Sharkey Smith."

"How come they got arrested?" Peter asked. So often these fights went ignored by the authorities, if they were even around.

"Oh, Marnie, you know her? She's Sharkey's girlfriend. Well, she got upset and called over here. Just happened Sheriff Tucker was in town and he went and broke it up. So they's outta commission till tomorrow. He'll let 'em go in the mornin'. They won't be feeling good, though," he added with satisfaction.

"How about the guy who got hurt, Sharkey?" I asked. "Is he okay?"

"Yeah. Old Doc Hennessy sobered up long enough to patch him up, I guess. He'll survive, anyway."

I'd heard about Doc Hennessy. He'd been an up-and-coming surgeon over in Miami until he became an alcoholic. Now in his seventies, he practiced in a haphazard sort of way. When he was sober, I'd been told, he was still a good doctor.

"Well, we won't have to worry about them shooting up Duck Rock for a while," said Peter "We'll be back out there by tomorrow."

"Oh, there's no need to hurry," Art assured him. "Ain't no call to fret yourself." He didn't like Peter to be too diligent, I think he felt it reflected badly on himself.

We settled down on Rosa's sofa. Rosamaria, who had quite woken up again, in that perverse way children sometimes have, came marching into the living room in her PJs and wanted me to read to her. It was *Good Night Moon*, newly published then, and I read it with pleasure.

I lay on the sofa bed that night, reassured by knowing the Chokoloskee people were contained, at least temporarily. I fell asleep thinking of the contrast of the clean, clear whiteness of Marco Island's beaches and its light-filled landscape with the mysterious murk of the mangroves and the unusual, sometimes hostile people they foster.

21

BANG! Bang, bang, bang. The sound of gunfire coming from upriver greeted us as we approached Duck Rock. Our alarm systems immediately went on high alert. Were they attacking Duck Rock? Were they shooting birds somewhere nearby? Peter was instantly galvanized. He became furious and, piling on the speed, we thrashed across the water as fast as our boat could go, shuddering and bumping. In a few minutes we reached the *Audubon* amid a swell of wavelets.

We had left Everglades at sunup that morning and sped through the haze across glassy waters without incident, until we'd heard those ominous shots. But now there was no sign of another boat or anybody at all and everything was quiet. Not for long. A few moments later we heard more shots, coming from the south. Peter decided they must be up the Huston River, a small tributary entering the Chatham not far away. Peter was gnashing his teeth in frustration, standing on the bow with his binoculars clapped to his eyes, sweeping the view from north to south like Ahab looking for Moby Dick. Then, as Peter was looking through his binoculars, we heard the sound of a boat growing louder as it came towards us. We both saw it at the same time—a large open boat with an inboard motor, three men sitting in the bow. If they had guns they were hidden. As they came around the bend and saw us, they seemed to hesitate for a moment, taking us in, and then took off, flying as fast as they could out to the Gulf giving Duck Rock a wide berth.

Peter was sure they were the culprits. "I'm going after the bastards," he said, leaping into the *Snowy Egret*.

"Oh Peter, don't go after them. You don't know for sure it's them and they're running away anyhow."

"I know it's them. I've gotta go. Don't worry, I'll be right back."

"But what are you going to do?" I wailed. My anxiety and admonitions fell on deaf ears, and he was away in fifteen seconds.

Fortunately, their boat was much the faster and Peter had no chance of catching them. He kept up the chase for good measure all the way to Pavilion Key, where he gave up and returned to our boat. I was greatly relieved to see him all in one piece.

"I'm pretty sure one of them was that one-eyed Brown fella," he announced as he climbed back aboard, "but I didn't recognize the others."

He was still furious, but the activity, though futile, had defused some of his rage. He hadn't managed to get the boat's number or name, but he had a clear description of it. I was happy nothing more had come of it and there had been no direct confrontation. We'd been warned repeatedly not to get into a face-off with the local gun-toters because, as Art had told us in his gloomy way, "They'd just as soon shoot you as them birds. It's a felony either way!"

"I'm going to go check around Duck Rock and just make sure everything's all right," Peter said, and got back into the small boat. Returning shortly, he reported no sign of shooting on the island, and he was further mollified.

"How about some breakfast, wife?" he suggested.

I already had the stove going and water on, so it wasn't long before we sat down to our bacon, eggs and coffee, accompanied by the old newspapers we'd gotten in Everglades the day before. Peace descended. The sun shone and even though the day was warming up, the humidity didn't seem quite as bad. Out on the water two herring gulls were squawking and fighting over a fish one of them had caught, flying up and down, one diving and chasing, the other evading, until finally the would-be thief gave up and departed.

As usual, our peace and quiet didn't last. Again we heard the sound of a boat approaching and this time saw the cheerful face of Mr. Tooke, on his way home from Everglades. He came and tied up next to us and climbed aboard.

"Got you a telegram," he said, handing it to me.

Opening it hurriedly, I found it was from my mother. She was arriving in Miami the day after next. I was filled with excitement. We'd have to go in to Everglades tomorrow, then on to Miami, spend the night, and the next day meet the train. What fun. We hadn't been to Miami for ages and I was ready for some big-city life. I wanted to do some shopping. Mrs. Tooke and I had the same birthday, and I hoped to get her a cover for her little gas-powered washing machine. I was hoping I could find one at Sears.

I thanked Mr. Tooke and offered him some coffee. While he and Peter sat with their mugs and cigarettes, Peter told him about the Brown raid. Mr. T said the Browns had been up the Chatham the day before, to visit one of the Gomez stills.

"It's a bad business," he said soberly, shaking his grizzled head. "Them Browns and Gomezes, they's dyed-in-the-wool villains. Art told me about them Gomez brothers gettin' into a knife fight last night. Don't do no good to stick 'em in jail. They ain't never gonna change. They just make trouble for us all."

With that he got up and was getting ready to leave, but before he went, he told us Art had sent a message that the tour was canceled this weekend. There had not been enough sign-ups. I would be sorry if the tours didn't succeed, but I was always relieved when one was canceled. After Art left, I set about preparing the boat for my mother's visit and for our trip to Miami to pick her up. Peter decided to repair the outboard motor with the new part he'd bought in Naples yesterday. To the surprise of both of us, the job turned out to be simpler than anticipated, and he had the motor putt-putting again in short order.

To give it a trial run, he decided to go up the Huston River and see if he could find any evidence of shooting there. He came back a short time later with a dead egret and a dark report of seeing a couple of other corpses floating among the mangrove roots up the river. He was in a terrible state of impotent rage and frustration.

"It's just so stupid," he ranted. "Those bastards don't kill the birds for food even—just stupid mindless shooting. They don't give a damn about anything. They were undoubtedly drunk, if what old Tooke says is true. They came up here, got drunk, saw we weren't around and just figured they could get away with it." I could see he felt guilty and responsible, as if he personally had failed to prevent this shooting spree.

"I knew we should have come back last night," he growled, thereby making me feel guilty too, because I'd been the one who had persuaded him that we could safely stay away just one time.

"But it's impossible to stay here every single minute." I tried to defend myself and Peter. "We have to leave to get supplies and they could just as easily come then. You had to get that part for the boat, too." He knew I was right but it didn't make him feel any better.

Peter spent the evening writing furious letters to Mr. Baker in New York, Charlie Brookfield in Miami, and to our friend on the Miami Herald, Mr. Andrews—none of which would really make any difference, but it allowed him to blow off steam, which was good for both of us. I typed his letters for him without my usual grumbling and tried to be reassuring in general. Even so, we didn't have a very happy remainder of the day.

Naturally, after that shooting incident, Peter was reluctant to leave the island unprotected again, but we had to go into Miami to meet my mother's train. The next morning the mood was still glum and clouded with disharmony. However, when we got to Everglades in the *Snowy Egret* we were met by Art, who was about to take his boat up the Chatham and moor up there for a while. He assured us he'd keep an eye on things.

"The Missus is sick of Everglades," he told us. "She always likes it better out there at Tookes' place. I can run the small boat out to Duck a couple of times, just so's people know someone's looking out for things."

With that reassuring development, we drove off across the Tamiami Trail for Miami with a clear conscience, and, for me at least, with a lighter heart. The drive was unremarkable, though extremely hot. Even with the open windows blowing air on us, there wasn't much relief. Once in Miami, we found a good cheap hotel and got a room with a bath (but no view). After a successful shopping foray, in which I got the washing machine cover, and Peter bought a seersucker suit for dress up occasions (even though we didn't seem to have many of those), we went back to the hotel and took long, wonderful baths.

That evening, we set forth on the town, the air was getting cooler and we strolled along wide sidewalks, mingling with a few tourists as well as a scattering of drunks and folks who appeared down on their luck. Back then there were no homeless people or panhandlers like you see today. We decided to have dinner in an Italian restaurant. Unfortunately, they only served wine, no drinks, which made Peter quite annoyed. I didn't mind so much, but I was noticing that Peter had started drinking probably more than he should at times, which would land him in difficulties later on. For now, though, it didn't seem important.

After dinner, we stopped in an exotic ethnic store that smelled of nutmeg and had clothes from Cuba and Latin America. Peter wanted to buy me something for my birthday, which was coming up soon, so I started trying things on. I hadn't bought any clothes for ages and I'd forgotten how affirming and fun it was for me. The clothes were hand-woven cotton and embroidered with bright flowers and designs. Choosing was hard, but I settled on a blouse with blue and yellow flowers, and Peter approved. We had it wrapped so I'd have something to open on my birthday.

Our night on the town ended in a small, rather dingy joint near our hotel. The walls had faded murals of palm trees and beaches, and there was a piano bar, except in place of the piano was a huge shiny organ. A young woman with long dark hair down her back played quite well and not too loudly, but it seemed to go on and on. We'd been up since 5:30 and were both exhausted, and when we got back to the hotel, we both dropped into bed and fell instantly to sleep.

My mother's train was due in at 8:30 a.m., so the next morning we hastened to the railway station. The train from New York came steaming in and hissed to a halt. We were on the platform, looking up and down the cars, scanning the crowd for my mother's familiar smiling visage. Peter spotted her first (that bird-watcher's focus), and we all three started waving and calling out and rushed into a giant three-way hug. My mother was flushed with excitement and her hat fell off in all the hugging. We picked up her cases (she knew how to travel light) and headed for the car.

I could never walk into a railway station without feeling a strong mix of emotions. Seeing my mother in this setting, brought back some of the fear, hope, anxiety, suspense, as well as a happy relief, associated with my childhood experiences. Railroad stations in the '40s had both romantic and tragic overtones. Think of all the great old movies with scenes of separations and reunions: "Casablanca," "Mrs. Miniver"—almost any war-time movie, for example. In my life there had been many dramatic and intense occasions in railway stations—going to and coming back from boarding school, seeing relatives and especially my father going off to the war, and then the relief upon meeting them on their return. These times are always fraught with emotion, both happy and sad, but none was so highly charged as when I said goodbye to my mother at age 15 and left England for what would turn out to be forever.

In 1940, after the fall of France, people said Hitler could now just walk across the English Channel and take England. Overnight our little island became a fortress, the beaches covered in barbed wire, antiaircraft guns pointed at the sky day and night. I had nightmares of goose-stepping Gestapo soldiers. Everyone was afraid. It was at this time that the idea was developed to send children to the United States and Canada, to escape the bombings in London.

My own odyssey happened very quickly that hot August, when my mother's friends in Philadelphia offered to take me in for the duration of the war. To my mother, worried frantic about the possible fate of her nubile fifteen-year-old daughter in the event of invasion, the offer seemed heaven-sent. When I was told about it, I was almost equally thrilled and terrified. The thrill won out, partly because I'd always loved the thought of America. The impression of which I had gathered from watching American movies, about how glamorous, exciting, and rich everyone was there. To my teenage self, America seemed a much more exciting and desirable place to be than stodgy old England. Of course, I hated the thought of leaving everyone behind, but all the grownups were saying the war would only last a year. I'd been away from home at boarding schools the last five years, which would make this separation easier. Or so the reasoning went.

In amazingly rapid order, a space on a boat was procured and papers, passport, medical exams, shots—all the official requirements—were supplied. Then a serious hitch in the proceedings appeared. Any child traveling to America had to be accompanied by an adult. Who would go with me? It looked pretty hopeless. The boat was sailing in three weeks. What to do? And then a miracle happened, one of those lucky chances that change your life. A friend of my mother's was at the butcher's shop when she overheard two women talking. One was saying that yes, she was leaving in a few weeks, taking her two nephews to America.

My mother's friend, in a distinctly un-English stroke of forwardness, said, "I couldn't help overhearing what you've just been saying. My niece" (she lied) "has passage on that same boat, but she has yet to find a sponsor to be with her. Do you think you could look after her, too?" Or words to that effect. After more conversation and negotiation, the woman, amazingly and incredibly generously, agreed. So, there was nothing to hold me back. I was going.

Word came one morning of the hitherto secret date of our sailing. We gathered at London's Waterloo Station, as families and friends weren't permitted to travel to Southampton, only the evacuees. Clumps of people stood around their baggage. The atmosphere was subdued, but determinedly stiff-upper-lip. I didn't want to cry. We stood talking brightly about the magazines I had brought, the provisions in my kit, the care of my baggage.

"All aboard!" This was the moment. All my bravado deserted me, I wanted to fling myself on the ground and cling to my mother's ankles, "No, no! You can't send me away!" I was only half conscious, out of my head, as I hugged and hugged my mother, my brother, my aunt, some friends, and then I was on the train, looking at them clustered outside my window. I waved and waved as we pulled out of the station. Then I began to cry.

Now here I was seven years later, a married woman settled in another country. A whole new life unfolding. One of the lucky ones, I had been saved from all sorts of grievous dangers and horrors. And, in defense of it all, here was my dear mother, coming to share in the latest adventure. As we walked across the parking lot, talking nineteen to the dozen, I looked carefully at my mother. In her early fifties, she looked much younger with her lovely English skin and pretty features. Her face was always so alive, and she had the energy of someone ten years younger. When she first came over after the war in 1946, she'd looked a little pudgy. She'd gained weight living on their poor diet of the war years (all that bread and potatoes, she said). Since coming to America, she'd lost all those starch-induced pounds and looked quite her slim self again.

We decided to go straight back to Everglades rather than hang around Miami. We could come back and do that later. I was dying to show Mum the extraordinary place we were living in and introduce her to all the people and circumstances that made up our daily lives. I knew she'd love it all, and to that end, she didn't disappoint my expectations. My mother was one of those great spirits whose zest for life and the ability to enjoy herself made being with her a continual delight.

So, we set off for Everglades while it was still the cool part of the day. The Tamiami Trail is always a spectacular sight, even when you're familiar with it, but for the first-time visitor it's quite overawing. There were alligators in the ditch and ducks and coots swimming around on it, egrets and herons roosting in the trees, and, on the banks, solemn and motionless man-sized wood storks stood guard. The noise of the frogs was constant. Mother marveled at everything. She was not really a birder, but she'd been around Peter and his family enough to appreciate their zeal and knowledge, and she was interested in everything.

By the time we reached Okeechobee we were hungry.

"Time for lunch," Peter announced. "And a beer," said I.

"I'm all for that," Mum concurred.

"Let's go to Joe's," I suggested. "It's better than the drug store in Everglades."

We settled onto the cracked plastic seats in the booth by the window, overlooking the swamp out back, and ordered conch sandwiches, which we washed down with a local beer. I was a little disappointed that there weren't any of our colorful local characters around. In fact, the place was empty, except for a couple of fishermen with whom we had a nodding acquaintance. Then we drove up and down the little dirt streets of Everglades to show it off to my mother. We would have visited the Leightys, but everyone was at school.

"Well, Mum, have you got your sea-legs?" I teased. "We're about to take off into the wilderness."

"Oh, yes, darling. I've always been a good sailor," was her reply. "Luckily enough since we were always around water," she added. So, we climbed into the *Snowy Egret* and drove out to Duck Rock. The ride was reasonably smooth, but unfortunately the weather changed from its sunny aspect and became cloudy and damp. By now, the sun was going down in a uniformly dark purplish gray sky. It seemed we were not even to be treated to one of our spectacular sunsets.

We climbed aboard and stowed my mother's things as best we could.

"The birds'll be coming in soon. In fact, they've already started," said Peter.

"Oh, this is so exciting," Mum replied. "I've been dying to see this ever since you wrote to me about it."

"I'm afraid the weather isn't cooperating," I said. "We aren't going to get the best view tonight."

"It looks like rain," said Peter. "I'll just make us some gin and tonics and we can sit on the roof to watch, hopefully it will hold off long enough."

Just when you want the scenery to look its best and to show off, it promptly does the exact opposite. Nevertheless, it was exciting as always to see the long lines of birds flying in, and there were many "pinks" planing in on their dark–red-tipped wings, swooping to a landing. My mother was not disappointed in her expectations.

After a little supper, we sat around comfortably on our gently rocking boat, and talked and talked. While the lantern swung above our heads and the mosquitoes whined outside the screens, we sipped tea and tried to catch up on so much time apart. There was news of my brother, (somewhat confusingly) also named Peter, the most notorious non-communicator in the family. I hadn't had a letter from him in a year. "He's finished his flight training," my mother now told us, "and now they've posted him to a naval air station in Scotland. He's frightfully disappointed. He was hoping for a carrier, of course."

There was news of my favorite aunt, my mother's sister Yevonde Middleton, a famous photographer in London. "Oh, Vondie," said Mum, "she's always complaining that business is dreadful, but actually she's got lots of clients and the *Tatler* always has her pictures in it. I've brought you the latest to see." She fished around in her bag and brought out a month-old *Tatler*, England's preeminent social magazine, with a lovely portrait of Lady Mary Cavendish right on the front page. I was thrilled. Vondie lived such a glamorous life in London, where she mingled with the rich and famous and even a few royals. This small window into such a different world was a reminder of other lives in other places, other possibilities beyond this watery, strange, alien, and isolated place. I had almost forgotten.

Finally, we were all too sleepy to continue. I had made up a bed on the cot on the screened deck for Mum. After brushing her teeth at the basin in the galley, my mother put on her nightie, braided up her long graying hair, and climbed into her not-too-comfortable bed for her first night aboard the good ship *Audubon*. Mum was always a good sport.

22

For the next few days, the rain, which had been threatening, came down in buckets. This was a disappointment, as it put a definite crimp in our sightseeing. On the other hand, it turned out to be a disguised blessing because we were running low on water and the downpours refilled our tanks. Between showers one day, we managed to get over to Turkey Key for ice and to show my mother some of our watery realm. Mum made a big hit at the fish house, the locals seemed more willing to be open with her, more so than they had ever been with us, maybe it was the age difference, but whatever it was, the Tompkins's seemed quite taken with my mother. Even surly Bob managed to twist his sour features into the semblance of a smile, and Nellie, his shy, long-suffering wife, got into a detailed conversation with mom about the relative methods of cooking snapper. Mother had what the Irish call "the gift of the gab," as if she had kissed the Blarney stone. She could always talk to anyone, from admirals to shopkeepers. After more visiting than I had thought possible, we fed fish heads to the coon and had entertained Blackie, their hysterically friendly dog, one last time, we took our leave.

The rain started again before we had gone very far. Since we were in the little open boat, we were all soaking by the time we got back to the *Audubon* and had to change our clothes. In that climate, between the humidity and the rain, nothing ever got really dry. Our cabin was festooned with damp clothes hung on chairs and on temporary lines slung from the "ceiling." We added our sodden jeans and shirts to the collection and awaited the time we knew would come, when the skies cleared, and we'd all be too hot again. Meanwhile, we sat around and read, and I updated my Journal, while Mum wrote letters.

Sure enough, the clouds did move away, and the sun came out hotter than ever. We could start showing my mother around. Once or twice we went into Everglades for groceries—"shockingly high prices" was my mother's comment. We had a lovely tea party with the Leightys. Rosa, being aware of the importance of tea in the life of the English, made us scones with strawberry jam and egg salad sandwiches. Rosamaria was fascinated by my mother's English accent and went around practicing saying aluMINium and toMAHto.

One day we chugged through the mangrove channels upriver to visit Mr. Darwin, bringing him beer and newspapers. I couldn't imagine a wider difference of backgrounds than those between my mother and Mr. Darwin. Mr. Darwin, however, rose to the occasion and behaved in a very gentlemanly manner, even quite gallant (in English, GALLant). It was a side of him we'd never seen before, and I was touched by how much effort he put into hosting my mother. He was not at all taken aback by the unexpected visit and offered us hearts of palm and crab gumbo that he'd cooked up, which were served in old soup cans. I was a little nervous about Mr. Darwin's cooking and only accepted a taste out of politeness, but was pleasantly surprised to find that it was actually really tasty. We had an all-around very enjoyable visit. My mother found Mr. Darwin very entertaining and his unorthodox lifestyle totally fascinating.

Of course, we took her to see the Tookes. Mrs. T had been very curious about my mother. In spite of her goodness of heart and sincere friendliness, Mrs. Tooke's curiosity and interest in people could sometimes make her a bit tactless. She was known to blurt out some uncomfortably personal questions to those around her whenever they occurred to her. I was a little worried she'd embarrass my mother with her comments, but I needn't have been. The two women got along quite famously and when Mrs. Tooke said, "So where's your husband run off to now?" Mother didn't seem to mind. "Oh, he's in the Mediterranean somewhere" she answered, without batting an eye.

A grand birthday party had been planned at the Tookes' to celebrate Mrs. T's and my joint birthdays. It was to be a midday dinner, one of Mrs. Tooke's feasts, and there was much anticipation and elaborate preparation. Several of their ducks were to be sacrificed as the centerpiece for the meal.

The Tookes' daughter Kathleen and young grandson Wesley had come from Tennessee to stay for a couple of weeks. Wesley was a sturdy young boy, full of fun. He had an adopted brother, Nate, the same age as Wesley but quite a different story. He'd been adopted by Mrs. Tooke as a neglected baby and was now staying with Kathleen for the school years. He had a long history of ill health, which, considering his wretched beginnings, wasn't that surprising. Unfortunately, unlike his fun-loving brother, he had a mean streak; he was always tormenting the cats and doing things like pulling wings off flies. I shudder to think what may have become of him. Both boys were staying with the Tookes for the summer. Kathleen was a lot like her mother, round and cheerful with black curly hair. No one ever mentioned her husband, who seemed to have strayed off somewhere.

I awoke on my twenty-second birthday in our small cabin, the boat lying motionless, settled on the mud of the Gulf bottom. It was low tide and the smell of the muck and the nearby Duck Rock filled the air. The sun was up, the birds had left, and my husband in his bunk and my mother in the screened cabin were still sleeping. Getting up slowly, I crept into the galley and tried to fill the kettle quietly, but pumping water out of a tank is not a silent task, and pumping up the stove to light the burner was also noisy. However, no one seemed to mind being woken up for a nice cup of tea. The thought flashed into my head that, since it was my birthday, by rights I was the one who should have been woken up with a cup of tea in bed, but never mind, I'd get my treats later. And indeed, I did. Over breakfast I was given many hugs and Happy Birthday greetings, and I opened my presents. There was the package from Peter with the blouse we'd bought in Miami, and to my delight he'd managed to add a pair of pretty blue earrings as a surprise. Mum had brought me a bottle of my favorite perfume from New York, which in those days was "Je

Reviens," and some nylons, still a relatively rare item.

"Oh boy, Mum, I'll be able to smell like something other than mangrove mud for a change!" I thanked her. There were cards from Donna and other New York pals. I felt quite satisfied by the special attention.

All this time the tide had been rising, slowly lifting the *Audubon* off the bottom to float quietly at her mooring, giving us enough leeway to cross over the mouth of the Chatham in the *White Ibis*. A few pelicans flew around over the still and shining water, and an anhinga sat on a branch of one of the nearby mangroves, wings outstretched, warming in the sun.

Our share of the upcoming birthday party was to supply drinks. We'd stocked up on soda and beer when we went in to buy groceries, and Peter had been seized with an extravagant impulse to buy a bottle of champagne. Finally, we packed everything into the boat, including the wonderful cover for Mrs. Tooke's washing machine, and we were ready to start upriver.

By the time we arrived, there was already quite a crowd of people milling in and out of the house, and the three hound-dogs greeted us with wagging tails and invitations for patting and ear rubbing. Mr. Tooke sat outside on the porch smoking his pipe, talking to his son Hamp, and to our surprise and pleasure Mr. Darwin was there too. It made my heart glad to see him all dressed up in a clean shirt and a pair of gray pants (even though they were ragged on the bottom), and he'd managed to get a whole pair of boots from somewhere. In fact, everyone seemed to have spruced themselves up and were wearing clean shirts and shoes. In deference to my mother, whom everyone recognized as "a real lady," the men rose to their feet and greeted us as we came up.

"Welcome, welcome," said Mr. Tooke with his sweet grin. "Hope you've got yourselves an appetite. Goodness knows what she's got cookin' up in there."

Peter offered beers all round and joined the group, and everyone lit up cigarettes.

Inside the house, Mrs. Tooke and Kathleen were bustling about preparing the meal. Mrs. T and I wished each other Happy Birthday and exchanged presents. She was delighted with the cover, and she gave me a photo album, "to put all them bird photos in," she said. I offered to help with chores, but she wouldn't hear of it and made my mother and me sit at the table while they cooked. The kitchen was piled high with works in progress. There were mounds of peeled potatoes ready for boiling and mashing, and Kathleen was mixing batches of cornmeal for cornbread. Mrs. Tooke was stuffing the three ducks and the wood stove was roaring away.

It was fiercely hot in there, so I was glad of the excuse to go outside, when Mrs. Tooke asked me to go out to the garden and collect some more greens for the pot. Wesley and Nate had joined the men on the porch and were cranking the old handmade ice cream maker, cranking and cranking the handle and arguing about how long their turns were. When I came back inside, my mother had managed to overcome Mrs. T's sense of propriety and was setting the table.

A short time later, Art and the Missus emerged from the *Spoonbill*, which was moored at the rickety dock below. Moving slowly, with the Missus leaning on Art's arm, they progressed up the path, leading their old deaf pug on a rope leash. Art tied the pug to a tree and joined the men, while the Missus came into the kitchen.

"Well, howdy," Mrs. T greeted her. "Have a seat." She gestured towards the table. My mother had already met the Missus, who because she was so deaf had a way of talking endlessly in order to avoid conversation. However, my mother, rising to the occasion, was able to shout into her ear every now and then and keep up her end of things.

The meal preparation was now coming to a climax and it wasn't long before the cooks announced dinner was ready. We all helped bring the dishes to the table, while Kathleen went outside to proclaim, "Come and get it!" Soon we were all settled around the vast old table, now covered with a blue checked tablecloth and a dozen deliciously smelling dishes. There was roast duck, biscuits and gravy, lots of greens from the garden and cornbread. There was a heaping platter of pork chops, a big bowl of mashed potatoes, and pickles and relishes of all sorts. We had just enough room to squeeze everyone in and we made quite a splendid party with Art and the missus, cheerful, grizzled Mr. Darwin, Hamp, Kathleen and the children, Peter, my mother and me, and of course the Tookes themselves.

"Help yourselves, everyone, don't be shy," cried Mrs. Tooke, and we all tucked in. Peter opened the champagne and there were Happy Birthday toasts. Most of the company had never had champagne before and didn't think much of it. However, they sipped for the toasts and then went gratefully back to beer. A huge decorated birthday cake covered with candles was brought in with a flourish, Happy Birthday was sung in several different keys at once, and Mrs. T and I blew out the candles. After consuming huge plates of cake and the ice cream the boys had made, the meal was finally over, and everyone leaned back and loosened their belts. Mr. Tooke brought out his secret stash of moonshine and everyone nipped on a shot glass. He called it white lightning, and that is just what it tasted like, pure and stinging, it burned all the way down.

The company, mellowed by food and drink, began telling ghost stories. Everyone had a story and they also knew there were supposed to be many ghosts and haunted houses in England. My mother was questioned about her experiences. She told a few chestnuts about headless queens wandering around the Tower of London carrying their heads, and about apparitions appearing and disappearing through walls. Mrs. Tooke told a story about how her father had seen a ghostly head, with red eyes and a wooly face, floating in the air as he drove his wagon home one night.

"Probably too much moonshine," said Mr. Tooke. "I don't hold with the notion of ghosts, no how." And everyone shook their heads and stoutly maintained they didn't believe in 'em.

"Says so in the Bible, ain't no such things," pronounced Mrs. Tooke, whose word-for-word belief in the good book was always her unassailable argument. On the other hand, they were all convinced that malaria was carried by a sort of miasma creeping out of the swamps, and not by mosquitoes, and their cures for warts were truly in the realm of fable.

"Get you the bleached bone offen a dead cow," Mrs. Tooke said solemnly, "rub it on your wart, and then go bury that bone and continue on your way— without looking back, mind—and that wart will just shrivel up and disappear in a few days."

You could also do the same sort of thing with a dish cloth, which you must steal from someone, and then rub your wart and bury the cloth. Then there was also a sure way to stop bleeding, she told us. You must recite the sixth verse of the sixteenth chapter of Ezekiel (or was it the sixteenth verse of the sixth chapter?) forwards and backwards and the bleeding would stop. She had wonderfully gory tales of people who chopped themselves in an artery and were all alone and bleeding to death, but who did this and, sure enough, stopped the bleeding. I'd say it was just lucky they'd memorized that verse!

It was getting late. Mr. Darwin was ready to go. He had brought some hearts of palm to Mrs. Tooke and in turn she loaded him down with avocados and papayas. Now he gathered his stuff together and took his leave. It was time for us to do the same. The sun was setting amidst a bank of stormy-looking clouds piled up on the horizon, but the trip down the Chatham was smooth and calm until we reached the bar at the mouth of the river. The tide had turned and was low again and we only just made it over.

By the time we reached Duck Rock it was almost dark and we could hardly see the stakes. The last of the birds had come in for the night, and we were all ready to turn in too. Peter lit the lamps and poured himself a nightcap. Mum and I declined, and Mum made a pot of tea. Listening to "Your Hit Parade" on the radio, we sang along now and then. It felt cozy and sweet, and fleetingly I wondered if perhaps it might be possible for Peter and me to continue living here after our first year was up. I wanted to believe so, but deep inside I felt it would never work for me.

23

I was thoroughly happy to have my mother visiting us, being with her every day, listening to her sing (she had a lovely trained soprano and would sing spontaneously whenever the mood took her), and just to enjoy the feeling of security I always had being around her. However, I had to admit, her constant presence put something of a strain on Peter and on our marital relationship. Not that he and Mum were at odds with each other, they got on quite well. The problem was the lack of privacy, and our sex life suffered for it. The circumstances of living in such close quarters on the boat, day in and day out, was beginning to feel like the proverbial pressure cooker. We were forced to be alone together too much of the time in too close quarters. With so little social life and few outside distractions, I sometimes felt like a caged animal. Petty personal habits (why was he always clearing his throat?) began to grate, magnified as they were by our solitary situation. I started feeling irritated with him, though usually he managed to be quite good tempered and cheerful. Even when I wanted to fight with him, I couldn't. He had a way of avoiding actual confrontation. This was a further frustration. We could seldom "have it out" with each other.

Another drawback to our physical intimacy was the awkwardness of the bunks and the general limitations of the physical setup of the boat. It was no wonder I began to be turned off. In those days, there was less openness about relationships in general, and in the England of my mother's generation one never talked about anything uncomfortable. Nothing negative was acknowledged. It was always, "Never mind, cheer up. Mustn't grumble. Keep your chin up." This strategy may have been great for getting through a horrible war and its miserable aftermath, but it was less effective for life's emotional ups and downs. So, nothing was easily acknowledged or talked about amongst the three of us.

In spite of it all, we bumped along and most of the time our life together was contented enough. Peter went off almost every day to Pavilion Key, by which he was more and more fascinated. He kept finding unusual birds, unexpected nestings, rare or hitherto undocumented mammals. He would come home full of excitement about his latest discoveries, which he then carefully entered in his little notebooks. Mum and I puttered and read and kept things going. I got quite proficient at running the small boats and in particular the outboard, *White Ibis*, and we would often go for a visit and to do the laundry up at the Tookes'. Mum and Mrs. Tooke continued comparing notes on life. Mrs. T loved hearing my mother's stories about living through the blitz.

"Them poor peoples," she would say, shaking her head. "Makes you thankful to be an American."

Art would come out of his boat and drink a cup of coffee or tea, whatever happened to be going. He would regale my mother with tales of his exploits as a boat captain (of a small fishing boat on the eastern coast many years before). He would watch her out of the corner of his eye as he was talking, to see how this naval officer's wife, (even if an ex), was taking in his tall tales. It was always pleasant visiting the Tookes and I was pleased and relieved that they were so accepting of my "proper" English mother.

Once, I took my mother over to the dark interior of Duck Rock. She was bound and determined to see it even though I warned her about its disagreeable aspects. She was too curious to heed me, though, so off we went. We managed to tie up to a big mangrove root and climb slipping and sliding into the interior, but after scrambling around on the scaly, slimy roots and breathing the fetid atmosphere for about half an hour, Mom's fervor was dimmed and she was ready to leave. "Fascinating, darling," she commented, scraping some heron guano off her shoe, "but I think I've had enough of exploring for one day."

Peter had begun working on a talk for the Everglades elementary school. Rosa had prevailed upon him to address the monthly meeting of the PTA on the subject of conservation. One night, when we were all sitting around in the Leightys' living room, the conversation turned, as it so often did, to the Everglades and the Ten Thousand Islands and what was to become of them.

"It make me so sorry to see how the government do not help the peoples here. So many poor. And the animals, too," she said, with feeling. "They are not caring about this place."

Ralph chimed in. He had a degree in soil conservation and he was appalled by what was happening along the Tamiami Trail, where the Army Corps of Engineers was digging ditches and canals and attempting to drain the swamp to make it available, for what? Farming? Housing developments? Ralph was a silent man on the whole, but every now and then he got going.

"Of course, the poachers are a problem," he said, "but as you must realize, they are small potatoes compared to the real estate developers and the people who want to see this whole area cleared and changed into a sort of pasteurized, sanitized version of itself. For tourists, mind you. Just for tourists. What kind of mentality is that?" He was contemptuous. This was long before Disneyworld at Orlando, but that was exactly the kind of development he was objecting to and unfortunately most of his predictions have come true.

I chimed in, "And the people who do live here, they are kept in the dark about what's happening. And, besides that, their daily lives are so challenging, they don't have time to think about the long-term consequences of issues like this on their livelihood."

Those living on the outer keys especially had little influence on anything. They had probably never voted in their lives. All they could manage, given their primitive circumstances, was to stay alive. It was subsistence living, struggling for the next meal, and with no time to think about much else. The townspeople, tradesmen and shopkeepers, had a little better time of it, but their lives were also quite limited. They lived largely uninformed, and ignorant of the goings on in the larger world around them, many folks still hanging on to longstanding prejudices and superstitions. Education was limited, many had not graduated from high school and the opportunity to go to college was almost non-existent. Opportunities were few to improve their circumstances, so how could they be expected to embrace conservation and other such radical notions? For many, the obvious answer to their woes was money from tourism, with little thought to what the price of that type of development would be.

Nevertheless, there were some folks who did recognize the dangers of such short-sighted solutions and were ready to speak up for the less popular idea of conservation and preserving the everglades, instead of development full speed ahead.

"Peter," said Rosa, "you must speak to the PTA at my school. They will be happy to hear you to talk about this, please. You could do something good with this."

"He's already doing something good here," said Ralph, who didn't want his wife to seem pushy, but Peter was quite willing. He came from a family of liberal thinkers, who had been advocates for conservation measures well before preservation and endangered species became a "cause celeb."

"I'll be happy to do it," said Peter, "but I'll need a little time to think about what I would want to say." I knew he was nervous about writing and also about public speaking.

"Mum and I'll help," I volunteered. "I should think between us we could come up with something."

And so, it was decided. A date was set and Peter got to work. He struggled quite a bit with the writing. Peter was not what we'd call nowadays a "head person." But he was willing to accept such help as we could give him, and between us we crafted quite a respectable presentation.

The day arrived and we drove into Everglades in the *Snowy Egret*, managing to stay dry, and walked over to the school. The PTA consisted of a dozen earnest parents and four teachers, including the principal. They seemed to be torn between being pleased with their progressiveness for sponsoring such a controversial subject, and some slight misgivings that they were espousing a dangerous cause. However, as my mother, Peter, and I presented ourselves at the school's general-purpose room, we found a small gathering of about twenty-five adults and several children of assorted ages. Rosamaria was showing off and being rather cheeky, hanging on my arm and prattling to Peter. Mummy and I sat in front with the Leightys, and Peter was on a chair facing us all. It was stuffy and hot, even though the big ceiling fans were turning slowly above our heads.

The principal, a kindly, rumpled man wearing a red bow tie, introduced Peter and explained the significance of the job he was doing for the Audubon Society. Recognizing his dedication to an important cause for the benefit of the rest of us. I was impressed to hear Peter's and my role thus described and I felt rather self-conscious. By the time he began to speak, Peter's nervousness had subsided and he read his talk in a firm, clear voice. People looked impressed. I was filled with a mixture of pleasure and pride and felt a new respect for him. He'd had to work very hard to come up with this presentation and it really *was* important. His talk over, we all stood around a long table and had juice and homemade oatmeal cookies, served up by the PTA Ladies Auxiliary. People were shy at first. Rosa and the principal were conferring. She wanted him to let her start a class in environmental studies.

"This is so important." She looked up at him with her big brown eyes. "Do you not think so?"

"Well, yes, of course, of course," he answered her. "Let me take it up with the Board. I think it could be a very good addition. The problem, as always, is I don't know if we'd have the money...," he trailed off thoughtfully.

"Oh, I'd volunteer, I'd love to teach it," she assured him. "I would have time." "We'll see," was his answer. "Let's talk about it again."

Peter had a circle of parents, mostly mothers, around him. They were also talking about a class.

"Even if the class doesn't get going right away," he was saying, "we'll make a special arrangement, so that anyone who wants to can come out on the tour to Duck Rock. Perhaps Charlie would make a special rate for the school." The mothers thought that was a wonderful idea.

"Don't you get lonely tied up out there all the time?" One of the younger moms batted her eyelashes at Peter.

He smiled his friendly grin,

"Oh no. We've plenty to do, haven't we, Chloe?" He looked over at me.

"Well, we keep busy, that's for sure," I agreed. "But it *would* be nice to go to the movies sometime," I added teasingly. The nearest movie theater was thirty miles up the Tamiami Trail in Naples.

Another parent wanted to know how long we were staying. I almost fell over when Peter said airily, "Probably for three years at least." This was the first I'd heard of it. I understood we'd signed on for a year, "to see how it went." Three years? Not bloody likely, I thought.

My mother was talking to a small circle, exchanging preferences for hot or iced tea. The ladies were amazed no one in England drank anything with ice in it.

"We just aren't in a warm enough climate, we don't need to ice anything," my mother tried to explain. "Our houses are cold and we are only just now getting refrigerators. We make do with stone pantries to keep things cool."

The talk ran down and we all filed out. Rosa invited us for a beer.

Art was with us. He was surprisingly complimentary. Instead of showing his usual jealous and denigrating side, he praised Peter and his efforts, which warmed my heart. Good old Art, it was nice to have him so supportive in the public arena.

"That Mr. Baker and them New York folks ought to be pretty happy about this 'ere talk, I reckon," he said. "Make 'em see we ain't just sittin' around collecting' wages, pokey though they might be." He was obviously going to share whatever glory Peter might be garnering for the Audubon Society, which was okay with Peter. He was too generous to try to shut Art out. Even though Art did make things difficult for us at times, with his constant grumbling and negativity, I figured it was all because he was basically anxious about his future, and insecure about himself.

Rosa was in high spirits, not only because the talk had gone well, but also because the principal had seemed receptive to her idea about a class.

She asked Peter again about bringing some of the children out to Duck Rock for one of the tours.

"Oh, they will so enjoy to see the birds and how they come flying at night to the little island. We must do this."

Peter promised he'd talk to Charlie the next day when he came out on the tour. "Now," continued Rosa, "you must stay for dinner with us before you go back out there." Which sounded like a great idea.

It was late afternoon on a Friday. The post office was still open, and we ambled over to get the mail. There was a small bunch of letters, including one from The Boys—Peter's two younger brothers, Hank and Tom, plus Walter, a first cousin. They'd all grown up together and were very close. The boys were still quite young, Hank and Walt being about eighteen and Tee, as Tom was known, only fourteen. They were on their way to California to visit relatives, planning to go via Mexico. They were hoping to get to Everglades in about ten days and wanted to stay for a week. Peter and I were delighted, The Boys were very dear to us, and furthermore they would bring news and gossip of our various friends, whom I for one, missed so much.

There was also a letter from our boss, Mr. Baker, telling us about the annual meeting in New York City of the National Audubon Society in October and inviting us to attend, all expenses paid. Would we like to attend? Would we? I was enormously thrilled at the mere idea. New York! The bright lights! Our friends and family! Whoopee!

Excited and buoyed up by the news in these letters, we returned to the Leightys' bringing beer and some wine to celebrate Peter's successful talk and our good news. After a cheerful, festive dinner, we set forth again in the *Snowy Egret* back to the *Audubon*. The sun had nearly set as we traveled across the rather choppy waters, huddled in our raingear to keep dry. There was a lot of bird activity as herons and egrets flew around heading for their various roosts. Gulls flapped along in small groups, and passing Pavilion Key, we espied an osprey swoop in for the night. Mum and I sat in the stern and sang old music hall songs at the top of our lungs. The sound of the motor drowned us out, and we could abandon ourselves, throwing our voices into the infinite space of the evening as we sped across the water, the foam from our wake now flashing pink and gold as the sun set. We were still singing and laughing as we approached Duck Rock and tied up. All but a few late stragglers had flown in for the night. Peter switched off the motor and silence settled over us as we clambered aboard and made our way to our bunks.

I wanted to confront Peter about the "three years at least" he'd answered so casually to that parent's question. But I decided to wait. I was tired, and we needed more privacy if we were actually going to have a disagreement. Instead we made love for the first time in ages. We felt close and happy, almost like old times. We tried to be quiet for Mum's sake, and I hoped she was asleep.

24

Time slowed to a leisurely crawl as the heat and the humidity increased, leaving us limp and inert. None of us could bring ourselves to do much more than the absolute minimum to keep daily life going. The slightest exertion produced copious sweat trickling down your back, from under your arms and around your waistband. Even sitting still, we were always slightly damp. On the boat, without electricity, the most basic chores took twice as long and in that unending heat were twice as onerous. Everything had to be done by hand. It was like living in the 19th century. To top it off, the bugs were so bad it felt like the return of the Ten Plagues.

On a more positive note, Mrs. T's cat had her kittens and now they were ready for adopting. We went over to see them on a muggy, rainy morning. They had their eyes open and were ready to be weaned. We watched them rolling around with each other, chasing and batting playfully with their tiny paws. One adventurous creature was trying to climb over the side of the basket and tumbled out onto the floor.

"That's the one I want," said Peter, and he scooped up the soft little ball of fur and cuddled him. The kitten just fit in his palm and it began purring loudly. I was so happy that Peter had been completely won over. In the face of such cuteness it hadn't been hard. Then it was my turn to pick. We wanted males but it's hard to tell with kittens. My famous aunt in London had a cat named George for years and years, and then one day George gave birth to five kittens. So, you never know. I chose one who had been chasing his own tail and now seemed ready to nap. Both of them were light gray tabbies with white chests and feet, so tiny they were hardly more than a squirmy handful. I thought they were beautiful, and we named them Castor and Pollux.

We took our new pets back to the boat, where I had already set up a cat box lined with newspaper and covered with crushed seashells. Castor was very good about it, but Pollux would get in and play with the shells and try to eat them— they must have still smelled fishy. I made them a bed under the table out of an old quilt, which they scorned, preferring to sleep in a cardboard box under the cot. They settled in quickly. They were a source of endless entertainment as well as great cuddles. Perhaps they were a sop to my dormant maternal instinct.

Meanwhile, I confirmed with Mrs. Tooke that Mum and Tommy could stay at her house, at least some of the time while the boys were here. As the day neared for the arrival of Henry, Walt, and Tom, I grew increasingly concerned that they would show up on a tour day and really confuse everything. They were supposed to arrive in Everglades on the next Friday, the day before the tour on Saturday. Peter drove the small boat into town to meet them, planning to spend the night there if they didn't appear, in which case he hoped to bring them out the next day. This was just one more instance of the primitive world of communication in those days that made logistical planning so uncertain.

All day Friday my mother and I waited on the boat for them to come, but by 6 p.m. we decided they weren't going to make it. They finally arrived the next day, an hour before the scheduled tour, exactly as I had feared they would, disheveled, unwashed, and exhausted. Here they were at last, our dear family, having traveled non-stop for the past twenty-four hours and apparently having had no sleep for three days, living on bennies and beer. Henry claimed to have been hallucinating as they drove the final miles along the Tamiami Trail in their converted Army weapons carrier. This was probably true, although Henry was prone to hyperbole and exaggeration.

Henry, sometimes known as Hank, was the eldest of the three, though elder by only a few months than Walt, his first cousin. Tall and dark, he looked a lot like Peter. Even Tom (sometimes Tee) the youngest brother, though blond and slighter, still had a family resemblance. The Scott gene was very dominant, they all looked like their father. Walter took after his own side of the family and had the wide shoulders and rangy build of his father, Will Helmuth. They were all of them immensely personable and likeable. The whole family had always had an indefinable glamorous aura about it. They attracted people effortlessly and were at ease with themselves and others in any situation.

We'd heard from Art that there were twelve people signed up for the tour this time, which would mean altogether too many people on the boat at once. So, thrilled as we were to see the boys, there was no rest for the weary, and Peter hustled them off to Pavilion Key to wait for the tour party to come and go. Mum was to stay on the big boat and help Peter with tour chores.

It seemed to be my role to go with our visitors on the island trip, so after gathering a few necessities together, we climbed into the *White Ibis* for the short trip to the key. The bow grounded with a sandy crunch about fifty feet from the beach as the tide was extremely low. We grabbed our stuff and waded ashore. Then, turning the boat around, Peter waved and sped back to the *Audubon*.

A crowd of fiddler crabs scuttled off as we approached and a flock of least sandpipers twiddled away down the beach on their matchstick legs. Unfortunately, in the confusion and hurry, I had left the 612 bug spray and the beer can opener behind. This was a major mistake and we paid dearly for it. Here we were—marooned, beerless, and at the mercy of gazillions of mosquitoes and sand flies in the scanty shade at the edge of the trees. We tried to get comfortable on our towels on the sand and ate our hastily assembled sandwiches. The sun beat down mercilessly.

"Sonofabitch, these no-see-ums are hell," complained Walter. It was true. The bugs were numberless and persistent and their bite a furious aggravation. I lit a fire, hoping to ward off some of them, but it didn't help much. Even smoking innumerable cigarettes and blowing smoke around ourselves wasn't very effective.

"Geez, can't we find a better spot?" was Hank's rather plaintive suggestion.

I tried to distract the visitors as best I could. We walked around the island looking for birds, we went swimming in the tepid shallow water, and we found a slightly better camping spot on the other side of the key where local fishermen had set up a crude shelter and a fireplace. Nothing really helped. Resigning ourselves to our wretched fate, we waited and waited through what was to be a long, miserable afternoon. Henry, Walter, and Tee were so tired they wanted nothing more than to sleep, but it was impossible because of the insistent attentions of the insects. Hank and Walt even made Tom bury them up to their necks in the sand, but they got too hot and had to be disinterred. We just had to endure as the hours dragged by.

At last, with almost hysterical relief, we heard the sound of the motorboat and saw Peter returning to rescue us. We climbed into the little *White Ibis* feeling like four Robinson Crusoes, fervently thankful our ordeal was over. Once we were back on the *Audubon*, my mother welcomed us with cold beer and the picnic supper left behind by the tour guests, and we all felt much better. The final irony was that there had been only four tourists after all and there would have been plenty of room on the boat for everyone. Our miserable afternoon had been totally unnecessary.

That unhappy and unnecessary afternoon was an unfortunate beginning to a visit fraught with mishap. Everything seemed to go wrong. We ran out of ice and for some reason there was none to be had at Turkey Key for two days. In that climate no ice was a disaster. Then too we were all quite crowded and uncomfortable on the boat, even though my mother and sometimes Tee (who didn't like being separated from the group) went to sleep at the Tookes'. Mrs. Tooke, with her characteristic tactlessness, kept making comments and remarks about Tom's small stature and wondered aloud why he "hadn't growed big like his brothers." No hints or distractions had any effect on her. Tom was just fourteen and for his age he was on the small side, which was emphasized by his brothers and cousin being quite large and well built. In later years, he caught up to everyone else, but meanwhile poor Tee just squirmed at Mrs. Tooke's unthinking remarks. Henry became allergic to the cats and was sneezing and snuffling and blowing his nose. One of the small boats developed carburetor trouble and started running sporadically and unreliably and finally quit. Fortunately, when it completely gave out, we were up at the Tookes', so everyone had a go working on it, but a planned trip to Gopher Key had to be canceled, much to everyone's frustration. The weather continued unbearably hot and there was no rain, so we began to run low on water. Circumstances seemed to conspire to make us all suffer.

But despite the drawbacks and frustrations, Peter and I were both very happy to have our beloved family with us. We all got along and enjoyed being together with great zest, even under the adverse conditions. Henry and Walt had just graduated from high school, Henry from Andover (where Peter had gone, too) and Walt from East Hampton High, where Tee was a freshman. Along with Peter, they had all been close growing up. Walt's father, the aforementioned and rather famous Will Helmuth, had initiated them into the pleasures of bird watching and natural history exploration since they were old enough to hold their own binoculars. So, despite the discomforts, they were naturalists at heart and appreciated the positive side of our unusual situation. In fact, both Henry and Tee went on to become natural scientists, Henry as a marine biologist and Tee as a plant physiologist. Walt went off on a tangent and became a film maker, but he remained an ardent camper and outdoorsman. They brought with them a strong whiff of home and the familiarity I'd been missing, which helped me with my homesickness. It was fun having them all on board—full of life, big and lovable and taking up all the space. Their visit passed all too quickly.

After Peter got the *Snowy Egret's* engine running better, we were able to go on expeditions up into the further reaches of the Chatham River. Peter wanted everyone to visit Mr. Darwin. We hadn't been to see him since we'd taken my mother there. Peter wanted his brothers and cousin to meet him, as he was such an interesting person and lived under such unique circumstances. Mr. Darwin's way of life was like going back in a time machine to the past century, an example of a way of living becoming more and more rare, as the last wildernesses are increasingly tamed and regulated. Also, Peter really wanted to set traps for the white-footed mice he'd seen the last time we were there. He was sure they were an undiscovered subspecies.

When we came putting up in the *White Ibis*, Mr. Darwin was tending his row of string beans tied up to rough stakes of mangrove branches. He straightened up to greet us as we scrambled ashore and handed him the beer and old newspapers we'd brought. He was pleased and didn't seem to mind the papers being a week out of date.

"It ain't the news so much, ya see," he explained. "It's jest good to read about your fellow humans' shenanigans. Keeps me from wanting to go back into that world, for sure." He winked and nodded.

We introduced him to our family. "Well, young feller-me-lads," he greeted them, "getting your fill of the swamp life, are yah?"

He asked after my mother. "That's one special lady," he complimented her. I think Mr. Darwin, whose first name I never knew, had some English experience in his background. He'd bring forth surprising expressions sometimes. He'd recognized my slight accent and for whatever reason began to address me as "Miss English." Perhaps "Chloe" was too familiar and "Mrs. Scott" too formal.

Peter said, "I've brought some traps along to see if I could collect some of those little mice, you know, the ones we saw last time?"

"Sure, you do your science, young feller. We'll take a walk up to the cistern and show your friends around this here old mound. The trail's gotten real overgrown though, and there's some trees down across it. It's hard to navigate. Bring your machetes, boys, you can help clear it." Of course, Henry and Walt had brought all their equipment and were thrilled to have a serious use for it.

They all set off and I stayed in the campground. The cooking fire had gone cold, so I revived it and put the filthy black pot on. I'd brought some coffee along, as well as the beer and papers, and I thought some good old camp coffee would hit the spot. When the water boiled, which took ages, I threw in some grounds. It was still boiling away when the work crew returned, rather hot and sweaty. Not surprisingly, they chose to drink beer rather than coffee. But the coffee would be good for later and Mr. Darwin was pleased.

"He showed us how to get the hearts of palm out, really great stuff," said Walter. They had each got one, so we'd have plenty for supper. Now if we could just catch a fish on the way home, we'd be all set.

Mr. Darwin told us his son, Lennie, was about to visit him. This was interesting news, he'd never mentioned having a family before. Lennie was also a fisherman, apparently, but he mostly worked up north on the shrimp boats. It was off season and he was taking some time out to visit his old dad.

"Yes," said Mr. Darwin, a little proudly, "he's all the time wantin' me to leave here and go north with him. He's got a house and all, but what would I do with myself? I ain't slep' indoors in fifteen years." He chuckled, revealing his toothless gums. He began regaling us with stories about his life in the Merchant Marine in the Pacific in the '20s.

"We was headin' for Okinawa," he started, "and the radio operator was pickin' up these storm warnin's to all shipping in that area about a monster typhoon headin' our way. We changed course directly and ran down south as fast as we could to get out of the storm's way. About three days later, we got back to our original course and what should we see but bits of flotsam and all kinds of debris floatin' all around. Then, up ahead, we spied a life boat driftin' in the current. There was still big swells, mind you, and we could see someone or something in that boat. When we come up alongside, sure enough, there was two Japanese fellers in the bottom of the boat, near dead of exposure and thirst. One of them was covered with oil, black all over he was, and their tongues was swollen and stickin' outta their mouths. Reckon they'd tried to drink the sea water. We hauled them aboard and they recovered. One could speak a little English, and he told us they was the only survivors of the *Mikyoki Maru,* out of Honshu, caught in the typhoon. I reckon that was some storm. The Mikyoki Maru was 50,000 tons with a crew of 65. All lost 'cept for our two. We heard later that several other merchantmen was sunk, too."

He could clearly have gone on for ages, but we had to be going. "I'll be back and check those traps in a day or so," said Peter, and we took our leave.

"Boy oh boy," Tee was breathless with enthusiasm, "I'm coming back here someday and build myself a hideaway just like Mr. Darwin. I *love* that place and that old guy. It's just what I want to do!"

We trolled on the way home and caught a couple of yellow jacks. My favorites. Dinner was assured.

25

Since the boys were on their way to Mexico, they had to have typhoid shots. This meant a trip into Miami, as our local doctor didn't have the vaccine. We needed water badly, plus the *Snowy Egret* still wasn't running well. So, a few days after our visit to Mr. Darwin, Peter decided to take the *Audubon* into town, where we could stay over and put the *Snowy* up on the ways and get the engine fixed properly while the boys went off to Miami.

Safely moored in town, we all went ashore and the boys proudly showed off their infamous vehicle to my mother and me. They had converted an army weapons carrier into an RV crossed with a Hummer. Painted in army camouflage, it stood high off the ground on huge wheels. They'd parked it near the Leightys', where it lurked, looking sinister and vaguely menacing. Nowadays, one might suspect it of being packed with wild-eyed, gun-toting survivalists. Back then, it was just army surplus. Right after the war there was a lot of army surplus around in the form of not only vehicles, but all manner of GI equipment to anyone who would buy it. In addition to the vehicle, they had spent a small fortune in one such surplus store, where they'd bought, among other things, pistol belts, "Woodsmen's Pals" (which included the most dangerous-looking knives, hatchets, and machetes), canteens, and even some sort of masks in case of sandstorms in the desert! Two hammocks were slung in the back for Henry and Walt, and Tee slept on a mattress on the floor beneath them. Their whole outfit, and the boys themselves, were the subject of much amazement and speculation amongst the locals.

The boys went on into Miami to get their shots, and Peter turned his attention to getting the *Snowy Egret* up on the ways. I set about filling the *Audubon's* water tanks from the hose on the embankment.

Mr. Darwin was there filling his water containers. Looking as disreputable as ever, he greeted me cheerily, "Hello there, Miss English." He told me he and his son Lennie had been fishing together.

"Got us some big tarpon," he boasted.

After I filled the tanks, my mother and I went to visit the Leightys, where my mother had become a great favorite and where she planned to stay overnight during the boys' last days here. Taking her up river to the Tookes' in the evenings and picking her up again in the morning had become rather onerous for everyone and besides, the Leightys had much superior plumbing!

Our three adventurers did not return until the next day, having had a great time in the big city. Where, they reported, they had gotten a lot of action in some dive they'd discovered.

"You should have seen the looks we got," Hank said. "The truck caused quite a sensation."

"Yeah. The cops even pulled us over. I think they thought we were smugglers or gun runners or something," Walter added.

Unfortunately, the boys were having a bad reaction to the typhoid shots and were feeling terrible, shivering and feverish. Besides which, they were hung-over, which made everything much worse. In fact, they were good for nothing except to go to bed and sleep it off, which they promptly did.

On the other hand, Peter and I had done all the chores, the boats were back to running smoothly, watered and fueled, with all our provisions laid in. We felt we deserved a little night life too. Especially me. The presence of my mother and the others had kept my mind occupied, but now they were leaving, the boys in a couple of days, and my mother in a week. I was not only sad, I was depressed. I was ready to leave too. To cheer me up, Rosa suggested that she, Ralph, Peter, and I go to the slightly notorious Almar Cafe up on the Tamiami Trail. She assured us they had a great jukebox there and we could dance.

"Come on. It will be fun. We will just be silly and forget to be so much serious." Dear Rosa. She had a great sense of living.

I was already persuaded, and Peter was game. He and I had been there before, and even though it was a bit rough and raunchy, we'd had a good time. I thought it would be even more fun to go with Ralph and Rosa. My mother offered to babysit, saying she was too old for juke joints, so Rosamaria was taken care of.

The four of us walked into the crowded, smoky bar with its minuscule dance floor. The juke box was blaring swing instead of the usual country music, and a few couples were jostling round on the dance floor. Squeezing into the last booth in the back, we ordered beers and then joined the dancers. How long had it been since I'd danced? I'd lost track. As I began, I felt a bit rusty, but then the music took over and filled me and moved me and I remembered who I was. I felt like the dancer in the movie "The Red Shoes," who had to dance till she died. ("I Could Have Danced All Night," indeed, though "My Fair Lady" hadn't been written yet.) It felt like heaven. Movement is the key to life, as Moshe Feldenkrais says. We stayed late, drank a little too much beer, and went home happy.

The following morning our boys were recovered, though Peter and I were slightly worse for wear. Nevertheless, we set off early for the trip back out to Duck Rock. The weather, which had been unchanging for several days, now took a turn for the worse. As we slid down the Barron River towards the Gulf, we could see huge storm clouds piling up on the horizon and the wind began to pick up. As soon as we cleared the lee of the land, the wind intensified and the old *Audubon* started rocking, pitching, and rolling.

"Better grab everything on the shelves," warned Peter. "This could get worse before it gets better."

The boys and I rapidly began securing everything that could fall down, including the ice box which had fallen on its face more than once in a hard blow. The squall came screaming down on us, blowing sheets of rain through the screens. "Get the shutters," I yelled. Between us, we wrestled the shutters into their slots to keep out the streaming rain blowing almost horizontally across us.

Peter was standing up at the helm trying desperately to see through the windshield and the furious rain which was becoming almost a whiteout. The water, gray and foaming, was whipped up into short, choppy waves as the *Audubon* labored along, lifting up on the crests and coming down with a thud as the wave passed beneath and left us in the trough. She had a very shallow draft in order to be able to travel in these waters at all, and when the water was rough like this she just bobbed like a cork. Peter was doing a great job steering us through the storm. Navigating amongst the mangrove clumps of these Ten Thousand Islands was tricky under the best circumstances. Everything in the seascape looked dismayingly the same and now with almost nil visibility, the task became daunting.

The pitch of the wind's howl rose higher as it came tearing across the water. Conversation was impossible. We could only hang on and hope for the best. At least, no one was seasick. Peter and I had had a few bouts of nausea in earlier days, but now we had our sea legs and were impervious. As soon as we'd hit the open water and the squall, the kittens had retired under the cot into their box, where they stayed, sleeping throughout the voyage. They seemed quite unperturbed. We wallowed on. A few sea gulls were having trouble making headway against the wind as they flapped across the gray, scudding clouds right above our heads. Further off, a pair of frigate birds sailed high on the wind, utterly unfazed. This was pure fun for them, sweeping along in the air currents above the water. We were only half way to Duck Rock and the storm was still hitting hard. Most squalls came blowing in from the west, across the Gulf, heading towards land and going away as quickly as they came. This one was lasting.

I was cold. The wind came through the shutters and rain was leaking in around them and under the door. After the terrific heat we'd been suffering, this cold was a violent contrast. We all put on sweat shirts.

The *Snowy Egret* was towing badly, swinging wildly from side to side on the tow rope. Peter yelled that he was worried it would come loose, someone had to get in and steer it. How could anyone get on board in this sea? The task looked impossible. Up ahead we could see Rabbit Key Pass coming into view. If we went behind the key, into the shelter of the pass, the wind would be quieter. If Peter could slow down enough, one of us could try to clamber into the smaller boat. All three of the boys volunteered, but Tee gave up quickly, knowing his small size would be against him. Walt and Henry argued briefly, until Peter, in his role of elder brother and captain, said, "Hank, you go. Put your slicker on. Walt and Tee can help hold the boat while you climb in. You'll have to haul her as close as you can and you'll have to be quick about it."

As soon as we were in the lee of the island in the pass, Peter slowed down. Walt and Tee clambered into the stern well, and with both of them struggling with the tow rope, managed with great effort to pull the bucking and careening *Snowy Egret* close enough for Henry to scramble over the stern and crawl across onto the deck of the smaller boat. Despite the pitching and rolling, he staggered to the stern and took the tiller. I was terrified, expecting to see one or all of them fall overboard any minute or some other disaster to happen, but all went well and I felt my anxiety level start to ease.

Now we just had to get back to Duck Rock. The moment we came out on the other side of the key where we'd been sheltering, the wind hit us again, but it seemed a little less strong, the sound of the wind a few decibels lower. I hardly dared hope so, but the clouds to the west seemed to be lightening and breaking up. Then a glimpse of sunlight showed momentarily, and a few minutes later it was unmistakable, the storm was abating. Already the water was calmer, in these shallows the water could change on a dime. The rain diminished and then stopped altogether. A huge surge of relief went through me and I realized how tense I'd been these past hours.

"We're through the worst of it, thank God," said Peter, "Light me a cig, would you, hon?"

I found a pack and some damp matches and we all lit up thankfully. Up ahead Duck Rock came into view, still just a line on the horizon. We'd soon be back to our safe haven. Fifteen minutes later we tied up to the stakes. The sun came out and began to dry us off. The air felt fresh and less humid, and we took the shutters down. I hugged Peter gratefully.

"You were terrific," I praised him. "Really. I was scared there for a little while."

"So was I," he grinned. "But I knew we'd make it. The *Audubon* is a seaworthy old girl, after all."

The boys were impressed that we'd all survived and Peter had done so well. We cracked open some beers and sat around the rest of the afternoon, playing with the kittens.

The next day was the boys last day with us. How quickly their visit had gone by. There was so much we hadn't had time to do, so many unexplored places left unseen, and now they were about to go off again in their vehicle to further adventures in other new places. We still had one day, though.

We all got up early the next morning to watch the birds leave at dawn. We all marveled once again at the ascending rush and whoosh of wings, as all the birds flew up and off in their thousands, rising up into the dawn-lit sky above the dark water, winging their way off to their feeding grounds.

Over breakfast a little later, we discussed possible plans for the day. "We could finally get up an expedition to Gopher Key, if you like," Peter suggested.

"The skiff seems to be running fine now, touch wood," he added.

We considered this for a while. The skiff was not really big enough for us all, but I desperately needed to do laundry, so I actually wanted to go to the Tookes'. If the guys went without me, they'd be better off anyway, especially navigating those shallow, narrow creeks that led to the inner pass to the key. After more discussion, they decided to go. Supplies were gathered, sandwiches made, beer collected, the 612 found, and everything stowed into various packs and bags—and off we went. They were going to drop me and my laundry at the Tookes' on the way.

As we drove upriver in the calm morning air, we were a tight squeeze and I thought it was a good thing I wasn't going along on the expedition. A few stray seagulls were flying idly towards the Gulf, and we could see and sometimes hear small songbirds as they darted in and out of the mangroves along the banks. Everyone was in high spirits as we came up to the Tookes' dock, where we noticed a strange boat tied to the pilings.

"I don't like the look of that," said Peter "It looks like one of the

Browns' boats." There was no one around either, which was a little unusual.

"Oh, it's all right, you go on," I urged. "Don't worry. Mr. Tooke will look after everything. See you later." I waved them away and they took off.

Gathering my bundle of wash, I started up the shell-strewn path, leading to the old house at the top of the mound. I found Mrs. Tooke sitting on the front porch looking tense. I could tell she was in a terrible state. Through the open kitchen windows, I could hear men's voices raised in alcoholic wrangling and yelling. Mrs. Tooke rose to greet me, seeming glad I'd come, and we walked away from the house. In a lowered, anxious tone, she told me that Red Gomez and a couple of the Brown boys had shown up early that morning. They had come with a boatload of stolen booze, including eight cases of whiskey and a dozen or more of beer. They'd been drinking ever since and were by now stinking drunk.

She was furious and upset because (a) they were drunk, (b) they were still drinking, (c) they were messing up her kitchen and had Mr. Tooke in there with them, and (d) worst of all, neither she nor Mr. Tooke dared throw them out. Not only were they unpleasant characters, but they could be dangerous. She told me that, if crossed, they would be quite capable of coming back when no one was home and wrecking the place, killing the chickens and who knows what all deviltry, possibly even setting the house on fire. I decided that under the circumstances, I'd wait for a more auspicious moment to start my wash.

We walked a way into the orchard and continued fretting about the situation. It didn't look good. I decided now would be a good time to use the outhouse, and while I was in there, I heard the sound of an approaching boat. I hoped it was the sheriff. I wasn't the only one who heard it—as I started to walk back to see who it was, Mr. Tooke and the three outlaws suddenly came lurching and stumbling out of the house. I was frightened and didn't want them to see me, so I hid behind a tree and watched them. I recognized Red Gomez and the two others as Browns, all obviously drunk. Their aspects were frightening, they were unshaven and their eyes were bloodshot. They were peering around with hostile and aggressive, but also slightly worried, looks. They also all had guns, which they were waving recklessly about. The Browns were holding Mr. Tooke by the arms, while Red had his face shoved menacingly towards him, apparently saying something threatening. Then they staggered away to their boat, cursing loudly, and took off in a cloud of blue exhaust smoke.

I came out of hiding as Mrs. Tooke appeared. Mr. Tooke, looking very shaken up, told us they'd stolen his gun and threatened him with murder and mayhem if he said anything to the sheriff, or anyone else who might come looking for them. We were all quite upset.

Then suddenly, it began to pour with rain. In all the excitement, none of us had noticed the gathering storm clouds. We quickly ran inside and Mrs. Tooke and I had some tea to calm our nerves, while Mr. T broke out his secret stash of white lightning. I accepted a small sip to be friendly and it did do the trick and settled my stomach. The rain continued in a steady downpour. The unknown boat had gone on by, to fish upriver presumably. The outlaws had spooked unnecessarily, but thank goodness they had.

A short time later, we heard the putt-putt of another boat and recognized it as the *White Ibis* with our intrepid explorers returning. A moment later they came tromping in, wet, cold and wretched. Once again Gopher Key had eluded them and they'd had to turn back. This time they at least got a glimpse of the interior lagoon before the rain drove them away. Mr. Tooke offered them some white lightning, while the ladies offered tea. It was no surprise which they chose. Even Tee was allowed a tot. Although, as Mrs. Tooke unnecessarily pointed out in her tactless way, "drinkin' and smokin' 'll stunt yer growth, and you don't need that..." However, she was quite rightly ignored and Tee choked down a shot glass of the wild stuff. After they had dried off a little by the stove, Mrs. Tooke outfitted everyone in dry shirts, and holding a couple of big tarpaulins over our heads, we dashed back to the *Audubon*. A rather ignominious ending to the boys' last day. But they were enthralled by the story about the ruffians and furious because they'd missed all the excitement.

Peter took it rather seriously.

"It's too bad old Tooke gave them his rifle," he said. "That doesn't bode well." "But he didn't give it to them," I protested, "they just stole it. If it came down to whose word to believe, well, it's no contest. The sheriff knows Mr. Tooke and he'd never take Red Gomez's word over his."

But we all knew we hadn't heard the last of this episode.

Back on the boat, the kittens greeted us with little mews of pleasure, running up to us with their tails up in the air and purring as we petted them. Everyone tried to get dry, which wasn't easy. It was still raining hard, big drops splashing down on the water in fat craters and drumming on the cabin roof. Visibility through the screens out to the mangroves of Duck Rock, and the larger vista out to the Gulf, was dimmed, gray, and colorless. I started dinner and we all opened beers.

"No bird watching tonight, I guess," said Hank glumly. "Too bad. I wanted to see them come in one more time."

As so often happened, his prediction was premature. The weather changed again. just at sunset, and the rain let up. The clouds piled up on the horizon, turning pink and purple in the sun's last rays. The returning birds showed up in all their glory, especially a spectacular line of about twenty scarlet ibises weaving towards us in a brilliant red line. Unfortunately, with the rain's cessation, came the no-see-ums in great clouds, and we had to retreat inside.

Dinner over, we cleaned up, the boys finished their rather haphazard packing, and we sat around the lamp-lit table telling tales and reminiscing—and I, for one, wishing they weren't leaving in the morning. They wanted to take off early, so reluctantly we all turned in at a reasonable hour, and were rocked gently all night by the water lapping against the side of the *Audubon*.

26

Early the next morning, Peter and our dear family piled their gear into the *Snowy Egret* and headed off for Everglades and points unknown. I didn't go. The boat was crowded and I hate protracted farewells (a well-known failing of the Scott clan). I felt bad enough as it was, but I managed not to cry until they'd gone, waving goodbye as they drove out of sight, a small blotch on the calm surface of the Gulf.

Their departure left me feeling hollow and sad. I busied myself with cleaning and tidying up. I played with the kittens and listened to the radio and tried not to cry. Being way behind in my Journal, I decided to distract myself by typing up some of the events of the past few days. The trouble at the Tookes with the Gomez's and Brown boys loomed large in my thoughts and my journal entry.

After a while, I noticed the tide had gone out and the boat had settled in the mud at a slight angle, making it awkward to move around. The kitties had gone out on deck and were playing around on the catwalk (aptly named), that led from the stern around to the bow deck, suddenly I heard a splash and a yowl and Pollux came tearing back inside. I hurried out on to the deck and peered over the side. Sure enough, Castor had fallen overboard and was thrashing around in the shallow water. He must have slipped off the railing because of the unusual list to the deck. Ordinarily, they were both extremely sure-footed. I leaned over and fished him out. He was dripping and furious, but I toweled him off and gave them both a treat, and he recovered quickly. Since Pollux had fallen in only last week, I hoped they had now both learned their lesson.

Around mid-afternoon I heard a boat and saw the *Snowy* returning. Peter came alongside, and he and my mother disembarked. I was so glad to see her. The world immediately became a happier, more manageable place. Peter reported that the Vehicle had been given a good send-off by the Leightys, Art, the postmistress and the drugstore man who happened to be standing around and had joined in. Peter also brought the mail, groceries, and news of the wicked scoundrels and their booze heist. Apparently, the Gomez-Brown gang had taken the liquor from a warehouse in Everglades that we didn't even know existed. Peter, who was deeply concerned about the whole misadventure, said that Sam Tucker, the redoubtable sheriff, suspected Mr. Darwin's son, Lennie, of being involved. He also thought it likely that the outlaws were holed up at Mr. Darwin's camp.

"I told him he was wrong there," Peter said stoutly. "I just don't believe Darwin would have anything to do with those guys." Peter was very loyal to his friends, but he could be a bit naive. I hoped the sheriff was wrong, but as far as Lennie being willing to help the thieves, I wouldn't have been all that surprised. The sheriff was sending Art Eifler and a deputy, Mr. Atkins, upriver to Darwin's place to try to persuade the villains, if indeed they were there, to give themselves up and pay for the stolen goods. He also planned to offer them leniency in exchange. It didn't sound very likely to me. I couldn't see those men surrendering or agreeing to anything. I guessed it was worth a try though. Peter was more disturbed by the possibility that he and I would be called as witnesses to testify, if it came to a trial.

"I sure as hell don't want to get on the bad side of all those people," he said to my mother and me as we sat drinking tea. "It's taken months to get any of them to see us as anything but enemies. I'd hate to see even the little bit of good will we've got built up destroyed. If we testify, it will all go up in smoke. These people stick together, right or wrong."

My mother was concerned about everyone's safety, but not unduly alarmed. "But darling, surely they wouldn't do anything to you, even if you were witnesses. I mean, what good would it do them?"

"It hasn't anything to do with rational thinking," Peter answered. "It's like clan loyalty and revenge, especially when they're drunk, they'll do almost anything."

Actually, we were more concerned for the Tookes than ourselves. They seemed vulnerable, and though I had great faith in Mr. Tooke's sturdiness and independence, still he was only one against three or four, and now they had his gun. On the other hand, he probably had another gun and he could get Hamp to come and stay a while. Plus, he had other friends and allies from around and about. I felt a certain security being under the wing of the Audubon Society, as it were—although, come to think of it, that hadn't helped much in the past when they'd shot those two wardens. I comforted myself that things were more civilized nowadays, but I wasn't completely convinced.

We sat around imagining wild scenarios of armed gangs shooting it out in the mangroves. It was anxiety provoking, but somehow quite removed from reality for me. This sort of thing simply didn't happen to people like us! A little later we saw Art and Mr. Atkins coming back into town. Apparently, they had found no one "holed up" at Darwin's. This boded both ill and well. If the suspects were not at Darwin's then our friends weren't implicated. On the other hand, it meant the villains were still at large and could be hiding anywhere—and worse, could still be a threat to all of us. Art waved but didn't stop.

The following morning, we decided to go up to the Tookes' to see if they knew any more of what was going on. Also, I'd never got that laundry done that I'd left there in the middle of everything, and Peter needed to work on the *Snowy Egret's* carburetor. The darn thing was acting up again and burning too much gas. Mr. Tooke was on the dock as we came alongside. He caught the bowline I threw him and he secured us.

"Well, I guess you've heard the news," he said rather dourly. "We're all mixed up in this mess."

We debarked and he invited us for coffee. Sitting on the porch with our mugs of coffee, we lit up and the Tookes told us more about the Gomez family. Red and his brother Virgil both had criminal records and had done jail time. Virgil deserted from the army and for six months went on some sort of crime spree before getting caught. Red was jailed for a year for beating up the sheriff. He drank to violent excess, stole whenever and whatever he could, and rolled drunks for their wallets—they were both very unpleasant characters. The Browns were of the same ilk: nasty lowlifes. They were the products of decades of disenfranchisement and lives without any education or prospects and not much hope. Mr. T thought one or two of them might even have wives and children. Poor things, was all I could think, doomed to travel on such an unfortunate path.

By now the fugitives were armed and probably drunk, dangerous, and getting desperate. They could not go back to Everglades because they'd be picked up at once. They'd have to stay hidden in the swamps unless they could take their boat south to Key West or somewhere equally distant.

Finishing their coffee, Peter and Mr. Tooke went to work on the boat. Mum and Mrs. Tooke continued chatting and I started my laundry. Hardly had I gotten the little Sears machine started up when we heard a boat approaching. It turned out to be Hamp and three friends, plus Mrs. T's grandson, Wesley. The Tookes seemed not only glad to see them, but relieved. I certainly was. I felt much better for the Tookes now that their large, competent son and his pals had arrived. After greetings and small talk, they spread themselves around the place and the afternoon wore on.

Suddenly another boat appeared—the Sheriff Department's big launch. The sheriff, Sam Tucker, and three deputies, all armed, were out hunting the Gomez-Brown band. We gathered by the dock as they came ashore. Sam Tucker was a large man with a big beer belly hanging over his belt. He was slow-moving, slow-talking, and he had squinty eyes peering out from under his hat brim, which was pulled low on his forehead. He had a reputation for "getting his man" and not always playing strictly by the rules. I wouldn't want him after me, I thought. Mr. Tooke managed to hiss an aside to us that we were "not to say nothin' about nothin'" to the officials. Shortly after, he and Mr. Tucker went into a huddle. I don't know what Mr. Tooke told them, but he must have warned them about Red having stolen his rifle. Anyway, Sam Tucker and his deputies all left right away, headed upriver to search in the little creeks and side waters for their quarry—not an enviable job. The fugitives had the advantage that they could see and hear the law approaching well before the law could see them. The whole event was unsettling and, worse, unresolved.

I hung my laundry on the line and bade Mrs. Tooke farewell.   Peter, Mum, and I climbed into the now (we hoped) repaired *Snowy Egret* and chugged back to Duck Rock. Once back on board, I went through the mail Peter had brought from town earlier in the day. There was a letter from his Uncle Will Helmuth. In earlier times, Will had practiced medicine in New York City and in East Hampton, on Long island. He'd retired early, in his forties, and now lived with his wife, Mardi, sometimes his grown children, and a dog named Monty.

Will had been, and still was, a major influence on Peter and his brothers. He had taken them all camping on many occasions, even as far away as Brownsville, Texas. There, at the southernmost point of the United States, a serious bird watcher could expect to find rare, seldom seen birds to add to their precious life lists that they were all so avid about. Will's influence was not just as a naturalist and birdwatcher, he had introduced the boys to many other areas of thought and inquiry as well. When I came on the scene as a teenager in the 1940s, I also came under his wing and he educated me in many subjects including politics, art and classical music. His politics were quite liberal, in contrast to the Scotts' father, who was a stock broker and a dyed-in-the-wool Republican. This caused frequent dinner table friction in the family when the kids were teenagers and full of revolutionary fervor. We all ganged up on poor old George, who told us all to "go back to Russia."

Will also taught us about psychology, which up till then I'd known practically nothing about. He encouraged us to read Freud, Adler, and Jung, among others. In the end, we all became interested in Wilhelm Reich, and Peter and I both had a round of Reichian therapy later in our lives.

Will's most recent sphere of interest was grasses. He was making a study of all the grasses of eastern Long Island, and of Suffolk County in particular, something which no one had done before. We were both very fond of him and I looked forward to our reunion. He was a lot of fun and told the most wonderful stories. I knew Peter was eager to show Will this amazing environment and to share with him all the amazing discoveries he'd made. He would arrive a few days after my mother left, so there would be no space problem. I have to confess, though, I did have a few moments of misgiving about his coming so soon on the heels of everyone else. I was feeling a bit overwhelmed by so much company, even though I loved them all. The situation that summer seemed to be feast or famine. First, we were alone too much and rubbing against each other, and now we were swamped with company and hardly a moment to ourselves. Well, I reminded myself, it would change again for sure and there'd be plenty of time later in which to catch up. If there was anything to catch up to.

For the rest of the afternoon Peter, Mum, and I all went over to Pavilion Key to look for birds and stretch our legs a bit. My mother spotted a black-whiskered vireo's nest, which got Peter very excited as black-whiskered vireos are terribly rare. (Mum didn't know it was a black-whiskered vireo's nest, of course, just that it was a nest.) The bugs weren't bad, and my mother and I wandered along the beach gathering shells. My mother had started a collection to take home not only keep, but to give to her friends as well.

"Some of these shells are just so spectacular no one would believe them if they didn't see them," she said.

We weren't talking much, just strolling along and feeling the slight breeze blowing across the water, breathing the salty air, our bare feet in the warm sand.

"I wish you weren't going, Mum," I said. "I'm going to miss you so much."

"Well, it's time to go, you know. I've loved being here with you, but 'all good things must come to an end.'" One of her favorite sayings.

"I just wish we weren't always so far apart," I said.

"I expect you'll be back before long, won't you?" She looked at me.

"Oh, I don't know. Peter seems to want to stay on, I think. But I sure don't. I mean, I thought we were here for a year, and then at the talk, I heard him say he thought we'd be here three years. Three years. I haven't asked him about it yet, but I don't think I could stand it for that long." I had an urge to tell her how much I was already wanting to come home, but I couldn't complain too much, I felt disloyal to Peter. She knew anyway.

"It's a hard life here, sweetie," she answered my unspoken thought. "I think you are doing a marvelous job, and I can also see why you wouldn't want to stay indefinitely. You don't have to, you know. When you've had enough it's perfectly okay to say so." This was an encouraging thought and it cheered me up. She was right. I didn't have to feel like a traitor to want to leave.

After a while we came back to the boat, where I went aboard to start supper. Peter and my mother continued on around to the far side of Duck Rock to see the baby pelicans. A short time later, just as I was cutting up onions for the chili, I heard them coming back. A moment later, I heard a splash and a shriek and, dashing up on deck, found that my mother had fallen in! She had missed her footing as she stepped from the skiff onto the stern of the *Audubon*. Fortunately, as the tide was low, the water was only chest deep. We helped her clamber out again, unharmed, but feeling most chagrined, and—worst of all—she had Peter's field glasses around her neck. She was dreadfully upset about this although Peter assured her, quite truthfully, they could easily be repaired by any good optician. Otherwise, she was none the worse for wear, if a bit wet. They came on board and we all had a gin and tonic to cheer her up.

27

The Eiflers were now moored at the Tookes', unfortunately, because of this, we didn't visit up there as freely or as often. Our relationship with the Eiflers was undergoing a sea change as it were, and although we hoped it would be only temporary, it was still discomfiting. Art and his old Missus had always been a little difficult for both of us. They were full of odd notions and could even be considered prickly. They were both jealous souls, especially Mrs. Eifler, marooned in her deafness. She was not ageing well and she was physically deteriorating rather rapidly. While Art was very helpful to us in many ways and was basically a kind man, his pessimistic outlook, and his paranoia about the Audubon Society, made him a difficult companion. Peter managed to get along with him; Peter could get along with just about anybody.

I was a more difficult case. Although I didn't mean to put on any airs and graces, my natural Englishness might have seemed a bit hoity-toity to some. Once people got to know me, though, most folks saw me as a regular sort. Mrs. Eifler, however, did not see me that way. To her it seemed, I was a threat. Unfortunately, Art appeared to have developed a yen for me.

At first, I was oblivious, but Mrs. Tooke, who loved gossip and intrigue, announced one day over a morning coffee, "That old Art, he's gotten a real crush on you, the old fool."

"Oh my gosh." I was dismayed. "How do you know?"

"Well, he used to say kinda bad things about you. Thought you was stuck up and kind of a snob. Not just you, either. He was down on Peter too, at first, thought he was just some rich kid didn't know nothin'. Now he's gotten over that and is just full of compliments, says you're both doin' such a good job, and you especially. He's got a real soft spot for you."

Art began stopping by our boat every time he passed us on the way in or out of town or going to Turkey Key. He'd stop "to see if you want anything," or on the way back he'd stop with a six pack or a box of crackers or extra eggs from the Tookes. I thought at first it was my mother who was the big attraction, but it became obvious in the way he paid attention to me that Mrs. Tooke was right. I was embarrassed more than anything else, embarrassed for him. But I couldn't think of a way to get him to stop.

One day when he came by, I was alone on the boat, since Peter and Mum had gone to Turkey Key. He climbed aboard, even as I told him they were gone.

"I'll just wait on him, then," he replied.

"They may not be back right away," I said "You know sometimes you have to wait there."

I was torn between wanting to make it sound as if they'd be right back and I'd be protected, because they might return at any moment, or telling him they'd be gone a while, in which case he should leave, but he might stay anyway, thinking he could be there alone with me for a while. Oh dear. Damned if you do, damned if you don't. I busied myself in the galley and though I didn't want to, I offered him coffee.

He stood around awkwardly in the main cabin making small talk. We'd hardly ever been alone in all this time. I stayed in the galley as long as I could, but finally I'd washed every dish and pot and I had to come up into the cabin. I tried making bright remarks.

"How's Frieda?" I started. "Mrs. T says she's been poorly."

"Well, poor thing. She's got the rheumatism in her joints, ya know. Makes it hard for her to get around."

I made sympathetic noises. "Has she ever tried taking comfrey tea?" I was improvising. "It's supposed to help your joints. Or maybe she could get some medicine from the doctor."

But in his typical way, he assured me they didn't believe in no doctors, they never could help much and always ended up costing an arm and a leg.

Then he looked at me admiringly and said, "I bet you never get sick, do ya? You look like a healthy young thing to me." He was evidently paying me a compliment.

"Oh," I said airily, "I'm pretty lucky with my health, I guess."

"Well, I jest hope Peter *realizes* what a lucky fella he is to have sech a healthy, pretty wife." "Thanks, Art...," I started to say, but he went on. "Where'd you get that red hair from, huh? I've allus been partial to red-haired gals." And he kind of leered at me.

"Well, this gal's taken, Art," I said hastily, moving away as far as I could get in the narrow space of the cabin. "I guess my red hair came from my mom. She was a redhead once. Oh, look," I said. stepping towards the screen door, "I think they're coming back." Indeed, I hoped fervently that little dot on the horizon was Peter and my mother.

As I walked around him as quickly as I could, he put out a hand and tried to touch me or grab my arm or something. Now, Art was a nice old guy, but the thought of him actually touching me made my skin crawl. I managed to dodge past and flee out the door.

"Now, you cut that out, Art," I said lightly as I left. "They're coming back."

Art harrumphed and finished his coffee. A few moments later, the boat drew up under the stern and Peter and Mum climbed aboard. Nothing had happened, really, but I made a silent vow never to let myself be alone with Art again. I told Mum and Peter about it later and made light of it, but it was still rather distressing and made everything so awkward.

Mum said, "Well, it's not too surprising really, under the circumstances." And when Peter asked her what circumstances she meant, she said, "Oh you know, everyone cooped up here with no distractions. He's at a vulnerable age, sort of late middle-age. Men get notions."

Peter was annoyed by Art's attentions to me, but since he was not a jealous type and it was all so ridiculous, he didn't let it bother him or interfere with their relationship.

I was unhappy about feeling I had to stay away from the Tookes due to the awkwardness I felt about being around Art. I really liked seeing them and they, in turn, became hurt when we seemed to be staying away for too long. Mrs. Tooke didn't seem to understand why I wanted to avoid the Eiflers.

"He just makes me so uncomfortable," I tried to explain to her.

"Oh, he's a harmless old duck," she scoffed.

"Yes, I know that, but he still makes me feel weird," I said.

Consequently, I was very glad when a few days before my mother left to go home to New York, Mr. T stopped by on his way to Turkey Key and invited us for "dinner." They knew Mum was leaving and wanted to say goodbye. My mother was glad she'd have a chance to make her farewells too. They had been most kind and hospitable to her.

We went up one morning a few days later. There was quite a crew of us sitting at the T's big round table, with the Tookes' son Hamp and their daughter Kathleen, plus her boy Wesley and the Tookes' adopted son Noel, all in addition to the three of us, plus the Eiflers. Despite the heat and the humidity, Southern hospitality demanded huge fried meals with several vegetables and side dishes, salads, and desserts, all in the heat of mid-day. Still, we managed to show Southern manners and ate a lot to properly honor the cook.

Talk turned to the Gomez-Brown robbery and its aftermath. There had been no official word about the status of the situation.

Art said, "They're up there near Hurricane Creek is my guess."

Mr. Tooke said the Indians had been by and told him they caught a glimpse of their boat beyond Alligator Bay. It sounded as if they were moving around. If anyone could find them, the Indians could. I wondered why the sheriff didn't enlist their help. Probably some racial thing.

Hamp thought the gang had taken off for points south, and I sincerely hoped they had. I wanted them to be gone. At least things had quieted down and they hadn't done anything alarming lately. It was heartening to hear that there was definitely no connection between the gang and Mr. Darwin or his son Lennie.

Dinner over, my mother said her farewells and we set off for our good ship *Audubon*. I was touched by how genuinely everyone seemed to have taken to my mother, appreciating her cheery spirit and kind heart.

There was still plenty of afternoon left, so we had time to do something if we chose. My mother suggested she'd like to go up to Mr. Darwin's again. Now that the place was cleared of the suspicion of being a haven for outlaws, it sounded like a good idea. Peter had been talking about going to see what he could find in the shell mound. He'd trapped one white-footed mouse there that was a variant and he needed to capture another one. He was hoping Will could help him identify this little gray morsel of life, at the moment floating in a jar of formaldehyde. We had some newspapers left from when Peter had taken the boys into town to bring as a gift, but we were rather low on beer. However, we decided we would sacrifice our last two bottles in the name of good neighbor relations and the advancement of science, so we brought them too.

The trip up to Darwin's was uneventful, though I couldn't shake a certain nervousness about running into the Gomez people. What if they were there after all? Happily, my fears turned out to be groundless. Mr. Darwin's son Lennie was there, however. A small, wiry young man, he was a younger version of his father, with the same cock-sparrow cheerfulness and ornery nature. He told us he was going home shortly, back up North to his regular life. We presented our beers and old newspapers, and my mother was helped ashore by Mr. Darwin, who could be quite courtly when he'd a mind.

"Oh ho," says he, "it's Mrs. English herself." Although my mother had told him her name was Rena (short for Verena, her rather Victorian given name) and assured him it was all right to call her by it, he stuck to his own names for us both and we remained Mrs. and Miss English respectively.

The afternoon was not too hot and the little encampment sheltered beneath the palms, palmettos, and gumbo-limbo trees, seemed full of tropic charm. We wandered around exploring for a while, and then went up the trail to the top of the mound. We'd heard you could sometimes find bones and other relics in these mounds. We started scratching around in the top layer of the moraine, the 2,000-year-old detritus of the Calusas. On the topmost layer the shells were almost all fossilized and then, as we dug down, the layers changed colors and the next one we came to was greenish, and then a pink one, and finally the shells just looked very old, and indeed *were* fossilized. We didn't really get very far down, as it was about twelve feet high—or deep, whichever way you think of it—and we failed to find any artifacts.

Peter set his traps and we ambled back to Mr. Darwin's camp. He'd rekindled his fire and insisted that we stay for camp coffee, but Lennie was anxious to be gone.

"I'll be back, Dad, never fear," he told Mr. Darwin. "I gotta see how my partners is doin'. Mebbe they owe me some money." And he nodded and winked just like his father.

As we ourselves were about to go, we heard an approaching motor. I froze. "What if it's the Gomezes?" I whispered to Peter.

Everyone was looking up the creek, but Mr. Darwin just grinned, "It ain't the Gomezes, ma'am," he said, "it's the Indians."

It was Tony Tigertail and two of the women, wearing their colorful dresses. I recognized one of the women as Mary, whom I'd met at the chickee when the deaconess took me to visit. The other woman was Littlefeather, who, unlike her name, was massively large and sturdy. Everyone came ashore and Mr. Darwin made more coffee. Our oddly assorted group sat around on the sandy ground, making conversation and drinking coffee out of tin cups. It was rather stilted at first, but then Peter produced a pack of cigarettes, which broke the ice. Everyone except my mother lit up and solemnly puffed away.

After a while they got down to business. Tony and the others had come to trade. On the slightly higher ground behind the shell mound grew two very large papaya trees. At the moment they were loaded with the big golden fruit we call Mexican papaya. These were what the Indians wanted. In return, they had brought a sack of hand-milled corn meal. It was a fair trade and quite simple, but these things could not be rushed and had to be accomplished in their own time and manner. There was discussion and consideration, nodding of heads, and counting of papayas, until finally everyone was satisfied. After solemn handshakes all round, the visitors putted off up the creek. It was time for us to be going as well.

The afternoon was wearing into evening and the light on the mangroves had turned golden, the shadows were lengthening and everything was still. We started up the motor, breaking the quiet and taking our leave of Mr. Darwin. Our run through the pass, all illumined now with the magic light of sunset, was like a passageway to an enchanted land. Once out into the Chatham river, we picked up speed and arrived back at the *Audubon* in short order.

28

The morning my mother left to go home to New York I realized, with a stab of dismay, I was probably pregnant. I was always quite regular and now I'd missed my period again. "Oh, God, what now?" My feelings tumbled like clothes in the dryer from dismay through a rapid turnover of excitement, anxiety, amazement and delight, and back to dismay. I didn't say anything to Peter or my mother or anyone else right then. I needed to think about it for a while and I wasn't feeling up to dealing with everyone's opinions and reactions.

Early that day, Mum, Peter, and I took the small boat into Everglades and then drove our little Ford straight to Miami. On the way we chattered and gossiped, but as we drew nearer to Miami, we all fell silent and I began to dread the actual moment of her leaving. Since the sleeper train to New York left at the crack of dawn the next morning, we were spending the night at our favorite cheap, but clean hotel on the waterfront. After the usual long luxurious baths, we went out on the town for a last evening of fun. Even though everyone made an effort, we were low-key and a little sad. I'd had so many separations from my mother during my relatively short life, and none of our partings got any easier. Even though I was now a grown-up and knew this separation wouldn't be for long, I also knew I would miss her just as much as I always did. All these partings had been hard on my mother, too. It was only after I myself had raised a child that I came to appreciate how painful it must have been for her to make the decision to send me to America. The choice to keep me at home, with the probability of air raids and a possible German invasion, or to send me off alone to America, not knowing when, or even if, she would ever see me again. I realize now how wrenching that must have been for her and how she must have suffered.

In the morning we drove to the station and settled her into her compartment, saying our farewells quickly. The train pulled away as we waved her out of sight, and then she was gone, on her way to East Hampton, where secretly I longed to be. As I'd known I would be, I was miserable and tearful.

On the way back to the Everglades, with a mixture of trepidation and excitement, I told Peter I thought I was pregnant. He was taken aback, but bless his heart, he was excited too. He stopped the car to give me a hug. I warned him we shouldn't get our expectations up too high just yet, it was very early on, and last year I'd had a miscarriage at four months. Furthermore, our circumstances were far from ideal for having a child. Actually, having a baby on our boat would be well nigh impossible, which would mean we'd have to rethink our plans to stay on the *Audubon*. The whole thing began to feel inappropriate and poorly timed. How could we have been so careless? It must have been that night we went dancing, when the boys got their shots. We continued talking about this new and perturbing turn of events all the way home across the Tamiami Trail, with my mood continuing to go up and down like a yo-yo.

This unexpected turn of events forced us to confront our life in the Everglades and to reconsider the future. What were we doing, really? Where would this job take us? What else could we do? The last time Charlie Brookfield had come out on a tour, he'd offered Peter a job in Miami for the winter, assisting with the new wild-life tours in Florida Bay. It would mean living in Miami during the winter months, when there was less urgency to guard the birds at Duck Rock. When I first heard about this offer, I was enthusiastic. I imagined living on land again, in town, in a house with running water, a bathroom, and all the comforts I'd been missing. My imagination played around a dozen fantasies. I'd take a dance class. I could have a piano. I'd get a sewing machine. I saw it as a possible rescue from our present life in the swamps and a feasible way for me to be able to stay on. The intensity of my enthusiasm showed me how deprived

I'd been feeling.

The offer was not firm and we really hadn't had a chance to think about it, and there were issues that would need to be addressed. For a start, it was contingent on approval from Mr. Baker and the New York headquarters, which was far from assured. Now, this likely pregnancy added another level of complication and concern, and I was becoming less sure I wanted to stay here under any circumstances. I didn't really fit in. Try as I might, it just wasn't for me. I felt so limited, partly because my politics and beliefs were not in line with those of the folks here. The racial prejudice and discrimination that seemed to be everywhere in the South in those days, was becoming unbearable. Our living situation may have held some amazingly unique and special qualities, but they could not compensate for the isolation and displacement I was feeling. Once the novelty of being here had worn off, a reaction had set in which by now was becoming acute discomfort. It occurred to me fleetingly that this pregnancy might be a way out. I didn't voice these thoughts to Peter however, and our discussion continued to roam amid myriad possibilities, needs, wants, and dreams.

Peter had no particular ambitions. Because he'd gone off to war so young, he'd never even finished high school. A scholar he was not and he'd never particularly wanted to go to college. He was a hands-on sort of guy and he'd learned a lot in the field, but academia left him cold. The notion of staying on in this job, perhaps dividing our time between Everglades and Miami, sounded good for Peter, but not so good for me. We were still going around and around about it all when we reached Everglades. I was filled with feelings of conflict and confusion and I missed my mother. I began to cry.

I was still sniffling when we drove up to the river bank where the *Snowy Egret* was moored. Peter did his best to cheer me up, so I dried my eyes and blew my nose and we stopped in to see Rosa. She tactfully refrained from remarking about my mottled appearance and offered us tea and cookies, which was absolutely perfect—for me tea is the great panacea for all that ails. My family used to quote from some long-gone Victorian ancestor, "Tea, the cup that cheers but does not inebriate!" After tea and a short visit, we had no excuse but to get going and head back to Duck Rock. Reluctantly, at least on my part, we climbed into the boat and drove home through the sunset. My spirits rose somewhat. The evening birds on their way to their various homes in the mangroves flashed now pink, now white and golden in the last light. The long-necked, long-legged cranes and egrets so graceful, accompanied by the occasional black anhinga. The ever-present seagulls and terns dipping and flying, always looking to catch a last bite of something from the sea. All a part of the complex natural world we shared, it's beauty and serenity seemed always able to lift my mood.

For a day or two I enjoyed the return to solitude after all the hustle, bustle and over-crowdedness of having constant company aboard. It was pleasant to have the primitive bathroom amenities to myself and to have only the two of us to worry about feeding. Life was a quiet round of the humdrum and unremarkable. But then the relentless heat, and the constant struggles with the basics in our cramped living conditions, began to get me down. I was undergoing hormonal changes, too, and my mood swings were sometimes disconcerting. Peter was patient and tried to be understanding and he had numerous ways to escape into his work. I did not. With a pang, I again realized how different our experience was of our life here. Peter was quite happy and seemed to need nothing more. I, on the other hand, was beginning to feel acutely unhappy, made worse because I couldn't tell him, and he couldn't see it or just didn't want to face it.

We had been asked by the NAS to write an article for the Audubon magazine. This was at least something we could do together. Sitting at our table in the morning while it was still relatively cool, we would think out loud and I would type up our ideas on the Olivetti. The cats loved it when I typed, and they would sit on the table trying to bat the flying keys. In addition to the fact that neither of us had ever written anything like this before, we were limited to 1,000 words. We developed a story idea, but immediately ran up against the word limit. Despite the difficulties, we struggled on. Our efforts came in fits and starts, but eventually we finished it.

One morning, a few days later, I came up on deck as the sun rose. The two cats, usually still asleep at this hour, were sitting motionless, gazing intently at something under the table. Bending down to look, I gave an involuntary shriek as I saw a large snake curled up on itself, staring, cold and impassive. Peter came rushing out of the head, buttoning his pants.

"What's the matter?" he asked, looking alarmed.

"Quick, catch the snake," I said pointing under the table. He was an expert at collecting creatures and had no trouble with this one. He scooped it up and bottled it.

"Probably came up through the scupper hole," he guessed. "Well, it's just a flat-tailed water snake, nothing to worry about." So that took care of that, and he went off to his morning exploration of Pavilion Key.

Looking at the horizon, I saw what looked like a cloud bank coming our way. The weather had been unusually dry the past few weeks. Rain squalls would come up, only to fizzle out in a short time. We were getting low on water and if we didn't get some soon, we'd have to take the big boat into Everglades. This shower looked as if it might help us out as it came closer and closer. Then, mysteriously, it just stopped and rained and rained about fifty yards away. I stood impotent and frustrated looking at it, willing it to come over. A short time later it began to move again and slowly approached. Aha, I thought, now we'll get some. But no, this contrary rain cloud just passed right over, scattering a few drops on the roof and settling down to pour about fifty yards to the other side of us. No way to chase it, either, for the tide was too low. Quite maddening.

This morning after Peter left on his explorations, I went down into the small cabin to tidy up. Bunks are not easy to make, tucking in the covers requires all sorts of gyrations. I was heartily sick of them in general. The idea of a big, soft double bed seemed an incredible luxury, a fantasy out of the Arabian nights. The head, tucked up under the bow beyond the bunks, had a door so low you had to duck to get through. On the outside of this door I had put a long mirror, the only mirror on the boat, besides Peter's little shaving mirror that he kept by the basin in the galley. I don't know why I hung it there. I certainly didn't get dressed up very often. I suppose I was clinging to some idea of how we used to live, when a mirror might be needed because one's appearance might actually matter.

I decided to have a wash, took off my clothes and examined myself in the mirror. I was quite skinny these days. I looked hard at my body, with its small high waist; was I gaining a little round the middle or was I imagining things? I was only seven or eight weeks pregnant, I couldn't be showing yet. It would be nice if my breasts grew, I thought. I looked at them critically, they were perky but small. I'd never had anything much in the way of breasts, they don't seem to go with ballet dancing, they just get in the way. Good legs, though, long and well-developed without being overly muscled, the way some dancers' legs are. Nice behind too, to make up for it. All in all, I was not too displeased with myself in the mirror. I took my stand-up bath and got ready for another day.

But my mind was not on the day, which looked like just another hot one aboard the boat. My mind was on the future, and especially on my pregnancy. Although I was experiencing some emotional ups and downs, they were not severe. I was lucky and never suffered from morning sickness. In fact, I felt very well, if rather sleepy, a lot of the time. It never seemed to occur to either of us for me to see a doctor, both for a general check-up and to confirm the pregnancy. There were no do-it-yourself pregnancy tests in those days and women were either guided by their own symptoms or saw an obstetrician.

I decided to write letters. I'd already written to my mother and told her she was going to be a grandmother, but I hadn't told anyone else about my "interesting condition." Peter was pushing me to tell his family, too (he was not much of a letter writer). But for some reason, I was finding myself reluctant. I was very fond of my mother-in-law, Mary, and she had always been supportive of Peter and me. I was sure she would be thrilled, but I was equally certain that George, his father, would be disapproving. He had thought all along we were too young to get married, and now to start a family when our situation was so precarious, would seem to confirm his worst fears. He was right of course, but at the time I didn't want to think so. I picked up some paper and threaded it into the Olivetti.

29

Hurricane season was approaching. The oppressive heat remained, but stormy weather with sudden gusty rains assailed us more frequently, and we paid close attention to the weather reports. The young birds had left their nests and now flew back and forth with their relatives to the feeding grounds.

The weekend tour program was coming to an end for the season, for which I was thankful, as they had become more of a chore than a pleasure. But one weekend was special. Rosa had finally managed to organize a field trip for her class from school, and on Saturday afternoon the *Spoonbill* and the *Snowy Egret* came skimming across the blue water towards us. In the first boat, Art and Rosa brought five little first and second-grade girls and boys. In the other boat, Charlie had as many, plus a couple of kids of friends from Miami. They were all wearing the required life jackets, which made them look like overstuffed munchkins. They were shrilly excited as they scrambled aboard the *Audubon*.

First off, everyone had to go to the bathroom. They were thrilled with the boat and all its features, and the head was no exception, with its funny low door and noisy hand pump used to flush the toilet. I was rather worried they would fall overboard or otherwise get into trouble, as they seemed to be all over the place at once. Everyone wanted to hold the kittens, and although Castor and Pollux were quite tolerant of being picked up, passed around, held upside-down and even dropped, they finally got fed up with the pandemonium and retired to their cardboard box under the camp bed and refused to come out again. Rosamaria, who had been on board before, was showing off a bit in her role of "old salt."

"Here," she told her little friends, "here's where you wash your hands," and she proceeded to pump water into our small wash basin to demonstrate.

After a brief rest and some sodas, everyone was ready to take off again and go exploring on Pavilion Key. Peter and I came along to help herd them all. We debarked on the white sand beach and the children ran around trying to catch crabs. Peter showed them some birds' nests in the interior and the remains of the turtle's nest, and they gathered as many shells as they could stuff in their pockets. The natural curiosity of the children made every minute a wonder. They discovered a baby nurse shark and a stingaree in the shallow water off the beach. The sparkling clear water and the rich smells of the mangrove mud seemed to fuel their energy as they ran with squeals of delight from one discovery to another. They could have stayed forever. Children don't seem to notice physical discomforts as much as grownups, especially when they are interested in something. After an hour or so though, even they got tired and we came back to the big boat. It was almost the magic hour, when the birds fly in for the night and soon everyone was eating their sandwiches and counting birds.

"Ooh, look, I just counted fifteen snowy egrets," said one savvy little girl.

"Here come twenty-four blue herons," said another.

The competition became fierce to see who could count the most of something. Many of the children had never seen any of these birds in great numbers, and some, such as the glossy ibises, they had never seen at all, and they were impressed. When several skeins of bright pink spoonbills arrived, they were truly awed. They all wanted to know why they couldn't go onto Duck Rock and see them and the baby birds up close. I sympathized, but had to explain that it would upset the birds if a whole bunch of people suddenly showed up in their home. Plus, I explained, there really weren't any babies left. I also described, that they probably wouldn't be able to see anything at all, actually, because all the nests were so high up in the branches. I didn't mention the hazards of scrambling around on the slippery roots, or the strong possibility that they would have undoubtedly tumbled into the water. They would probably have thought that would be all part of the fun.

Tired but happy, they all headed home again, having learned something important about their own back yard. Rosa was delighted with the outing and Charlie thought he'd try to get some of the Miami schools to participate and make special trips available.

The children's tour made me think about children in general—my own in particular. Maybe I could have a child here after all, if we were land-based. In so many ways, this was a remarkable place. A child could grow up here and become truly connected to the environment and the creatures in it. If only things could have been a bit more civilized. Becoming a parent was such a responsibility. I really didn't feel ready to have a child anywhere.

When Uncle Will finally did arrive, he too showed up on a tour day. Art brought him out from Everglades, throwing us into a tizzy when we saw the boat on the horizon, because we thought it was the tour come early. I was in a filthy bathing suit, and I'd only gotten the boat halfway cleaned up. I retired in a panic into the cabin to get dressed and then I heard the familiar voice.

"Hi Peter. I finally made it to this godforsaken place. You don't make it easy to find you, do you?" He laughed his characteristic wheezy chuckle.

I thought I was hearing things. We hadn't expected him for at least another day. It didn't matter, we were just thrilled to see him. I came rushing up from below and we all hugged happily. It turned out the telegram we'd sent him had arrived after he'd left home and had then been forwarded to his motel on the road south from New York. He'd sent us one from somewhere in North Carolina, which got to Everglades the same day he arrived. In fact, Art brought it with them when they came out. So, once again the primitive communications of the time had failed us.

Despite his obvious pleasure at seeing us and at being here at last, I could sense there was a shadow over him. We made coffee and the four of us sat around the table and began to catch up. The reason for Will's demeanor became clear when he told us that Art had met him in town that morning with another telegram, informing Will that his old and ailing mother had just passed away. She had been ill for some time, so her death was not unexpected, but it was still a shock. Will had called home from Everglades, ready to jump in his car and drive right back up to New York, but everyone in the family assured him there was nothing he could do now, and he should stay here with us. So, torn though he was, he had decided to stay.

He pulled out one of his horrible cigarettes called Home Runs, which were rolled in brown paper and smelled like nothing so much as a bad cigar rolled in rope, and looked at us across the table, his kind eyes twinkling, while he quizzed us about our life in the subtropics on a boat.

"You guys know how lucky you are, don't you?" he said." You've got a rare opportunity here for some real research. I'd give my eyeteeth to get into a situation like this for a while."

Peter nodded. "Yeah," he agreed, "I've been waiting for you to get here. You won't believe what I've been finding."

Will looked at me.

"And what about you?" he asked. He understood I wasn't much of a natural history researcher.

"Oh, there's lots for me to do," I replied vaguely. "This is really such a wonderful place."

But that wasn't the whole story, which of course he knew. Will's understanding was comforting, I didn't have to pretend anything around him. Still, my pride kept my stiff upper lip in place, I was reluctant to whine and complain. It would have felt disloyal to Peter, too, so I kept my misgivings to myself. We didn't have time right then to go into anything very deeply anyway. The boat was a mess and I had to get both it and myself ready for the tour, which was due shortly.

Will stayed for three weeks, and he and Peter spent many happy hours together discovering amazing wildlife, and exploring their unique habitats, found only in this strange and magical place, called the Florida Everglades. Slowly, the boat began to fill up with jars and bottles filled with various grasses from all the keys they explored. There were jars on the table, on top of the fridge, on any available shelf or level surface, not to mention ranks of bottles on the floor. I could hardly get into the galley. Will spent his evenings carefully writing down all his findings. Apparently, just as there had been no work-up of the mammalian life on the keys, there was not much of a botanical record either. Everything Will recorded was breaking new ground. Unfortunately, these findings from the Everglades were never published and have since been lost.

Peter and Will had so much fun together that I sometimes felt left out. Even when I went along on their excursions, I couldn't really participate, and I got bored with hanging around on some hot, mosquito-infested place, looking for birds or checking out grasses. Still, I went along rather than be left alone every day.

Then one day on Will's last week, as we were coming back from an expedition to Gopher Key, I felt a sudden strange wetness between my legs. At first, I thought a wave had splashed into the boat, but then, looking down at myself, I saw to my horror I was bleeding profusely. I began cramping and immediately became hysterical, as I realized I was miscarrying. Peter and Will tried to calm me down, as we sped as fast as the outboard would carry us back to the *Audubon*. Once there, we threw a few belongings into a case, grabbed the kittens, jumped into the *Snowy Egret* and dashed as fast as we could to Everglades. Though I was still bleeding and cramping, and suffering from great anxiety, I was reassured by the fact that Will was a medical doctor, and while he was concerned, he didn't seem to think I was about to bleed to death or otherwise come to an early end.

It was a tense ride into town, as we were racing the tide to get there. I sat hunched and miserable, clenching everything together, scarcely breathing as we careened across the choppy water. Every bump seemed to jar my whole body as if jolted by a roller coaster. Luck was with us however, and we just barely scraped over the shallows to make it safely up the Barron River.

It was too late to go on to Fort Myers, so we all stayed the night with Rosa. She loved being of help and immediately knew how to make me feel comfortable. She got me a hot water bottle and some Midol, and the cramps subsided. She also insisted I drink some warmed gin, which I took straight. She said it was what her abuela always gave her when she had menstrual cramps. I didn't argue, and the dose relaxed me. Of course, everyone else decided they needed a shot too, so we were all quite merry by bedtime. I slept well, and the next morning the bleeding had slowed down. We got up early and drove north to the hospital in Fort Myers. We were in separate cars, as Will was going to drive his battered old Chevy back to New York the next morning.

Driving north, Peter and I were alone for the first time since the whole contretemps had begun, and although he was always something of the strong silent type, he was stirred enough to express some of his feelings. He reached over and took my hand and squeezed it.

"Chloe, I'm really sorry about all this," he said, "but I know you're going to be okay. This isn't as bad as the last time, and I know you'll be okay again. We'll be able to have a baby later. This just wasn't the right time." And he told me he loved me and how much I meant to him.

I was touched and it warmed me to realize that, even though he was off in his own world a lot, he did really care about me and about us. We drove on up the highway and I felt closer to him than I had in long time, and some of my anxiety died away.

Will knew an Ob/Gyn in the hospital in Fort Myers, who was an acquaintance of a friend of his, which was a comfort—though as Will said, "there are no guarantees this guy's any good, but at least we've got some connections. My friend is head of Ob/Gyn at New York General, so we can pull rank if we need it!"

Dr. Beckwith turned out to be a Southern gentleman, and despite looking grumpy much of the time, he had a hidden heart of gold, and his hands were always warm and gentle. He had a great touch, and that's good when you're a gynecologist. I trusted him right away, which was a relief. The hospital was small, and had a dedicated staff, who had all been working there a long time and the hospital had a close, family feel. It was such a contrast to the way many patients are cared for today in our high tech., impersonal world. Of course, as it was smaller, one could have greater attention, but even apart from that, the attitude was leisurely and kindly, with no rush to get the patients in and out in the shortest possible time. The calm, relaxed atmosphere helped calm my nerves. Dr. Beckwith told me I needed a D&C and he kept me in the hospital overnight. He told me I would be fine, but he recommended I not get pregnant again while on the boat. Not bloody likely, I thought. I was put in a semiprivate room, where, fortunately, there was no other patient, and I thankfully settled into the tidy white bed and someone brought me a hot cup of tea.

Will, who had been staunchly standing by and supporting us through the ordeal, had to leave. I was being well taken care of and he now had to go and face his mother's funeral.

"Don't get into any more trouble, you two." he said, "I'll be looking forward to seeing you when you come up in October. Let's hope we don't have any real hurricanes before then!" We bade him fond farewell. I hated to see him go. He had been, and always was, such a comfort and support to us.

The next day I was released from the hospital. I was fine, but tired. We decided to stay another night at the motel where Peter had been sleeping. The kittens, who had been with us all this time, loved it and spent most of their time curled up on the bed. It felt good just to lie around and be able to take a shower and not have any work to do. I needed time to sort out my feelings about this "spontaneous abortion" as it was designated, being too early on to be a miscarriage proper. Even though Peter had been supportive of the pregnancy, and although he didn't say so right then, I knew he thought it was probably all for the best that it had ended. The more I thought about it, the more I came to see it that way too. I had been pregnant for so short a time, I had barely gotten used to the idea. There had been problems surrounding it from the start, and after all, it was true we could easily try again when we got back on land. Or so I comforted myself.

My feelings were still mixed when we got back to Everglades, and I was so glad to see Rosa. She greeted us warmly and was very sympathetic.

"Are you sad?" she asked gently. "You must not be too sad. For a little while you will be sad and then you will be happy again and make many babies."

Her sympathy made me cry, and I missed my mother. There wasn't much time to indulge in my feelings, though, as Rosa reported there was a hurricane on its way, which meant no rest for the weary. We had to dash out to the *Audubon* with all possible speed. We had told Rosa the truth of what had happened, but we told everyone else I'd had "threatened appendicitis." I didn't want to have a fuss made over me, and appendicitis was less loaded than a failed pregnancy. But we hardly had time to think about it anyway. Because of the threatening hurricane, we had to get all the boats up to Hurricane Creek as soon as possible, and with that in mind we sped straight to the Tookes' without stopping.

30

We got to the Tookes' around midday and found Art waiting for us on the *Audubon*. When we'd taken off to the hospital five days ago, in our hurry we had left the boat in a terrible mess. We were quite touched to find, that good old Art, had not only cleaned up the boat, but had resupplied the ice and changed the water in the turtle's bowl. He had his good side, I thought. He greeted us in his usual dour way.

"Well, you're back in time for the hurricane, anyway," he growled. "Everyone's up listenin' to the radio." He jerked his head in the direction of the Tookes' house. We walked up the shell path and joined the group around the old portable radio that was crackling away on the kitchen table.

With the Tookes' son, Hamp, and grandsons, Noel and Lester, plus Mr. Dobbs from Mormon Key, as well as the Tookes, Art Eifler, his Missus, and us, we just about filled up all the space in Mrs. Ts' kitchen. Peter and I were greeted like returning prodigals, and I sensed an unspoken curiosity about my condition. No one knew about my pregnancy, and now we told them our story that I'd had "threatened appendicitis."

Mrs. Tooke, in her characteristic way, remarked, "Well, hope everything's okay with you now," and launched into a lurid story about her cousin's burst appendix.

The radio crackled on, and the announcer informed us the velocity of the storm had reached a hundred miles per hour and was heading inland.

Mr. Tooke didn't think we'd get this storm. He was betting it would head off to the east, and a big discussion ensued. Some folks wanted to go up to the safety of Hurricane Creek, while others were willing to wait and see. The creek was used by everyone around because it was deep and wide and the mangroves were tall enough to give shelter to many boats from even the fiercest storms. There were scary tales of past hurricanes going around the table, "like the one where the wind reached 150 miles per hour, and the water in the creek rose so high that the boats were exposed above the tree tops and blown away."

"That's the only thing you have to worry about up here," Art informed us. "High water. Just keep yer fingers crossed we don't get the strongest blow at high tide."

I would keep all fingers and toes crossed if it would help. This hurricane business made me very nervous. Peter trusted Mr. Tookes judgment and decided to wait and see. Art, on the other hand, said he was going to take the Missus and go, just to be on the safe side. So, he and Mr. Dodds untied their boats and left. The wind had risen considerably and was now blowing very strongly. Even tied up at the Tookes' dock, our boat was rocking hard. Then, about 10 PM, just as I was about to suggest that maybe we should head up the creek, the radio announced that the storm had changed course, passed on and was headed for Texas. We all breathed a collective sigh of relief and went to bed, we were exhausted.

In the morning people started back to their home moorings. We might have escaped this storm, but it certainly wouldn't be the last. It was late afternoon by the time we finally returned to our mooring at Duck Rock. I felt relieved to be back "home," tied up to our three stakes in the mud, even though the water was still rough from the residue of the storm. As the tide went out and the boat settled into the mud, the rocking stopped and we were stable. I was looking forward to some peace and quiet after the turbulence, both outer and inner, of the past week.

The birds flew in, seemingly undisturbed by the strong wind, as I was starting to make supper. I was still a bit unstrung by all the past events, and as I was starting to fire up the devilish stove, I burnt one of my fingers badly enough to have to stop and deal with it. Suddenly, I felt very sorry for myself and burst into tears. I cried and cried, and though Peter bandaged me up, gave me hugs, brought me a drink, and finished making supper, I was inconsolable.

I was crying for myself, for the way things were turning out, for the loss of the baby, and for the need of comfort and security which wasn't being met at the moment. I was crying for my mother, for my past and my future, and as I cried, the deep well of sadness expanded until it seemed to include every unhappy thing that had ever happened to me. I guess I just needed to "cry it out."

I finally calmed down a bit and felt somewhat better, the way you do when you've had a good cry. I was just washing my face when we heard a boat approaching. We hoped it was just a fisherman on his way to get ice, and our hearts sank when the sound came closer and closer and then stopped, and a voice came out of the dark.

"Ahoy there, Scotts. You've got company."

It was Charlie from Miami with his boyfriend, Dave. I was dismayed, to say the least, but there was no help for it. I hoped I didn't look too swollen and awful as the two men came aboard. Fortunately, the light from the swinging overhead lantern wasn't too bright. We had met Dave before. A slight, blond man with a crew-cut, he was very witty and charming and he soon cheered us up. If they guessed they hadn't come at an ideal moment, they ignored it, and poured us all drinks from the bottle of dark Cuban rum they'd brought along, which also helped with the cheering up. They had come from counting spoonbills on Marco Island. After a big blow, the Audubon Society liked to get stats on all the rare species in the region. They confided it was also an excuse for a weekend getaway from the rigors of big city life in Miami. They stayed for supper and we had a much more pleasant evening than we had been headed for without them. They spent the night on their boat, tied up to our moorings.

In the morning, the weather had calmed down to near normal, and Peter set off to Gopher Key with our guests. Declining the invitation to join them, instead I spent the day working on the article for the Audubon magazine. We had actually finished composing it, and now I just had to type up a clean copy and send it off to New York. In all the ups and downs of the past weeks, I had quite forgotten about the Audubon Society conference. Now, thinking about the Society and New York, I realized suddenly, with an ecstatic lurch of my heart, that the conference was only a few weeks away. Oh joy! New York, New York, it's a wonderful town. I couldn't wait. I had the radio on, and right then it started playing Artie Shaw doing "Begin the Beguine" and I just had to get up and dance around in the crowded space of the cabin. The kittens fled under the bed, but I couldn't stop till the song ended. Oh *yes*, sang my heart. I hoped I wouldn't be too overwhelmed by the city when I got there. I'd been on the boat nearly nine months, and the grandeur and sheer density of New York might be daunting. I didn't believe so, I thought to myself. I will really love every single minute of density and grandeur, oh yes. Not to mention all the automobiles, buses, exhaust, grit, noisy crowds, Central Park, and of course all my friends and the family and wonderful East Hampton with the ocean, the beach, and the clean, salty dunes, whiskered with dune grass and bayberry bushes. I couldn't wait and would utterly love every overwhelming moment of it.

Later Peter returned with Charlie and Dave, who then headed off into the sunset back to Everglades. That night, Peter and I again tried to discuss our future. He had become enamored with the idea of writing and illustrating articles for nature magazines to make a living. He wanted the independence of working for himself. I understood the concept, but was not sure he had the expertise to carry it out. I didn't think either of us had, though I didn't say so then. In the mean time though, what to do? Stay here? I didn't want to. He did. The discussion was inconclusive as so many of our talks were.

We went to bed in our little bunks and Peter read to me from a book about bats. We were using our gasoline lantern to conserve the boat's limited batteries and at one point he flapped his arms to illustrate the flight of a bat and hit the lantern. With a horrid crash it fell to the floor and we were plunged into instant blackness. I held my breath expecting an explosion. Nothing happened. We were lucky. We could have had a terrible fire, but for some reason the gods were with us.

Peter laughed a little shakily. "Well, that's all folks, I guess reading is over for tonight."

We both laughed hysterically in our relief. I climbed into his bunk and we cuddled for a while by watery moonlight.

The next morning at breakfast, an ominous report informed us another big storm was brewing in the Caribbean. We spent the following two days close to the radio, storm-watching. This hurricane seemed to change direction all the time. We didn't have the technology of today's weather stations and satellite observations to count on. In those days, intrepid pilots went up and flew around, even through these tropical disturbances to get a fix on them. There were no computers to help predict a storms' course or behavior. It was all by guess and by gosh, and everyone had their own opinions. All we knew for certain was the storm was big, and already had winds up to one hundred forty miles per hour. I was worried about it. The uncertainty and unpredictability were what made me most nervous.

Peter didn't worry much. In fact, I was afraid, among other things, of his being too casual and not getting the boat up to Hurricane Creek in time, waiting till the tide got too low to navigate or getting stuck out in open water and being blown away. I had a whole inventory of scenarios of possible disasters. While we waited, life went on. The bad weather made living conditions even more uncomfortable than usual. The boat rocked constantly, and at low tide, when we sank into the muddy bottom, the boat often settled at an awkward angle so that everything sloped. When that happened, I worried about the wind becoming so strong as to blow us over altogether. All we could do was wait for the tide to lift us up again.

A couple of days later, we heard that the hurricane was heading for Palm Beach, less than a hundred miles away. The storm was big, they reported, five hundred miles across with winds already up to a hundred and sixty miles per hour. At almost the same time, up sprang a brisk northwest breeze which grew steadily stronger. Peter decided we'd better head up to the Tookes' right away, so we untied, and after making sure our smaller boats were properly attached, headed up-river through the steadily increasing winds. Is this it? I wondered. Now that we were actually moving, I was less worried—and the last hurricane hadn't been so alarming after all.

We got to the Tookes' in the late afternoon and there was already an undercurrent of concern and increased activity. We tied up our three boats behind Art's houseboat, *The Flying Dutchman*, and noticed his *Spoonbill* was missing.

"Huh," said Peter "wonder where he's got to? I should think he'd want to stick around with the weather like it is."

No sooner had we moored than Mr. Dodd and his wife, Elsie, appeared towing their old houseboat with their big speedboat. They didn't stay long. Mr. Dodd was antsy to get going up to the safety of Hurricane Creek and shortly took off again.

Mrs. Tooke was in her kitchen when we walked up to her door. She told us Mr. T was off fishing and Art had gone to Miami on business. I didn't know whether their combined absences made me nervous or reassured. Perhaps if they weren't concerned about the big blow, I needn't be either, but on the other hand, I would have liked them to be there, as they were so much more experienced than we were.

There was nothing to do but wait. We sat around on the boat listening to the weather reports when we could get them. The radio wasn't working very well and kept cutting out or drifting. Just as we would find a station giving the weather, in would come some boogie-woogie or one of the Miami evangelists. Finally, tired of the whole thing, I went up to the Tookes', where I found Mrs. T making candy.

"You're just in time to help me pull the taffy," she said, welcoming me in.

I'd never done it before. Pulling the sweet-smelling, warm, sticky taffy was entirely beguiling and when it was all finished, we sat around and ate it. Bits dropped to the floor and were eagerly gobbled by the dogs. Gossiping and eating candy, I was overcome once again with the feeling of the unreality of our situation. Here we were, sitting up a river in the middle of absolutely nowhere, pulling taffy while waiting for a hurricane. I couldn't assimilate it.

Finally, around 6:30, Art returned from Miami. The weather still looked anything but ominous, the wind was blowing a bit hard, but the sunset was luminous and calm. Peter immediately went into a huddle with Art about what they should do.

"It's a big storm all right," Art said, "and it's just about bound to hit us. We gotta get these here boats up Hurricane Crick, and soon."

Peter agreed. They would take the big houseboats up first, get them situated, and come back for me and the Missus. Except the Missus refused to be left.

"Ach, nein," she bellowed. "I'm comink wis you, Art, you ain't leavin' me anywhere." I was torn between wanting to go with Peter and wanting to stay here in the Tookes 'comfortable house.

Peter said, "Why don't you stay here, honey? You can keep Mrs. T company and I'll come back for you. We're just going to be moving boats around, backing and forthing. You'll be better off here."

"But couldn't I help?" I said dubiously, feeling a little guilty.

"Not really, there'll be plenty of guys up there to do the heavy work. Don't worry, I'll be back as soon as I can to fetch you." Even though I was nervous, I decided to stay.

He knew how I felt, and I trusted his judgment, but I hoped he would be back soon. I didn't like being separated when I didn't know what was going to happen. On the other hand, the Tookes were surely the most experienced at this sort of thing and they gave me a feeling of security. So, the two men and the missus took off with the boats and I went back up to the house to be with Mrs. T. It turned out to be a long night.

31

We sat chatting in the kitchen while Mrs. Tooke started her husband's supper: fish balls, greens, cornbread, and coleslaw.

"Lord knows when he'll get home," she said. "He's out there with Hans Andersen down to Mormon Key. Could be hours yet, specially if they's catching anything."

"Isn't he worried about the storm?" I asked.

"Bless you, no," she chirped. "We've been in a dozen big storms afore. Ain't nothin' goin' to happen yet awhile." Mrs. Tooke was always so reassuring.

"But Peter and Art seem to think they have to get up to Hurricane Creek right away," I said doubtfully.

"They've got all those boats and some of 'em belong to the Society and all. I guess they feel responsible. Plus, Art's sort of an old woman sometimes," she chuckled.

Then she went out to put the ducks and chickens to bed. I went to help her round them up and shoo them into their pens. After a lovely russet sunset, it was growing dark. The wind shook the tree branches and rattled the banana fronds. The supper was all cooked, but no sign of Mr. Tooke or Peter and Art. Mrs. Tooke and I had something to eat while we listened to the radio. The storm was approaching, but moving slowly, growing in intensity as it came. Hurricanes build up more force the slower they progress, so at this rate it could indeed become a real monster. We washed the dishes and took the radio into the bedroom and lay down. The wind was banging around the house, and we could hear boats moving in the distance.

"Hamp's supposed to be bringing Kathleen pretty soon," said Mrs. T.

"Wonder where they are?"

She thought she heard Hamp's boat, the *Helen*, but she was mistaken. Then we heard the sound of a hot-head motor. My blood froze. Only one boat sounded like that—the Gomez boys'. Oh, no—they had reportedly been seen over on Chokoloskee Island. The law still hadn't been able to capture them.

"That sounds like them Gomezes." Mrs. T sounded worried. "It'd be jest like them to come around now. Prob'ly think they's no one home and they can jest take whatever they want."

Neither of us admitted to being scared when we heard the motor stop. She turned down the little oil lamp and lowered the shades. I bravely took the flashlight and peered around outside briefly, saw nothing (for which I was intensely grateful), came back in, and locked all the doors. The dogs, who had been making a terrific racket, were now quiet again. We turned off the radio and strained our ears for sounds of intruders, but all we could hear was the rising wind.

"Well, let's turn in," said Mrs. Tooke, and with that she barred the door with a great heavy board fitted into slots on either side that Mr. Tooke had made years ago during another crisis with some outlaws. On the wall nearby was a shotgun.

"You see that?" she pointed to it, "They want that. They've got one of our guns, and now they want that one, too." I shivered. I didn't need to ask who "they" were. I asked if it was loaded.

"Oh, yes," she replied, "Mr. Tooke allus keeps it ready," I was reassured. I couldn't imagine myself firing it at anything or anybody, but I bet Mrs. T could.

Time passed, the dogs remained quiet, and I began to relax a bit. Lying there in the dark, I once again found the whole situation surreal. I wished Peter would come back, and I wished I'd gone with him in the first place. The wind continued to rise, howling around the house, banging the shutters, and whistling down the chimney. Mrs. T was snoring. I dozed, still clutching the flashlight.

I awoke with a jump, hearing another approaching motor. It slowed down, and then the engines were cut and it stopped. I got up, and after a struggle with the barricade, went into the kitchen. I heard someone approaching up the path.

I called out in quavering voice, "Peter?"

But there was no answer, and then suddenly there was a silhouette in the light from the kitchen door and someone tried the handle.

"It's me, open up," said Mr. Tooke, and I threw open the door. How reassuring he looked, standing there smiling with the yellow light from his fishing hat streaming in the door.

"Boy, am I glad to see you," I said. Mrs. T came bustling in when she heard his voice.

"Where you been?" she asked.

"We caught us six thousand pounds of mullet"—he was jubilant. "Got to get it to the ice house afore it spoils."

"But what about the storm?" I worried.

"Oh, we got time, I reckon, iffen we hurry."

Mrs. Tooke insisted he eat something before he dashed off again.

"Did you hear a hot-head a while ago?" she asked him.

"Yeah," he said, "it was Dutch Futch going down to the fish house."

Everyone seemed to have been fishing. Mrs. Tooke and I laughed at ourselves for our idiotic fears, even as we breathed sighs of relief. It had just been old Dutch Futch after all, not the dreaded outlaws.

This was a night of coming and going. Not long after Mr. Tooke left, Peter returned. I was so relieved that when I went to let him in, I snapped, "Where the hell have you been?" I couldn't understand how it had taken so long to get the boats fixed up.

"Sorry, hon. It just took forever up there in that creek with so many boats trying to get situated. We had to help some of the guys with their moorings, and oh, I don't know. Anyway, we're here now."

He looked a little tired. I was sorry I'd snapped and gave him a kiss. "Well, I'm sure glad you are. We've been shivering in our beds here thinking we heard the Gomezes, but Mr. Tooke said it was just Dutch Futch."

Mrs. Tooke came out in her housecoat, and we sat on the porch talking about the storm and all the people who might be out there in it.

"Wonder what Hamp's doin'," said Mrs. Tooke. "Cain't imagine where he's got to." The night was very dark, the clouds had gathered and thickened, rain spattered loudly, but intermittently, and the wind was raging through the mangroves, their leaves straining. A little while later, Hamp and Kathleen finally arrived. They had gotten stuck on a sandbar for hours. They were tired and cold, but otherwise fine. Hamp had caught a big load of fish up at Gopher Key which he'd had to leave there. It was a great fishing night, probably something to do with the approaching storm.

Peter and I said good-bye to the Tooke family, and set off for Hurricane Creek. The ride was a nightmare. I was wearing shorts and a tee shirt and got drenched immediately by spray and rain, which meant I was cold and shivering all the way. It was totally dark, and I was sure we'd never find the narrow opening in the mangroves that was the entrance to the creek. I should have had more faith, because Peter found it straightaway, and we putted upstream to our mooring place. We tied up past several other boats, most of them darkened, with no people to be seen.

The moment we entered the shelter of the creek, the intensity of the wind dropped dramatically, and the sound was dampened. Relieved by the relative lull, we climbed thankfully aboard the old *Audubon*. Peter opened a bottle of whiskey, and gave us each a tot, before we collapsed into our bunks for what was left of the night.

Early the next morning, the wind woke me, roaring through the trees. The sound was a continuous tumult, insistent and disquieting. Even sheltered in the thick, high mangroves as we were, the wind reached down to us, blowing through the screens and swirling around on deck. Twigs and branches were breaking off, raining down through the air, landing on the roof of the cabin, banging and rattling. Leaves were flying into the water, plastering themselves to the sides of the boats. Although it was 9 o'clock in the morning, the sky was still a predawn dark, leaden gray.

Looking ahead up the creek, I could see the line of boats tied to various mangrove trunks. There was Dutch Futch, Hans Andersen, and then the Dodds' old clunky houseboat. The Eiflers were behind them, and we were behind the Eiflers so that we were last, but we were anxiously waiting for the Tookes to get here and tie up behind us.

"Where are they, what could they be doing?" I said nervously to Peter, as we drank our cups of tea. The boat was rocking and rolling, and every now and then, bumping against the mangrove tree we were tied to which made tea drinking more of a challenge than usual.

"I guess they're just not too worried is all," he answered, "but they better get here soon by the sound of things."

We had one ear on the radio, and one eye on the barometer, which was sinking fast. The latest radio forecast had the storm moving toward the coast and expected to hit Del Ray Beach, between Palm Beach and Miami. Only 78 miles separated us from Miami, and the diameter of the hurricane was reportedly 500 miles. Moving slowly as it was, it kept building up force, though once it hit land it would begin to weaken. Even so, by the time it reached us, the storm would still be carrying quite a punch. My stomach was in knots. I wondered what everyone else was feeling. There was a sense of excitement and anticipation among the men. Action at last. It was sure a change from the humdrum of daily life here in this watery world. Most of the men were out in their boats, cutting away threatening branches, double-securing all the ropes, and making sure everyone's hatches and entryways were tightly battened down. All the lines had to be re-adjusted frequently, to allow for the rise of the water, and to keep the boats from banging into each other or the trees.

The women clustered together on their boats, cooking and gossiping. I felt almost a sense of holiday at the novelty of the situation, and despite the dangers all around us, there was a party atmosphere. The threat made us feel besieged, drawing everyone closer. No one seemed unduly concerned about the storm, they'd all experienced many storms in their lives. Peter, though, was getting worried about the Tookes, and wanted to go and see if they needed help. He asked Art if he'd like to go with him, but Art surprisingly, said no. He'd gone down there at 7:30 that morning and found the whole family still in bed.

"I bet Mr. T got annoyed with Art and told him off," Peter said with a grin. "Anyway, I guess I'll wait a bit longer."

Then, at about midday, here came the Tookes, with Hamp and Kathleen aboard, chugging up the creek. They pulled up and got moored in behind us. I was very relieved, and immediately felt safer. Mr. Tooke was such a competent, sensible man, he always knew the right thing to do, and Mrs. T, so cheerful and sanguine, I felt we could rely on their support completely.

The barometer was down below 29 inches, the wind blowing ever harder, with fierce gusts that made the boats feel as though they would be ripped off their moorings. The latest weather report told us the storm had hit the coast with winds up to 95 miles per hour and gusts of 120 miles per hour. These were serious numbers indicating great possible damage. Rain was now coming down heavily, soaking people and property alike in a deluge. We put up the shutters along the windward side, which helped keep us dry.

I was too keyed up to eat. Peter was off helping Art with something, and I scrambled over to the Tookes' boat to visit. It would be less nerve-wracking to be with them, I thought, much better than to be sitting alone on the *Audubon*. There was no proper land in this mangrove hideout, so we had to get from boat to boat either by hanging on to tree trunks and slithering along on the roots, which the wind made even more hazardous than usual, or crossing over by climbing from boat to boat. I chose the boat route. The moment I set foot outside the cabin, my poncho was blown out behind me, and I was immediately soaked. I struggled across from our bow deck to the Tookes' stern, hauling myself along by the mooring ropes. I arrived looking like a drowned rat, but it was worth it.

Mrs. Tooke and Kathleen were sitting around drinking coffee.

"Come sit over here," cried Mrs. T handing me a cup, and I joined them on the banquette built into the galley bulkhead. Their boat had some amenities our old houseboat lacked. She gave me a towel to dry my hair, which was dripping down my neck.

"What a night you must have had," I said to Kathleen, "stuck on a sandbar in a rising storm. Sounds nightmarish to me."

"Oh, Hamp tried to get through Sandfly Pass, but the water was too low. That *Helen* draws a lot of water, and we just couldn't get over the bar.

He shouldn't have tried it, but there you are." She smiled. "Anyway, no harm done. The boat's okay and we managed to get some sleep. I was just glad the kids weren't there." I remembered they'd gone home to Tennessee for the start of school, and Kathleen had lingered behind.

"You weren't worried?" I persisted. I was amazed that anyone could be so casual about what to me was such a scary situation.

"Oh, no, not really. We had time enough, and we weren't going to get swamped or anything." Kathleen was off-hand.

"That Hamp," chimed in Mrs. Tooke. "He's not one to take chances as a rule. That old sandbar must have moved." This was quite possible, as I knew.

"Did Mr. Tooke get his fish to the fish house?" I hoped he had. It had been such a big catch that I knew it would be worth a lot of money, and the Tookes could certainly use it.

"Oh, bless you, yes," she replied, "though we don't know if they's enough ice to hold it through this storm till the run boat can get there and get it."

Such was the life of a fisherman. It was like farming, you were constantly at the mercy of the vagaries of wind and weather.

After a while, Peter and Mr. Tooke came back and told us to come aboard Art's boat, where Frieda had made chili for everyone. We all scrambled over to the Eiflers boat. By this time, it was nearly three o'clock and I was hungry—you can't stay keyed up forever, I realized. I had grown used to the noise of the wind and rain, and the choppy rocking of the boats, and my fears had idled down to just a general feeling of uneasiness.

The Dodds were already there, and the boat was getting quite crowded, with people sitting on the bunks or standing around. I looked at the gathering, and once again, a feeling of unreality swam over me. Here was Peter, with a three-day beard (I thought it made him look like Humphrey Bogart), Art, who, oddly, was looking uncharacteristically tidy, as he'd gotten a haircut when he'd been in Miami, Mr. Tooke, short and rotund, cheerful despite his sleepless night, and Mr. Dodd, whose bright blue eyes gave his creased face a youthful aspect. The men were all clustered in the forward cabin talking shop. How strange, that even during hurricanes, it seemed the men and women separated themselves at gatherings.

"All them fish could be spoiled," Art gloomed. "Ain't it just typical of the weather? Life's a bitch and you cain't win for losing sometimes."

"Just hope the fish house don't blow away," said Mr. Dodd. The fish house, being situated out in the gulf on stilts, was very vulnerable. Still, it had survived big storms before.

The women were visiting and organizing the food. Mrs. Tooke was helping with the chili, Kathleen was deftly stacking plates on the fold-up table, old Mrs. Eifler, wrinkled, and nervous, was talking constantly, giving directions at the top of her voice, which no one paid any heed. Mrs. Dodd sat by her calmly, in a carefully mended shirt and old pants rolled up to her knees. She had deep-set dark eyes and was still a beautiful woman, despite her age. Then there was me, sitting there in my old jeans and striped tee shirt, feeling unkempt, and out of sorts, having had no time for a bath in three days.

The chili was ready and, as we gulped it and drank beer, the whole event took on an unlikely party atmosphere. There was much speculation about the fate of some of the other fishermen, and whether or not the run boat would get swamped before it could find shelter in the harbor. We all listened to the radio as it chattered on and off about the storm's progress. By now it had passed through Miami, and we could expect the strongest winds soon. The high winds would be followed by a lull, as the eye passed over us—after which the wind would pick up again, and we would have to worry about the rising tide. We were so vulnerable, really, even in the moderate shelter of this creek. Our little boats felt like peanut shells offering only the most minimum protection.

Meanwhile, the beer had made me sleepy. None of us had slept much the night before, so Peter and I and Kathleen struggled back to our boat, clambering across the decks. Kathleen and I lay down in the cabin for a while. Peter wrote notes. He was very worried about the birds, of course. What would this storm do to all those thousands of them trying to shelter on Duck Rock? He went out to loosen the ropes as the tide was rising. Kathleen and I dozed.

But the raging storm, the rocking boat and the general discomfort of

it all made resting difficult. A sudden crash on the cabin roof woke me
with a start. For a moment, I was disoriented and thought I was in an air
raid, like the ones we'd had in England. I gave up on trying to sleep and
got up again. The barometer was now down to 28.92 inches, an incredibly
low level. I thought the eye must be close, and indeed, suddenly the boat
stilled and the wind and rain had stopped. A weak sun shone blearily
between the remaining clouds. It was an eerie sense of stillness, in the
ensuing silence, everyone came out of their boats and looked around.

We were in the eye of the hurricane, an area of relative calm in the
center of the storm, it was a short respite that would pass over us in an
hour or so. Then the winds would come back again, and mayhem would
return, only this time blowing from the opposite direction, it felt very
disorienting and bizarre.

"If them winds get here at high tide, we'll have something to worry
about," said Art, looking up at the narrow bit of sky we could see above
us.

The quiet and sunshine made the mess of broken branches and debris
on the water seem like a giant incongruity.

"It ain't going to," said Mr. Tooke positively. "I reckon we're gonna
squeak by this time." "Hope yer right," Art growled. He respected Mr.
Tooke's experience, but he still wanted to be the one who knew everything.
I was glad he didn't, pessimist that he was.

"Well, I guess we're half way through, only a few more hours of all this
to go," said Kathleen, and taking advantage of the letup, she climbed back
to her parents' boat.

At around 5:30 the storm came roaring back, its fury unabated. By this
point, for me somehow, the really scary feeling had passed, and I had
stopped jumping out of my skin every time a branch crash-landed on the
roof. I was still apprehensive about the tide, but Mr. Tooke had been so
reassuring, I had to believe him. Darkness came early and I lit the lamps.
Peter put up the rest of the shutters to keep the rain out. Even though we
were still rocking mightily back and forth, with the rain pouring down and
the wind howling outside, we settled down into a relative coziness. Peter
warmed us up with a shot of his whiskey, and I warmed up some left-over

spaghetti. The kitties came out from their lair under the couch and curled up in my lap, while I read my latest Ellery Queen mystery.

I was too blurry-eyed to read for long. We turned in, and exhausted from the stress of the storm, we fell asleep. Peter had to get up again once or twice during the night to adjust the ropes, but I didn't move.

32

In the morning, the weather was still wild and unsettled. Rain and wind alternated with brief clearing spells, and the air was chilly. After a quick early breakfast, we set out in the *White Ibis,* taking Art and Mr. Dodd with us. We were headed down the Chatham River to check on some friends of Mr. Dodd's.

"I'm wonderin' how the Squires made out," he said. "They went up Parson's Creek. Don't know why. It ain't real thick in there."

We were all concerned about Mr. Darwin, alone on his little hummock, at the mercy of the water and winds. Since Parson's creek was on the way to Darwin's place, we decided we would check on him too, if the Squires hadn't heard anything of him.

In the morning's dull light, broken branches dangled from trees and the surface of the water swirled with debris, ripped from the mangroves by the wind and rain. The water was choppy and high, reaching half way up the mangrove trunks. As we drove past the Tookes', we saw that the water was up over their dock. The wind blew cold, and by the time we reached the Squires' boat I was damp and chilled. Mrs. Squire, a skinny little woman who appeared to have a resilience of iron, assured us they were well.

"We could use some coffee, if any one of you has extra," said old bleary-eyed Mr. Squire.

"Bring your boat by our house," Mr. Tooke invited them. "I 'spect we still got some." The Squires had heard nothing of Mr. Darwin.

"We have to see if he's okay," I urged, so we continued downriver to the narrow creek leading to Mr. Darwin's.

The water seemed even higher here in this dense area of mangroves. I began to really worry. His shell mound was low and his camp was right on the edge of the creek. We chugged slowly along the passage between the tangled mangroves, the many fallen branches slowing us to a crawl. Rounding a bend, we came upon what had been Mr. Darwin's shell mound. Not a sign of the camp remained. The water had come up to the top of the mound and washed everything away. The uprights from his lean-to lay in a scattered heap, the campfire site was obliterated. Hanging from a mangrove was the tent in which he'd kept supplies. Bottles and cans were lying scattered among the mangrove roots. His boat was gone, though, and hopefully that meant he'd gotten away in time. There was nothing for us to do there, so we made our way back down the narrow channel to the Chatham River and headed back to the Tookes'.

"Well, he'll be back, you mark my words," predicted Mr. Tooke. "He been through this afore, but I would have thought he'd have looked for higher ground to set his camp."

"These old guys," Art said, "they don't want to change. They like things the ways they's always been."

Listen to who's talking, I thought unkindly.

"Yep," Mr. Tooke agreed.

"I hope he made it to his son's place," added Peter.

"Well, we'll know soon enough, I reckon." Mr. Tooke was referring to the amazingly quick circulation of local news by the grapevine of roving fisher folk and travelers through the region.

By the time we got to the Tookes', we were wet through, and I was shivering with cold. Tying up at the flooded dock, we scrambled out into the knee-deep water and waded up the path to the house. The kitchen was crowded with us, the four Tookes, and several others. Mrs. Tooke was feeding everyone breakfast. Blessed Mrs. T, given the opportunity she would feed the world.

"You look wet to the bone," she greeted us. "Sit and have some coffee," adding, to me, "I'll get you one of Hamp's shirts to wear. At least it'll be clean and dry." I drank my coffee and began to warm up.

A few minutes later in came more fishermen—the Weekes brothers, Luther and Daniel, and Dutch Futch—all bundled up in their yellow oilskins. More greetings, exclamations, and coffee. Everyone was glad to have the storm over, and apparently with little serious damage. The Tookes had escaped with only one small corner of the roof having torn loose above the kitchen, that was now leaking into a bucket.

A short time later, Hamp and the Weekes boys, who'd been fishing before the storm, went off to check the nets and boats they'd had to leave at Gopher Key. Hamp was worried that their catch would be spoiled before the run boat came back, but he was determined to get it to the ice house as soon as he could anyway. Then Peter and Mr. Tooke decided to check out Turkey Key and the fish house with the Tompkins, who were planning to return home from there after making sure all was well. Everyone else except Mrs. T and I went along.

"I got to get this place cleaned up," she said. "I reckon Turkey Key can get along without me lookin' at it."

"I'll stay and help you, if you like," I volunteered. "I don't feel much like going out there again in all that wet." Besides, I felt it was the least I could do.

We swept the water out of the kitchen and then climbed the rickety stairs to the attic to fix the leaky corner. The attic ceiling was so low we could only stand up if we stood right in the middle. In the corner where the roof had torn away, we had to bend double. Mrs. T squatted on her ample haunches and wielded the hammer as I handed her the nails to tack a piece of canvas over the hole.

"Well, that'll keep some of it out anyways, until we can fix it proper," she pronounced. The rain was still pelting down, but the canvas seemed to be working well enough. Downstairs again, we stoked up the fire in the cooking stove, which was barely smoldering. The wood on the porch had gotten wet, but between us we got the fire perked up and blazing away. The dogs and cats came in and lay down gratefully next to the fire to get dry for the first time in two days. The chickens and ducks had survived, wet, but safe.

"All them men will be back directly," said Mrs. T. "I'd better peel some potatoes. Ain't got much around here today. The storm washed out most of what was left of the garden."

"I've got some hot dogs," I offered. "They should be eaten up. My ice is down to a nubbin."

When the men—Peter, Art, and Mr. Tooke, plus Hamp—came back, they brought several mullets and some cans of baked beans with them, which helped round out our rather meager dinner. The report from Turkey Key was that the ice house was unharmed and nothing had been damaged anywhere that they had seen.

"I jest hope Harold's right about the run boat. If it don't get there by tomorrow, them fish are gonna be stinkin' to high heaven," said Hamp. He had left his catch there, hoping to salvage a portion of it. Peter had also brought us some ice and a couple of snappers, so we would have supplies for the next day at least.

It was another twenty-four hours before we started up the *Audubon* and ventured out to Duck Rock again. As soon as we'd tied up, Peter took the outboard and putted over to see what damage the island had suffered.

"Want to come?" he invited me.

"No thanks. I think I'll just tidy up here, I haven't done any housekeeping for days. We will have to go into town soon too, we're out of just about everything."

"Okay, we can go tomorrow. I'll go over to Pavilion and get some fish for dinner. Or maybe they'll have some at Turkey Key."

"If they have any milk, we need some." All we had left was the canned milk which I hated. The day felt dark and mournful, which matched my mood. Birds were flying back and forth around the key. From here it looked okay. I started to clean things up. At least with all the rain the water tanks were full.

My thoughts were not on the boat or this place. I was filled with images of family and friends—my mother, Will, the cousins—my loved ones whom I missed so much. I could no longer pretend to myself. I had to get out of there, not just for the Audubon convention in a couple of weeks, but for good. There, I'd said it to myself at last. *I did not want to come back here.* I got a stomach ache when I thought about it. I felt if I couldn't go home soon and stay there, I'd go crazy, or have a nervous breakdown or something.

Peter would just have to understand. I felt awful about him, that's why I had the stomach ache. He really loved being here. On the other hand, if we wanted to have a family, and I supposed we did, we couldn't stay on the boat anyway. The thought I didn't allow myself to think, the thought that was buzzing just below the threshold of my awareness, the thought I was pushing away with all my might that I dared not admit to myself, was that the real trouble was in my relationship with Peter. We were friends, we had a lot in common, but I had married him for security and for his family, whom I loved dearly and who had become a surrogate family to me, the family I'd never had. I even used to joke about it when we were engaged and after we were first married, that I was marrying Peter for his family, hoping it wasn't really true and that no one would believe it.

When we'd met, both aged sixteen, I'd been briefly romantically inclined towards him. He, on the other hand fell in love. I was never "over the moon" over him, he never made me crazy with wanting him, never took me out of my self, wild with excitement. I was totally inexperienced, and had great longings for some ideal of romantic love, what my mother would call "une grande pashe." Yes, that's what I thought I wanted. That notion of love sold to us all in books and movies. All those Jeffrey Farnol romance novels I'd read as a girl growing up in England, for instance. But I couldn't think about any of that now, and as I was much too insecure even to imagine separating, I felt I had to make it work. Mainly, I had to make Peter understand that I couldn't stay here any longer, and that if he loved me, we'd have to go home.

All the while I had been thinking about our lives, I had also been washing, mopping, and cleaning up. I couldn't do laundry in this weather, nothing would dry. I had rinsed out some underwear and hung it above the stove in the galley hoping that would help it dry, but it was depressing. It looked like some awful tenement.

I heard the putt-putt of the returning *White Ibis* and a few moments later, Peter climbed aboard. He looked pleased, and his easy competence made me feel warmly towards him.

"Well, the outside trees got blown about a bit. Lots of nests destroyed. Some young birds killed. The interior is quite undamaged though. On the whole the island seems to have come through fine. I'll have to do a count when the birds come in tonight," he reported.

Then he went off to check out his beloved Pavilion Key. Bad weather and big winds invite interesting bird-watching. Birds were sometimes blown off course by big storms, and there was always the chance of seeing an "exotic," some poor creature pushed a long way from its familiar habitat. The sky had lightened a bit. I was feeling better, but not better enough to talk about New York and all that yet. Suddenly, I remembered I had missed an appointment with the OB/GYN in Fort Myers. The appointment had been for the very day after the hurricane. I could not possibly have gotten there. The storm had hit Fort Myers too, so probably everybody's' schedules had been disrupted. I would have to make another appointment the next time we went into Everglades.

Peter came back from Pavilion Key feeling ill. He had managed to get some fish for us all, cats and turtle included, and he had seen flocks of painted buntings and redstarts, which were very unusual for around here. He also seemed to have developed some sort of intestinal upset, and all he wanted to do was go to bed. He undressed and climbed into his bunk. He was shivering and feverish.

"Here, put on your flannel shirt," I insisted, "you've caught a chill." I made him a hot water bottle and some strong tea.

"Put some whiskey in it, wife."

"You've probably got a fever," I demurred. "I don't think it's such a good idea."

But he insisted, so I put a little in. Probably wouldn't hurt, really. Our thermometer had broken, so I was only guessing about the temperature. I hadn't had much experience nursing the sick.

At sunset he got up to count the birds. We sat on the cabin roof watching the always dramatic and beautiful spectacle. Their numbers seemed down, though I was only guessing. Peter, clicking away with his counter, confirmed this later with his official reckoning of roughly 45,000.

"I guess some of them are still back in the swamps or got blown north," he said after most of them were in, safe for the night. "They'll be back in a few days." And with that he returned to his bunk. I lit the lamps and started supper.

"I'm not hungry. The smell of that fish is turning my stomach," he groaned. It was rare for Peter to lose his appetite. "Well, don't eat then," I said. "Just try to get some sleep. You're exhausted. We all are. You'll be better in the morning." But he wasn't. He must have caught a virus of some sort, because his miseries continued on for a couple more days.

We were quite out of staples and one of us would have to go and shop soon. After a restless night, I got up and prepared to take the White Ibis over to Turkey Key, where I could at least get the bare minimum of supplies. Although I was quite comfortable by now with the small boat and could get to Turkey Key and back safely, I was reluctant to go out in the unsettled weather, and choppy water. So, when at the very moment I was about to leave, Art Eifler stopped by on his way to Everglades and saved the day, I could have hugged him. Of course, I didn't, though Art seemed to have recovered somewhat from his crush on me. He hadn't been coming by or hanging about lately, which had been a relief. Still, I wouldn't want to stir things up or give out the wrong message. He was in a hurry and didn't want to stay long enough for coffee.

"Jest wanted to check on you," he said. "Make sure Duck didn't blow away. Gotta get to the ways and see if that Jerry got the part for the Spoonbill I ordered. If the bridge didn't wash out at Ochopee, he should have it by now. Sorry you're poorly"—this to Peter. "Gimme your list and I'll be on my way." I handed him my grocery list and the last of our cash.

"Art, would you look up the Leightys while you're there?" I asked him, "I'm a bit worried, I haven't heard a thing about them."

"Sure," he agreed. "I 'spec they's fine. Everglades didn't get much damage, I heard," and he was gone.

It felt like a day off. Peter was still languishing in his bunk, so I started reading to him. We were in the middle of *Robinson Crusoe,* but our reading sessions, when we took turns reading to one another, had been interrupted by all the weather-related emergencies and extra work. Now I started in at my favorite part, where Crusoe finds Friday. The boat rocked mildly, the sky lightened, and a reluctant sun shone through the clouds enough to dry the towels I'd spread out on the cabin roof. I read for a while and Peter dozed off.

When Art returned with our mail and sundries, he told us the Leightys and everyone were fine, but also that there was another hurricane on the way.

"Better come on back up to the Tookes'," he advised. "Looks like we're going to get some more weather."

I was appalled. Would we have to go through all that again so soon? Art went on upriver, and a bit later the tide was high enough for us to untie the *Audubon* and chug up the Chatham once again to the Tookes'. Their dock was already full with Art's boats and the Weekes brothers', so we had to moor across the river, tying up to a mangrove.

"Geez, what's that horrible smell?" Peter wrinkled his nose in disgust. He'd rallied enough to drive the boat up to Tookes, but now he was heading for the bunk again.

I didn't know, but the stink seemed to be coming out of the mud. Something stirred up by the action of the hurricane, I supposed. I looked across the river at the other boats, I couldn't believe my eyes. What on earth? They had all turned an uneven, sooty black.

"Peter, come look at this," I called. He groaned, but came up the companionway steps. "What the hell?" he exclaimed. We peered over the side at the *Audubon*, and, sure enough, we'd turned black too. "Oh, hell— looks like we've got our work cut out for us," he complained and went back to bed.

I decided to go and see what Mr. Tooke recommended. I rowed across the river and walked up to the house. The Tookes were sitting outside talking to the Weekeses. They all laughed when I asked about the paint. According to Mr. Tooke, the paint had oxidized or some such and nothing would scrub it clean. "You can't paint over it either," Mr. T went on. "Nope. You'll just have to get yourself some paint remover. It's a real pain in the arse," he added in one of his rare moments of vulgarity. My heart sank. We'd be working at it for weeks.

As soon as Peter recovered, I came down with it, and I in turn took to my bunk. I felt horrible, rather as if I had a bad hangover. As the Weekes's had left, we moved the boat across the river to the Tookes' dock and Mrs. T plied me with herbal remedies, bringing me chamomile tea and concoctions of slippery elm bark and nettle. The latter tasted awful, but it cheered me up to be mothered.

To our great relief, the hurricane went north and left us alone. All we got were more squally cold winds and choppy water. My "collywobbles" only lasted twenty-four hours, the weather improved, and we chugged back downriver to our station, and tied up to the three stakes at Duck Rock, of which by now I was heartily sick and tired.

33

"I could stay here and work for the Audubon Society for as long as I want, I think, I'm pretty sure they'd always have something for me to do," Peter said. It was a few days later and we were in the midst of one of our rambling, inconclusive discussions about the future.

"But what will happen when the place becomes a national park?" I countered. "They won't need wardens any more."

"Well, there's always Miami and the tours," he mused, referring to Charlie's offer. "I bet the Feds will run them too." I didn't want him to find any loopholes. "Besides, we couldn't live on a few summer tours. If they ever happen."

I hated to admit I was sick of the place, and he hated to admit he might have to look for some other situation. What would he do? A desk job? Hard to imagine him in an office. Peter was an outdoors kind of guy, most at home "in the field," a naturalist's naturalist. But times were about to change, and even outdoor guys who had a bent for field study, would need higher education and degrees. He didn't even have a high school diploma yet; the war had messed that up. If he were to have any sort of future, he'd have to get an equivalency certificate at least.

We had a little over two weeks before we went to New York for the Audubon conference. I still hadn't completely acknowledged to Peter how I felt about returning here after the conference. I felt guilty about even having such negative feelings. My English stiff-upper-lip and "mustn't let the side down" upbringing interfered with the idea that I had needs too. In the '40s, wives were expected to follow their husbands and put their own preferences aside.

In the meantime, there was much to get done before the New York trip. The boats had to be scraped and painted because of the storm's weird blackening effect and the interiors needed scrubbing. The wretched pump that flushed the head had been acting up and was now almost completely non-functional. Plus, we had to finish the two articles we'd been struggling with for months, one for the *East Hampton Star* and one for the *Audubon*. Peter was still writing a report to be delivered at the conference and I had to go to the doctor in Fort Myers for a follow-up exam after my miscarriage six weeks before.

Going to Fort Myers was the most fun-sounding choice, so I focused on that first. I wanted some cute new underwear. My sneakers had holes in them, and Peter had used the last dishcloth for an engine rag. Mr. Tooke wanted to go too. He'd been having trouble with his teeth, and he had decided to have them all out, which sounded like a draconian solution to me, but I knew that a lot of people chose to do it. Dental care was expensive and hard to come by in that part of Florida, and so, in the interest of saving money and getting rid of potential problems once and for all, Mr. Tooke was "all in." It made me shudder even to think of it. Then Art decided he needed to come too, to look for lumber he needed for the *Spoonbill*. It looked as if an expedition were building.

Fort Myers was seventy-six miles up the coast. In order to get an early start, we spent the night before at the Tookes', and left before dawn in Art's boat, as ours was still wet from painting. As we sped into Everglades on the first leg of our journey, we passed Duck Rock just as the birds were leaving, flying up by the thousands and heading for the interior. Though I'd watched it from the boat many times, I'd never seen this phenomenon from any distance before. I was even more awestruck at the scale of the numbers and the incredible density of the cloud of birds as they flew off.

"They've all come back, I'm glad to say." said Peter looking at Art. "They were down a bit after the storm."

"Oh yeah," said Art, "always happens after a storm. Looks like pretty good numbers now, though."

Art didn't say, as he might have, that their numbers were up also because we had been so conscientious in our protection. He'd been jealous of Peter's dedication from the start.

"Yeah, I counted sixty thousand yesterday, give or take. I think some birds have come over from other keys," was all Peter said. The birds soon learned where it was safer to be. We sped on into Everglades.

Rosa Leighty was up, even though it was still early. "Come in, come in," she greeted us. "I make you coffee." We crowded into her little living room. Since everything in town was still closed, this coffee would set us up till we could get breakfast on the road. We didn't linger, the men were determined to get going. I wanted to stay and chat, but that would have to wait. We thanked Rosa for the much-needed coffee and piled into our little Ford and headed for civilization.

In the slanting rays of the early morning light, the Tamiami Trail appeared green and mysterious. Alligators basked along the canal banks, ignoring our passage. Where there weren't alligators, big wood storks stood on one leg, drowsing, too early for fishing. In the cypress trees with their festoons of Spanish moss draperies, egrets posed among the branches as warblers and small finches flitted in and out. Near the hamlet of Hammock Landing we stopped at a diner for breakfast. The sign "No Coloreds" made me want to get back in the car and leave. The others argued to stay.

"Won't find no place along here that don't keep out the colored folk," said Art, but Peter sided with me.

"There must be some place," Peter replied. "Let's go on a little bit." Amid grumbles from Art, we continued on a few miles further, to the outskirts of another small community, where we found another cafe. There was no sign, at least, but there were no black people either. However, I conceded, and we had a huge Southern repast complete with ham 'n' eggs, grits 'n' gravy, and biscuits.

At Naples, the canal ended, and the landscape changed. Now we looked west over white sand beaches and beyond to the expanse of blue Gulf water, while on the other side were sugar plantations and farm lands. None of it looked very prosperous. The fields were weed-grown and the vegetation appeared scraggly. At last we approached the mouth of the Caloosahatchee River, where we turned inland and drove the last few miles into Fort Myers. It was a small, country town, as sleepy and slow-moving as the river flowing along its northern edge. Its main industry was boating. Fishing boats, pleasure boats, sailboats and motorboats—every conceivable type of craft—lined the river banks. Boats need upkeep, and boatyards and boat-builders were everywhere. Seagulls flew up and down the estuary following fishing boats, raucously claiming any morsel that fell into the water.

We parked by the river and walked into town. I needed a phone and so did Mr. Tooke.

We found one on the street in front of the library.

"You go ahead, Missy," Mr. T. said, so I called the doctor's office. No answer. "I'll just go in later," I said. "They'll probably be able to see me." I wasn't concerned, anyway it was just a checkup, and all my insides seemed to have recovered. Mr. Tooke had better luck with his call, and he went striding happily off to get his teeth pulled.

The day was hot, but not uncomfortably humid. We strolled back toward the river to look for the lumber for Art's *Spoonbill*. The smell of wood was pungent and fragrant as we approached the lumber yard. Sawdust hovered in the air and lay in piles under the saws, which were whining and screeching as they tore through the planks, making conversation well-nigh impossible. Art was picky. After trying three places, he gave up and grumped back to the car.

"Drop me at Sears," I said. I was anxious to be rid of these tiresome men and get going. Among other things I needed a hat, I'd forgotten mine, and the day was warming up, and besides, I was dying to get my new, cute underwear.

Peter was tired. He'd been up late the night before working on his paper for the convention, and he'd had one too many whiskies in the process. He had brought our temperamental radio in to be fixed and was looking for a part to repair the pump for the head. We agreed to meet in an hour.

At lunch time we all four gathered at a cafe Mr. Tooke recommended. It was a place renowned for its fish. A huge anchor marked the entrance, and inside, the walls were hung with fishnets and old buoys. It's lucky I like fish, I thought, the amount of it I eat nowadays. Then I thought of how we would soon be in New York and of the many other kinds of food we could eat and of my mother's wonderful shepherd's pie, and going to all our favorite restaurants in the Village. The excitement that came with thinking these things made me feel expansive and happy. We all had a beer.

Mr. Tooke arrived and all his teeth had really been pulled. I had been kind of hoping he wouldn't go through with it, but the dentist had pulled them all, right then and there. He seemed fine, though, and was apparently feeling no pain. He said he hadn't had many teeth left, anyway.

"I can't chew much," he explained cheerfully, "but I can slurp some clam chowder." Peter was feeling better now that he'd had a beer, "hair of the dog" and all that. Only Art was still grumpy and complaining.

"This here town ain't what it used to be. Can't get nothin' I want." He would have gone into one of his diatribes about the decline and fall of practically everything, except Mr. Tooke forestalled him and changed the subject.

"Now, Art," he said, lisping a little without his teeth. "You shoulda come with me over to Joneses' boatyard. They got everything over there. They even got these Monel nails, somethin' new. They's got threads like a screw in the middle. Reckon they won't never come out. Here, got me a handful."

He reached into his pocket and pulled out the nails to show us. Art sniffed at them, but I could see he was at least curious. Peter examined one.

"Good idea," was his comment.

After lunch I saw the doctor briefly, and he told me I was quite well again, which I already knew. Our errands now completed, we piled back into the car for the drive home. When we reached Everglades two hours later, we still faced the long ride back to the Tookes', but since it was early evening, we didn't have to rush. The men went to the drugstore for a beer and to catch up on the local fishing news, while I went to visit with Rosa. Of all the people in Everglades, Rosa and Mrs. Tooke were the two I felt the closest to and who I was really going to miss when we actually left this place. At the time it didn't occur to me, but they were both in their own ways mother substitutes for me. Although Rosa, being closer to my own age, was more like a big sister, one who was wise, cheerful and kind. Now we sat in her living room, while I told her all about our excursion. Rosamaria and her friends were running in and out and Ralph was off somewhere preparing for class.

We talked about the upcoming New York conference. Rosa looked at me suddenly. "You comin' back here, no?" she queried. I was startled. She had sensed my ambivalence and confusion about the place, the job, our whole situation. I longed to confide in her.

"Well," I hedged, "we may. I'm not wild about it here, really."

"Is very difficult for you," she sympathized. "Is such an isolated place. No many people to talk to. I myself cannot stay much longer. We, Ralph and I, we want so much to go to Puerto Rico. Soon we will, I hope."

"I feel torn," I admitted. "Peter really likes it here."

"Well," she said, "if you don' come back, I understand. I miss you, but I understand." I felt comforted. She did understand, and she didn't think I was a bad person.

Just then Peter came in. "Gotta get going," he said. "Art's champing at the bit."

I jumped up. "Oh, okay. Did you put our stuff in the boat?" I wanted my new things, the now-fixed radio, my hat, the groceries, and especially my cute underwear. I couldn't wait to wear the panties covered in small flowers and the lacy pink bra.

We shoved off, Art driving. We had to stop by Hemp's boat downriver to get Mr. Tooke's laundry, and then we were truly off. All went well until we started through Rabbit Key Pass on the inside route and ran aground. We managed to get off the sand bar and started up again slowly, only to hit bottom again about half a mile further on. At that point, Art gave up and let Mr. Tooke take the helm.

We raced home without further problems. Peter was sitting up on the bow deck letting the evening air blow over him, while down in the cabin, I was so tired, I kept dozing off, only to be jarred awake by the boat hitting a wave. What am I going to do in New York, I thought, if one day in a little country town like Fort Myers wears me out?

34

There remained only a week before I was to go home. I planned to go on ahead of Peter, who was staying till the last minute to finish up some work. Although I didn't emphasize the point, I was looking forward to some time alone. In fact, I was brimming over with excitement and happiness. Oh, to be home again in good old, dirty old, wonderful New York! The week seemed endless with much to be done.

I had yet to tell Peter I didn't want to come back. I was trying to avoid it, but it was no good trying to fool myself any longer. I was not cut out for this life. The mere thought of returning plunged me into misery. Perhaps if I'd had a deeper interest in natural history, had different needs—in fact, if I were a different person altogether—I could find satisfaction here, but I wasn't. I was the way I was, and no amount of wishing or struggling to change was going to make any difference. It was very distressing to me to finally admit this to myself, and then to force myself to face it.

I would have to be strong, I was not good at standing up for myself or my needs and I was afraid of being a disappointment to Peter and the family, but, well, I was sorry. The whole situation was too primitive for a long-term commitment, we would never be able to start a family living on that boat. I felt strongly that to stay on would not be good for either of us, and certainly would not be good for our marriage. It had been a great adventure, but like all adventures, it had come to an end, at least for me. I didn't care if we didn't have any future plans. I would just have to convince Peter that, surely, something would turn up. We had plenty of family support and connections. There was the GI Bill. Peter could bite the bullet and go back to school. We were still young, with endless opportunity awaiting us. We'd just have to trust that our future would unfold somehow.

Thus, my thinking and self-justifying ran on. Looking back, my feelings seem quite obvious and understandable, but at that time I was simply in a muddle. I had to try explain myself to Peter as best I could.

Even as oblivious as he could be sometimes, Peter had been aware of my growing dissatisfaction. My unhappiness was obvious and it was affecting our relationship. I felt like I was failing in my own idea of who I, the dutiful wife, was supposed to be. My discomfort had me taking my frustrations out on Peter. I was also feeling very guilty that my "shortcomings" would then put the total burden of finding another job on him. Even though we both knew that sooner or later, Peter was going to have to get an education and/or find another way to make a living, it still made me feel guilty and selfish.

So, I was apprehensive about taking my stand. I was afraid to tell Peter once and for all I wouldn't come back. I waffled.

"What would you think if I said I really don't want to come back?" I ventured during our next discussion about what we were doing.

"Oh, I dunno. I guess I might say you just need a vacation. I mean, after all, we haven't had a real break since we got here." He sounded very reasonable. I jumped on this idea.

"Yes, that's true, maybe a vacation is exactly what we both need. Maybe going to New York for a break will be enough, and I'll feel different afterwards," I agreed.

I really didn't believe it entirely, but I still couldn't bring myself to say so. I had to see. Perhaps a vacation would do the trick and I'd feel fine about coming back. We left it at that for the time being.

In the interim, I busied myself cleaning up the boat and getting all our bedding and clothes laundered. A few days before I was to leave, we went upriver to the Tookes'. The weather had been, and continued to be, horrible, cold and damp with a chill wind blowing all the time. Not good laundry weather. Mrs. T was as welcoming as ever, and while the wash chugged away on the porch, we sat in the warm kitchen and drank coffee. After a while, Peter left to go check on the birds at Gopher Key.

"I'll be back in an hour or so," he said cheerily as he took off.

Mrs. T fixed me with her beady eye. "So, you're leavin' us," she began. "When are you comin' back?"

"We're supposed to be back in November," I replied, "but we don't know exactly when. Peter may come back before I do."

"That sounds a mite iffy to me," she said slowly. "Are you sure you really want to come back? I mean, you. I know your Peter does. He's a real naturalist type of fella."

Lord, I thought, am I so transparent? Does everyone know how I feel? First Rosa and now Mrs. Tooke. She didn't wait for an answer.

"Seems to me like this ain't really a place for you, leastways not for long. 'Sides, I know you're missin' your folks an all."

I didn't want to let her know she was right. I offered up the convenient excuse I was hiding in.

"I just need a vacation, I think," I said, trying to sound as if I believed it.

"Well, you're young yet. You young uns gotta go your ways," she replied neutrally. She made it sound less questionable, and in fact, quite natural.

I felt comforted. I hung up the wash hoping it would dry enough so I could take it back to the *Audubon* and damp iron it dry with my new Coleman iron that ran on kerosene.

When Peter came back, Mrs. T loaded us down with eggs and papayas, oranges, and avocados. I felt genuinely sad to be saying goodbye. For the first, and only time in our friendship, we hugged. I knew I might never see her again. I felt like crying, but then she'd have guessed I wasn't coming back and I didn't want that.

I shook hands solemnly with Mr. T. "Say good-bye to Hamp for me," I told him. "I hope you catch lots of fish."

Mr. T's eyes twinkled behind his little glasses. "Now, don't you be gettin' into no trouble up there in that big city," he smiled. "But have a good time, anyways."

Art and the Missus were back in Everglades, so we could say goodbye to them later.

When we got to Everglades, we'd also be saying our goodbyes to the Leightys and the other people we'd been involved with all along, the fish house folks, the drugstore guy, and the couple who ran the grocery store. Of course, none of them knew we might not be coming back, so from their point of view this was a very minor parting.

"Want to come with me to get ice?" asked Peter when we were back at the boat.

"Not really." I said. I didn't want to go through the charade again, saying my false good-byes.

"Okay." He waved as he drove off.

I started ironing the still-damp laundry. I was humming along with Peggy Lee on the radio as she sang "Fever." A steady bubbling of happiness, like an underground spring, coursed through me as I worked, thinking about going home.

We were planning to stay in the Scotts' family house in East Hampton. It was on Main Street across from the town pond. It was nicknamed the Box, not because of its shape, but for the box hedges surrounding it, and I loved it. It was a New England saltbox, with small rooms wallpapered in various floral designs. It was cozy and charming. Off the living room was a glassed-in porch with an orange tree in a big pot, and sitting there on sunny days, even in winter, you felt as if you were in the tropics. The senior Scotts were staying in Hewlett, up the Island, for the time being, so we'd have the house to ourselves. All our friends would be able to come and stay with us. It would be one long house party. Which is exactly what had happened on our honeymoon. After our wedding in Pennsylvania, we went to the box, and the very next day, various of our New York friends showed up and just stayed. Our honeymoon was short, as Peter was about to be inducted into the army, but it was one hell of a party.

The day I was to leave for New York, the weather cheered up and became gloriously warm and golden, with that special fall light glowing over the landscape. As usual, we were going to stay the night before the actual departure in Miami to catch the early train. Driving the *Audubon* into Everglades for what was to be the last time for me, I sat out on the front deck for part of the ride, soaking up the light and smells. The frigate birds flew above as we started off, and as we passed Pavilion Key an osprey sprang up out of the largest mangrove and dove into the water. Everything seemed especially fresh and sparkling, and part of me regretted leaving.

We reached Everglades before noon and the tide was running high as we approached our mooring place under the palms. We went over to say goodbye to the Leightys. It was Saturday and Ralph was home. I brought some of the booty from the Tookes to give to Rosa as we couldn't possibly eat it all before it spoiled.

"Oh, thanks. Is so nice and fresh. You must stay for lunch with us. I have made tortilla soup, we will have big salad, and then we can have papayas and ice cream for dessert."

Who could refuse? We didn't need persuading. I was all packed and ready to go. The boat was clean and tidy, and everything was as shipshape as I could get it. The lamps were full of kerosene, the icebox full of ice, and the water tanks were full. Peter would be fine for the next few days. I had nothing to do. Lunch would be great.

"We will take good care of Peter when you are going," said Rosa, "so he won't be too lonely." I knew she didn't intend to make me feel guilty, she was just offering me some reassurance. I was glad they would be there for him if he needed anything, although I didn't really think he would. Everything tasted so delicious. Rosa's soup was one of her specialties.

"You must give me this recipe," I told her. "I barely know how to make tacos. Is it hard to make? It warms your insides."

"Oh no. Is easy. I write you the recipe after lunch."

"Well, we'd better get going, wife," said Peter after we'd finished the scrumptious dessert.

"Oh, don't you have time for some coffee?" said Rosa.

"I guess we'd better get going. We have to say goodbye to the Eiflers, too," was his reply, and he went out to put my bags in the car. Rosa and I looked at each other, and I knew she knew I wouldn't be back. We hugged.

"Have a wonderful time." She meant it. "I hope everything will go well for you."

"I'll miss you," I said lamely. "I hope you get to go back to your home too before long. And thank you, thank you so much for everything. You've been so kind to us." Rosamaria gave me a big hug.

"Be good," I said to her as she wrapped her skinny little arms around my neck. "Keep up your bird watching."

"I wish you weren't going," she said.

We made our way over to the Eiflers' boat. Art was hanging around outside on the grassy bank.

"Well, so you're off to the big city," he said. "Have a good trip. Don't do nothin' I wouldn't do. Har har."

"I want to say goodbye to Frieda, too," I said. I stepped aboard the *Spoonbill* and saw her sitting in her usual chair on the deck. I wasn't very sorry to be saying goodbye to her, but she did look sad and unwell that I had a momentary pang of sympathy for her.

It evaporated rather quickly, though, when she said, "You know, they should have asked me and Art to go up there. He's the senior warden, ain't he? Ach. You-all ain't hardly got your feet wet. Cain't imagine why they'd be askin' you. 'Tain't right, to my way of thinkin'."

I was taken aback by the venom in her voice.

"Well, Frieda, I just came to tell you good-bye. I'm sorry you feel like that, but it's nothing I could do anything about. Perhaps they'll ask you next time," I added rather lamely. I didn't remind her that Art was supposed to be retired.

She simply snorted and said, "I hope you don't get robbed up in that place. It's a wicked city, I hear."

I was glad to get away. I climbed in the car and we waved to Art and the Leightys, who had come out of their house as we set off. Driving up the little dirt streets, I was already feeling a tug of nostalgia for this odd corner of Florida, with its palms and flowering vines and shrubs, the sun pouring down, a special quiet and peace pervading it all. The Tamiami Trail had never looked more beautiful as we drove across it, with the water lilies blooming in the canals and birds perched thickly in the trees. Alligators basked, ducks paddled, and the sky was a deep clear blue.

Once in Miami, we got a room in the cheap hotel we favored, and set out to have dinner, this time at a seafood restaurant Charlie Brookfield had recommended. We sat at a small table in a corner and I looked around. The decor was plain, but elegant enough to feature real tablecloths, cloth napkins, and a candle on each table. It was a little expensive for us, but it was my last night and we were prepared to splurge. The waiter brought our drinks, a martini for Peter and a Scotch on the rocks for me. We each lit up a cigarette. Our conversation was desultory—I was preoccupied with thinking of how to tell Peter my true feelings.

"When do you think you'll actually get to East Hampton?" I began. We'd talked about this before, of course; I was just filling the silence.

"If I get an early start on Wednesday, I'll get there on Friday, if I don't have car trouble, and I'll come straight to East Hampton. Then we'll go to the city and stay with Donna or someone for the conference. Maybe the Helmuths' apartment. You can organize that when you get there."

I gathered up my nerve and said, "You know, I'm feeling more and more like I don't want to come back." Oh, why was this so difficult? Why couldn't I simply say it?

"You'll feel different after a week in New York." Peter just didn't want to hear this. "Maybe. But what if I still don't?" I kept trying. "You know, we could stay in the city for awhile and you could go back to school and get your high school equivalency certificate or whatever it's called. I could get a temp job or something, and then we'd just see what would happen next," I suggested.

"I know I'll probably have to get that certificate eventually," he replied, "but I just don't want to do it now."

"Well, okay, but you might have a hard time finding something you like to do in the future without it."

"I like what I'm doing right now, and I don't need a diploma for it."

"But Peter," I said desperately, "we can't stay here forever. No matter what, I don't want to live here. I want to be in New York or at least nearer to the family and all our friends. Don't you, really?"

"Okay. Look, let's make an agreement. I understand that you don't really want to come back very much. (At last, he'd heard that part.) How about we say we won't decide for sure until after the conference. We'll leave it open until then. How does that sound?"

I agreed. It was fair enough after all. Even though I was sure I knew what I wanted to do, I would try to keep an open mind. I tried to forget about it for the rest of the evening. We drank a little more than was good for us, and we danced until late.

In the morning, we went to the station. After all the friends and relatives we'd seen off aboard the New York Express, now it was my turn and I was the one who was leaving. We kissed goodbye, and I found my seat in the sleeper compartment.

"'Board!" The whistle blew and we chuffed out of the station accelerating as we went. I waved out the window, and then settled down in my window seat next to an anonymous-looking middle-aged woman, who I hoped wouldn't be chatty. I wanted to be alone with my thoughts, but actually my mind was buzzing and unfocused. I gazed out of the wide, dusty window and watched Florida go by and become the past. The steady rhythm of the train made me sleepy and I dozed off. When I opened my eyes again my mind was clearer. We were coming into the first of our stops, Fort Lauderdale. I watched as passengers got on and off the train, saying goodbye or hello, struggling with bags and belongings, making the transition from one set of conditions to another. Transitions were sometimes the hardest part of life, I was thinking, but no, I thought again, the hardest part is just before you make the decision, before you actually start the transition process. The bottleneck of indecision was the most unbearable for me.

Now, here on the train going home, as I watched the telegraph poles snapping by, I felt the decision had been made. Now, I just had to follow through and deal with the consequences of that decision, whatever they might turn out to be. I was determined that this homecoming would be happy and not filled with regret.

Our stay here had been so full of challenge and new experience. I had definitely felt tested by circumstance. Most of the time I felt I'd risen to the challenges we'd faced, from the uncomfortable and inconvenient living situation on the boat, through my endless fears of the primitive environment, to dealing with recalcitrant motors, gas tanks full of fumes, dangerous stoves, and lamps full of flammable liquid, not to mention about a billion mosquitoes. I'd managed to cope with scorpions and snakes, with hurricanes and storms, and even scary villains with guns—all experiences I never would have dreamed I could deal with before we arrived in this strange, watery corner of the world.

On the other hand, I had been privileged to be part of an ongoing and noble experiment to help preserve and protect this very same challenging environment and its extraordinary inhabitants. I thought of the breathtaking dawn flight of the birds of Duck Rock every morning and their return at sunset. I thought of the beauty of the beaches with their bounty of shells, and of the mysterious murky interior of the mangrove islands with their never-ending re-creation of new life. I thought of the kindly, generous Mr. and Mrs. Tooke and of course, of Rosa and her family—Rosa especially, with her generosity of spirit, her love of life, and her non-judgmental, unconditional support and understanding she had so selflessly offered me. The thought that I'd never see them again was painful and I vowed to write and keep up.

I opened my mystery and read as the train clickety-clacked over bridges, whistled at crossings, rocked on through open spaces, and steamed into stations. Night fell, and I had dinner in the diner with some fellow travelers, but I didn't feel up to more than polite exchanges. After dinner, I walked back to my car and found my bunk had been made up. I had an upper, and I climbed into it and lay for a while, gazing out as the passing lights glowed and flashed against the window.

Another day on the train and I was starting to feel restless. I walked up and down the aisles, and stood for a while on the back platform, watching where we'd been disappear behind us. Georgia, South Carolina, North Carolina, Virginia, Maryland, Pennsylvania—now we were really in the urban built-up North, the scenic south long gone. Finally, the conductor walked through announcing, "Grand Central Station. Last Stop. Grand Central."

My heart raced. I reached for my bag in the rack above. Who would be meeting me? Several people had said they intended to—my mother, my in-laws, Uncle Will. I knew I'd be met by loved ones, and whomever they turned out to be, I would be in the arms of family. A new phase of my life was about to begin. I didn't know what shape it might take, and at this moment, I didn't care. I was home.

Epilogue

We did not live happily ever after. Following the Audubon Society conference and after many painful scenes, including tears and hysterics on my part, we decided not to return to Florida. Peter quit and we moved to New York City, where we lived in a fifth-floor walk-up apartment on the West Side near the Tenderloin. Apartments were hard to find and this was the best we could do. It was a "railroad" flat with all the rooms in a line opening one into the other and with no central heating. We heated it with a huge old kerosene stove which was bolted to the kitchen floor. The whole place always smelled of kerosene, including our clothes. Peter went to school, got his high school diploma, and then took a job with a newly started company calling itself E-Z Stick. It was the first peel-off-and-stick labeling device, now known as "post-its," to come on the market. Peter was supposed to learn the business from the bottom up, with the expectation that he would finally become part of management. But he hated it, and I didn't blame him. He was definitely not suited to the business life.

A year later, our daughter Jennifer was born and we moved to an apartment on Minetta Lane in the Village. Not long after, I got back into dance. I discovered modern dance, which was burgeoning rapidly in those early years. I took classes with everyone I could find, from Martha Graham to Hanya Holm, Merce Cunningham, and Alwyn Nikolais.

After three years of struggling, Peter quit the E-Z Stick job and joined with a local "bonaker" (native Eastern Long Islander), Milt Miller, and became a fisherman. We moved to Springs, a few miles outside of East

Hampton, where he and Milt built us a house on eight acres of mostly cranberry bog and bayberry bushes. At the time the whole area was swarming with early Abstract Expressionist painters. Jackson and Lee Pollack were our neighbors and we were good friends with Robert Motherwell and his first wife, the beautiful Maria. Larry Rivers used to come over and play our old upright piano. The partying, especially in the summers, was intense.

Milt had a boat, and in the summertime, he and Peter fished for bluefish at night. Sometimes they fished off the beach for striped bass, on a crew that might include writers John Cole or Peter Matthiessen, who were also fishing for a living in those days. In winter there was clamming and scalloping. Many's the time I stood in a cold drafty shed along with the other scallopers' wives, shucking scallops and filling gallon jugs with them for market. Our hands would get blue and cracked despite heavy rubber gloves.

This life lasted for a few years, during which time I commuted regularly to New York City where I continued dancing, performing, and teaching. In those days, before the freeways were built, the commute was three hours long. Driving home one night after performing with the Paper Bag Players, I ran into a snowstorm. I was the only car on the road and I was too terrified to stop. I kept going slowly, praying as the snow piled up and blew against the windshield. I finally arrived home at 4 a.m. in a state of collapse. This put a damper on my commuting for a while, but didn't altogether stop me.

Despite a life full of interest and diversion and wild fun, Peter and I were suffering. We found we were incompatible in many ways. I felt there was no center to our relationship. Where there should have been strength and cohesion there was a hollow. It was nobody's "fault," we just seemed to be growing apart. Our year of Reichian therapy which may have helped us individually, was not enough to save our marriage. With enormous and painful reluctance, I moved out and took Jennifer with me to New York City. My old friend Donna had become an editor for the Literary Guild. Previously, she had worked for Twentieth-Century Fox and she helped me to get job there as a story editor. As I had no idea how to do it, she wrote the first few synopses of the books I was assigned until I could get the hang of it.

City life, and especially New York city life, with a young child was not easy, and I craved the country. So, in 1956 I picked up and moved us to Menlo Park, California, where Peter had family who could help us get started.

Peter and I remained good friends in spite of everything, and he subsequently followed us out to California with a new wife and child. He settled near his mother in southern California, and Jennifer was able to spend more time with him. Tragically, in 1959, not long after he had been up to Menlo Park to visit us, he died in an automobile accident. Telling Jennifer was the hardest thing I ever had to do.

Peter's love of nature and his interest in natural science live on in the family. Both of Peter's brothers became professionals in the field, Henry as a marine biologist, and Tom as a plant physiologist.

Our daughter, Jenny, inherited Peter's happy-go-lucky streak and his special way with people. She and her husband, John Teton, have three children. Their daughters, Sage and Zoe, have entered the fields of law and medicine, respectively; their son, Ben, is a wildlife biologist, one of seven members of the extended family to have become biologists since Peter brought me to the Everglades in 1946. After living in Menlo Park for fifty years, I moved to Oregon to join them, all of which is another story— many, many other stories—altogether.

Acknowledgments

My daughter, Jennifer Scott Teton, and numerous others provided invaluable feedback on the text of this book. I am grateful to them all and want readers to know that any mistakes herein are mine alone. I am thankful as well to my son-in-law, John Teton, for his help in preparing the book for publication and designing the cover illustration with graphic artist Michael Ray Allison. More than seventy years after the events related in this book, I remain grateful to my then-husband, the late Peter Scott, for taking us on that extraordinary adventure.